LEAN SIX SIGMA LOGISTICS

Strategic Development to Operational Success

by
Dr. Thomas Goldsby • Robert Martichenko

J.ROSS
PUBLISHING

Copyright ©2005 by J. Ross Publishing, Inc.

ISBN 1-932159-36-3

Printed and bound in the U.S.A. Printed on acid-free paper
10 9 8 7 6 5 4 3

Library of Congress Cataloging-in-Publication Data

Goldsby, Thomas J.
  Lean Six Sigma logistics / by: Thomas Goldsby & Robert Martichenko.
    p. cm.
  Includes index.
  ISBN 1-932159-36-3 (hardback : alk. paper)
  1. Business logistics—Management. 2. Six sigma (Quality control
standard). 3. Process control. 4. Inventory control. 5. Waste
minimization. 6. Industrial efficiency. I. Martichenko, Robert, 1965–. II.
Title.
  HD38.5.G63 2005
  658.4′013—dc22   2005011208

Phone: (561) 869-3900
Fax: (561) 892-0700
Web: www.jrosspub.com

TABLE OF CONTENTS

PREFACE

As logistics and supply chain professionals, we all have one thing in common. This commonality is that time is a scarce resource, one that must be treated as a treasured commodity. This means that we must choose wisely when deciding what books to read or what avenues to pursue for professional development. With any luck, when we do invest our time in reading an industry book, we will walk away with one or two "golden nuggets" that can help us with our day-to-day responsibilities and challenges.

As the authors of *Lean Six Sigma Logistics*, we certainly kept the above in mind as we developed the framework for this book. To begin, we continuously asked ourselves whether a certain topic or theme was relevant to today's logistics and supply chain practitioner. We continuously asked ourselves whether each point passed the "so what?" test.

Consequently, we spent significant time up front developing the framework for the book. Using the serene background of Benson Lake in Eastern Ontario, Canada, we devised what we believe to be the key drivers for all logistics processes. This was no easy task. First of all, we must consider the two authors: one practical-thinking academic and one academic-thinking practitioner. Many times, we debated theory versus practicality and, oddly enough, many times the academic argued for practicality and the practitioner argued for rigor of theory! What lesson did we learn from this? The first was that theory relates directly to strategy. The second lesson is that practicality relates to tactical realities. To be sure though, we recognized that strategy and tactics are both required to achieve anything of significance. We must know what we want to accomplish and we must understand how to accomplish it!

A majority of our discussion surrounded the topic of "flow." Not flow from an inventory point of view, but rather the flow of the book itself. We continuously reminded ourselves that readers must be able to see the book as a whole, such that by the end they will say, "I see it, I get it!" And, therefore, the Logistics Bridge Model was born.

The Logistics Bridge Model is a compass and map. It will help us to set a strategic destination and direct us on the operational journey. It is not a step-by-step "how-to" guide, but rather a path for critical thinking. In our opinions, it is critical thinking that is required in logistics and supply chain management today. We need to be able to look at operations differently. We need to understand what value is and what waste is. We need to leverage value and eliminate waste. That is the primary purpose of this book.

In all sincerity, we appreciate your valuable time and we hope this book will help you to achieve your professional goals and organizational objectives. As well, we hope you will embrace the Logistics Bridge Model and enhance your ability to look at your supply chain with a critical eye and vision for improvement.

Thomas Goldsby and Robert Martichenko

ACKNOWLEDGMENTS

Writing a book might be compared to any number of challenging yet rewarding experiences. We have likened it to a great mountain expedition. Mountaineering is regarded as one of the most grueling pursuits of human endeavor. Writing a book and living to tell about it may not be far behind! Yet, we recognize that many people have helped us in our expedition.

We would like to acknowledge our many friends and colleagues for their support of this effort. In particular, we would like to thank Douglas Boyd, Brent Buschur, Pascal Dennis, Michael George, Craig Germain, Michael Goldsby, Steven Gran, Stanley Griffis, Jack Hines, Ted Stank, Glen Wright, Ike Kwon, Pamela Ruebusch, Helen Zak, Rachel Regan, Steve Scholten, Dean Dixon, and Richard Holland for their invaluable support and dialogue. We would like to thank David Kmet, Tom Taranto, Antonio Tong, and Sarah Valles, all graduates of The Ohio State University, for their research assistance over the past five years. A special thanks to Sarah for her contribution of visual illustrations used in the book.

From a writing perspective, we thank Drew Gierman and the team at J. Ross Publishing. A huge "thanks" to Carole Boyd and June Martichenko for converting very rough drafts to near-final copy. We thank Fred Moody of *Logistics Quarterly* magazine for encouraging the pursuit of writing on supply chain issues.

A warm thanks to Joe and Sujane Goldsby. Perhaps most importantly, we must thank our spouses, Kathleen Goldsby and Corinne Hines, for looking after the most important aspects of life while providing us the luxury of engaging in mountain climbs. And last, but not least, we would like to acknowledge our wonderful children: Emma, Aiden, Emilee, and Abigail, who taught us that "you can work on the laptop and be the tickle monster at the same time."

To close, we have realized that writing a book is comparable to climbing a mountain not only in the preparation and process but also in the outcome. For in reaching the peak of the mountain, one does not enjoy the view for long before realizing how many more peaks have yet to be climbed.

ABOUT THE AUTHORS

 **Dr. Thomas J. Goldsby** is Associate Professor of Supply Chain Management at the University of Kentucky. He previously served on the faculties at The Ohio State University and Iowa State University. Dr. Goldsby holds a B.S. in business administration from the University of Evansville, an M.B.A. from the University of Kentucky, and a Ph.D. from Michigan State University.

Prior to entering academe, Dr. Goldsby was a Logistics Analyst for the Valvoline Company. He previously worked for the Transportation Research Board of the National Academy of Sciences in Washington, D.C. and as a research fellow at the University of Kentucky Transportation Research Center. He has also served as a consultant to manufacturers, retailers, and logistics service providers.

Dr. Goldsby is an expert in the areas of logistics strategy and supply chain integration. His research has been published in leading academic and professional journals. He serves as a frequent speaker at academic conferences, executive education seminars, and professional meetings, having delivered programs throughout North America as well as in South America, Europe, and Asia.

A competitive marathon runner, Dr. Goldsby resides in Lexington, Kentucky with his wife, Kathleen, and two children, Emma and Aiden. He can be reached at Tom@logisticsprof.com.

Robert Martichenko is President of *LeanCor LLC*. Headquartered in Florence, Kentucky, *LeanCor* delivers logistics and supply chain management services to companies embracing Lean manufacturing and Six Sigma in order to eliminate organizational waste.

His over ten years of transportation, consulting, and third-party logistics experience includes multiple operational launches, including the "green field" start-up at Toyota Motor Manufacturing Indiana. He complements his years of logistics experience with a bachelor's degree in mathematics from the University of Windsor and an M.B.A. in finance from Baker College and is a trained Six Sigma Black Belt.

Mr. Martichenko is also directly involved with the Council of Supply Chain Management Professionals, the Lean Enterprise Institute, the Supply Chain Consortium at Saint Louis University, and *Logistics Quarterly* magazine.

Born in Timmins, Ontario Canada, he resides in Kentucky and enjoys family time with his wife, Corinne, two wonderful daughters, and assorted pets. He can be reached at Robert@leancor.com.

Free value-added materials available from
the Download Resource Center at www.jrosspub.com

At J. Ross Publishing we are committed to providing today's professional with practical, hands-on tools that enhance the learning experience and give readers an opportunity to apply what they have learned. That is why we offer free ancillary materials available for download on this book and all participating Web Added Value™ publications. These online resources may include inter-active versions of material that appears in the book or supplemental templates, worksheets, models, plans, case studies, proposals, spreadsheets and assessment tools, among other things. Whenever you see the WAV™ symbol in any of our publications, it means bonus materials accompany the book and are available from the Web Added Value Download Resource Center at www.jrosspub.com.

Downloads available for *Lean Six Sigma Logistics: Strategic Development to Operational Success* consist of Lean and Six Sigma tools, an algorithm for calculating total logistics cost, discussion notes to accompany the GoldSMART case study, and extensive slide presentations on key principles and concepts, including the Logistics Bridge Model.

SECTION 1.
LEAN SIX SIGMA
LOGISTICS:
WHY BOTHER?

WHAT IS LEAN SIX SIGMA LOGISTICS?

Lean Six Sigma Logistics. Although it may sound as if it would require a year-long training course to do the topic justice, most logisticians are in fact using Lean Six Sigma Logistics techniques without realizing it. As the competitive environment changes the way we do business, companies are embracing Lean and Six Sigma initiatives to support cost reductions and quality improvements. Although Lean and Six Sigma programs were separate initiatives in most organizations initially, today's firms see that Lean and Six Sigma do not compete against but rather complement each other and provide for dovetailing of continuous improvement activities.

But what does this have to do with logistics? The quick answer is "everything." Once grounded in Lean and Six Sigma principles, the logistician will realize that logistics, Lean, and Six Sigma form a natural union. This union leverages the strengths and weaknesses of each discipline to create a cultural and operational model that will aid the logistician to solve age-old issues while improving operations and contributing to business success at all levels.

Where does one start when dealing with a topic as complex as Lean Six Sigma Logistics? Mathematicians have shown us that Y is a function of X, so if we truly want to understand Y (Lean Six Sigma Logistics), the best place to start is with the Xs. In this case, the Xs we need to understand individually are logistics, Lean, and Six Sigma. Once we can envision the three focus areas on their own, then we can see how they come together, allowing the whole to be greater than the sum of the parts.

WHAT IS LOGISTICS?

There seem to be as many definitions of "logistics" as there are logisticians. And this is not a bad thing! Why? Because logistics is so far-reaching and yet so integrated into our businesses that it is hard for one definition ever to meet the challenge of summing up what we do in a few short sentences.

Although logistics does involve internal operations and stretches to up- and downstream trading partners in the supply chain, it is fair to say that any definition of logistics will need to involve the management of inventory, whether it is in the form of hard goods (materials, people) or soft goods (information). If there is no inventory to move around, there is no need for logistics.

WHAT IS LEAN?

"Lean" concepts are deeply rooted in the Toyota Production System. In its purest form, Lean is about the elimination of waste and the increase of speed and flow. Although this is a high-level oversimplification, the ultimate objective of Lean is to eliminate waste from all processes. According to Lean theory, at the top of the list of known wastes is excess inventory. More simply, we need to eliminate any inventory that is not required to support operations and the immediate need of the customer. In this book, we identify excess inventory along with six other potential sources of waste in logistics: transportation, space and facilities, time, packaging, administration, and knowledge. Clearly, each of these resources — all necessary for logistics planning and execution — becomes waste when not utilized effectively to generate: (1) the greatest possible value in the eyes of customers and (2) healthy return for the company.

Lean and the Logistician

The impact of Lean on the logistician is significant. A common misconception of the Lean philosophy is that it only finds application in manufacturing settings. The goal of Lean is to eliminate waste, decrease work-in-process inventories, and, in turn, decrease process and manufacturing lead times, ultimately increasing supply chain velocity and flow. Lean also has a vital cultural element to it that is crucial to the logistician, the concept of "total cost." The Lean practitioner does not focus on individual cost factors such as transportation or warehousing, but rather focuses on total cost. With inventory carrying costs representing 15 to 40 percent of total logistics costs for many industries, making decisions based on total cost has dramatic implications for the logistician.

Unfortunately though, many organizations never embrace the total cost concept fully, as poor decisions are made continually based on traditionally visible cost drivers like transportation, warehousing, and per-unit purchase prices.

WHAT IS SIX SIGMA?

Six Sigma is a management methodology that attempts to understand and eliminate the negative effects of variation in our processes. Based on an infrastructure of trained professionals (black belts), Six Sigma delivers a problem-solving model armed with "voice of the customer" utilities and statistical process control tools. Define-Measure-Analyze-Improve-Control (DMAIC) is a map, or step-by-step approach, to understand and improve on organizational challenges (see Chapter 21). Six Sigma–trained employees will work on "projects" using the DMAIC model to reduce variation in processes and to attempt to achieve "Six Sigma quality," a statistical reference to 3.4 defects per million opportunities.

At the heart of Six Sigma is the principle of variation reduction: If we can understand and reduce variation in our processes, then we can implement improvement initiatives that will center the process and ensure accuracy and reliability of the process around customer expectations. For example, an average order-to-delivery cycle time of five days may reflect a variation between two and eight days. It is this variation that leads to customer nonconfidence and the resultant inventory buildup and/or loss of sales.

Six Sigma and the Logistician

The concept of variation reduction is paramount to the logistician. As stated above, logistics is about managing inventory, and managing inventory is about managing variance.* If we look at the different types of inventory, we will plainly see why variation plays such a vital role in how we manage inventories throughout the business and the supply chain.

For example, safety or "buffer" stocks are inventories that we need to hedge against unknowns (i.e., the variations from the norm). That is, we maintain safety stocks because of variation in supplier quality, transportation reliability, manufacturing process capability, and customer demand patterns. In other words, if we can understand and control variation in our processes from supplier to

---

* We use the following terms interchangeably throughout the book: variation, variance, and variability.

customer, then we will be able to reduce our reliance on the buffers dramatically. In this regard, logisticians need to think of themselves as actuaries, like those who develop rates for automobile insurance. Actuaries look at key variables — the age of drivers, gender of the drivers, types of vehicle driven, measures of past behavior (e.g., speeding tickets and accidents) — and then they determine insurance rates that reflect the variability in the data. This is precisely why the sixteen-year-old male who drives a sports car will have the highest insurance rates!

Logisticians are no different than the actuaries in this analogy. For demographics and sports cars, the logistician substitutes supplier competence, transportation reliability, and demand fluctuation. Then the logistician determines the "insurance rate," using inventory as the unit of currency. The problem here, though, is that too many logisticians are treating their companies like teenage drivers when, in fact, the company performance is more like a middle-aged soccer parent who drives a minivan. A down-to-earth example of this is when a manufacturer has leveled demand from a supplier who is an hour down the road from the plant, yet the manufacturer continues to carry twelve days worth of that supplier's parts in inventory! Why? Most likely the answer is twofold. The first reason is that the leveled flow (and therefore low variability of demand) is not understood; the second reason is more emotional. The emotional part of the equation is simply that industry is addicted to inventory. Make no mistake about it — industry has an addiction to inventory. and as with any addiction, inventory is something that most companies cannot imagine living without.

WHAT IS LEAN SIX SIGMA LOGISTICS?

Now that we have explored the three elements of Lean Six Sigma Logistics, we need to put them together to appreciate fully how they dovetail and complement each other. Summarizing from the above, recall that:

1. Logistics is about managing inventory.
2. Lean is about speed, flow, and the elimination of waste.
3. Six Sigma is about understanding and reducing variation.

Therefore, Lean Six Sigma Logistics can be defined as:

> The elimination of wastes through disciplined efforts to understand and reduce variation, while increasing speed and flow in the supply chain.

The Logistics Bridge Model

Both Lean and Six Sigma lend distinctive disciplines and tools to logistics. Using these disciplines and tools will allow an organization to uncover and deal with wastes and inefficiencies. Although Lean and Six Sigma tools are very powerful, we need to remember that for Lean and Six Sigma to work in logistics, a fundamental mind shift must occur. This mind shift requires that we first begin to make decisions based on the concept of "total logistics costs," and second, we have the courage to eliminate waste in its various forms. This may sound simple, but reality will prove otherwise. Organizational norms, management tradition, and financial accounting methods will fight against "total cost" and will continue to support our natural tendencies to create waste. The purpose of this book is to provide a template for the design and implementation of a logistics strategy based on Lean and Six Sigma principles. We have called this template the *Logistics Bridge Model.*

The Logistics Bridge Model is a model that can be used as a *compass* for the logistics professional. That is, it will provide direction and insight on how to solve today's logistics challenges and set the course for ongoing success. At the heart of these challenges is the need to bridge our suppliers with our own processes and then bridge our processes to the customer. All of this must happen while we face competitive and shareholder pressures to reduce costs and increase market share.

The Logistics Bridge Model teaches us that Lean Six Sigma Logistics is made up of three main principles. These principles are:

1. Logistics Flow
2. Logistics Capability
3. Logistics Discipline

Logisticians can draw from these three principles to design their own, personally tailored solutions to meet the specific challenges faced by their organization. Our goal is to provide the logistics professional with *guiding principles* that can be used to solve any logistics challenge that might be faced. To accomplish this, we have divided the book into four sections.

In Section 1, we continue to explore the importance of excellence in logistics and supply chain management. Section 2 examines the wastes that are all too often created in the absence of Lean Six Sigma implementation. Section 3 provides the details of the Logistics Bridge Model, the guiding principles to Lean Six Sigma Logistics. We illustrate the key tenets to logistics strategic visioning, tactical development, and successful operational execution. Section 4 introduces key methods and tools that can be utilized for strategy development, problem solving, measurement, and Lean Six Sigma Logistics implementation. Toward the close of the book, a real-world example is provided as an exercise in critical thinking and problem solving related to Lean Six Sigma Logistics.

As the authors, it is our hope that this book will provide you as a logistics professional with the "golden nugget" for which you have been searching. Whether you have responsibility for a distribution facility or a global supply chain, *Lean Six Sigma Logistics* has much to offer. The same holds true whether you work in the commercial sector, for a nonprofit organization, or for a government entity. At a minimum, we trust that you will learn new principles that can be added to your current operations and strategy. At best, the logistics professional can use the Logistics Bridge Model to design, develop, and implement a comprehensive logistics strategy.

## 2

THE IMPORTANCE OF LOGISTICS AND SUPPLY CHAIN MANAGEMENT

If you were asked to generate a list of the world's best companies — companies that enjoy sustainable growth and healthy margins — which would you include? Would companies like Wal-Mart, Toyota, 3M, and Dell come to mind? How do companies like these somehow manage to stay ahead of the curve, to lead where others must follow? What is it that makes companies like these stand out from the crowd? Is it that their assortment and quality of products clearly outshine those of competitors? Possibly. Is it that they communicate the inherent value of their products better than their competitors? Maybe. Is it that they enjoy considerable channel power and negotiate favorable terms with suppliers? Perhaps. Is it that their supply chains and integrated logistics operations provide distinctive competitive advantage? Definitely. While these pillars of modern-day business achievement provide desired products at a good value to customers, all four have their supply chains to credit for much of their success.

DISCOVERING THE DARK CONTINENT OF LOGISTICS

How is it that logistics and supply chain management can make such a difference? After all, isn't logistics "merely" a company's management of material, product, and information flows in the supply chain? Those who work in the field of logistics recognize the difficulties associated with getting the right product to the right place at the right time in the right quantity and condition at the lowest possible cost. It involves not only a lot of heavy lifting, but also deep thought and decisive action to provide promised service at the lowest cost. Back in 1962, renowned management guru Peter Drucker once referred to logistics as an untapped source of innovation and opportunity, calling it the economy's "dark continent."* Four decades later, logistics management is only somewhat better understood among business practitioners and the general public. It is regarded as an afterthought among many companies, a necessary cost of doing business that has little viable input on corporate strategy. Yet, ask the CEOs of the leading companies noted above what role logistics plays in their enterprises. Excellence in logistics provision not only supports the missions of these companies but, in fact, also serves as a focal point in their very competitiveness. Take Wal-Mart, for instance. How well does its model of "every day low pricing" stand in the absence of cross-docking and economies of scale in transportation, keeping costs below those of rival retailers? And, at the end of the day, what good are "every day low prices" if the products are not on the shelf in sufficient quantity and quality? So, it is not only the low prices but also the exceptional service that differentiates Wal-Mart from rivals.

Too often, companies fail to deliver on the implicit promises that are made to customers. What is worse is when an *explicit* promise is left unfulfilled. Consider the promotional advertisements and fliers that appear in newspapers almost daily. What happens when the retailer promoting the product depletes its inventory? If the retailer is lucky, customers facing the empty shelf will accept a rain check or the promise to accept the order at a later date when inventory is replenished. However, in many instances, the customer knows that he or she can take the promotional flier to a rival store that will honor the deal offered by the first retailer. What might such an experience mean for the future relationship between the retailer and that particular customer? For one thing, the retailer is likely to order greater quantities of product in the future to overcome the stockout situation. However, the customer may not return in the future, knowing that a rival store down the street will honor the deals promoted by the first store. In this instance, the second retailer actually benefits from the promotions of the first store. Meanwhile, what happens when the consumer in question tells a few people about this experience? The impact of that original stockout can be amplified dramatically as others consider similar action in the future, bypassing the promotion-happy retailer in favor of the customer-responsive one. So, simply adding inventory is not the answer but, in fact, is a big step backwards.

---

* Drucker, Peter, The economy's dark continent, *Fortune*, pp. 103–104, April 1962.

Wal-Mart enjoys fewer product stockouts than its competitors not because of higher inventories but because of better inventory management achieved through high-frequency replenishment. Order cycle times (the time from order placement to order delivery) are forty-eight hours or less for U.S. stores, allowing store shelves to be replenished as much as four times faster than competitors. Not only does frequent replenishment of stores support in-stock objectives, but it also provides for "fresher" products. Like availability, the *timeliness* of product delivery have become a key differentiator in many markets. "Freshness" is obviously important for perishable consumer products like fruits, vegetables, dairy products, baked goods, and infant formula, but now it is also commonly advertised as important for products like soft drinks and beer. The waste of obsolete inventory is created when supplies are left unclaimed at the time of their expiration.

To take the concept of timeliness a step further, it is important to get the goods in the hands of customers while the product is in peak demand or "hot." This is especially true of fashion goods or products with very short life cycles. Getting the product to market first can often serve as the make-or-break moment for many products and perhaps the make-or-break moment for entire companies when their future hinges on a critical product introduction. Customer loyalty finds its roots in the first experience that customers enjoy (or despise) with a product and company. Being first to the market with a product or service that meets a previously unmet need offers a way to establish satisfaction that, over time, leads to loyalty. The benefits accrued by having loyal customers are well documented, including openness to new products, interest in collaboration, resistance to competitors' claims, price stability, and lower cost of sales.

Being first to market means having the first crack at being the industry leader. Logistics plays an important role in support of bringing innovative products and services to light. By effectively coordinating material flows with suppliers and managing distribution with intermediaries and customers, the logistics organization can help the company to "make the boat" rather than miss it. Along with a thorough understanding of internal operations, this physical connection to suppliers upstream in the supply chain and customers downstream allows logistics to assume a leadership role in the realm of supply chain management. This relationship is described next.

THIS THING CALLED "SUPPLY CHAIN MANAGEMENT"

Beyond the management of physical inventories and information in the domain of logistics is the way that products are developed, marketed, and sold. Add in the relationships formed with suppliers and customers and you have supply chain management.* When viewed in this light, supply chain management is clearly much more than logistics. This integration of a company's planning and execution functions represents not just a way to achieve efficiencies, but a holistic strategy for doing business.

While much talk has surrounded the concept of supply chain management, very few companies are seizing the potential found in broad-scale adoption. Why? First, the concept of supply chain management is not well understood. Much debate has surrounded the very meaning of the term, with a lack of consensus existing even today. Even the functions that belong in supply chain management have been debated. Another reason supply chain management is not widely practiced is that it is not easy to accomplish. As noted, it involves coordination of planning and operational activities throughout the company as well as coordination of activities with suppliers and customers.

Interestingly, it is often easier to achieve the coordination with *outside* members of the supply chain than within the company. For that reason, companies are often inclined to start with suppliers because they can always tell them what to do! They might even have great success in bringing customers around to their way of thinking, but achieving collaboration among a multitude of functional areas *within* a firm — well, that is another animal entirely! However, to enjoy any big, sustainable gains from supply chain management, a company must first get its own house in order. Supply chain management is about working the levers of a company and getting them in sync with the levers of trading partners in the supply chain. Manipulating the levers of the outside parties will only get you so far, and the gains may not be sustainable if you are unwilling or unable to work the levers within your own four walls. That is why the change must come from within the company first and then transcend to the up- and downstream parties. It is no coincidence that the leaders in supply chain management tend to be companies that have strong cultures that emphasize cohesive, coordinated action. They also tend to be companies that others, including their own suppliers and customers, look toward for leadership, making it viable for integration to occur at the cross-enterprise level.

This cross-enterprise level of integration has been met with much curiosity and skepticism. Some have even speculated that competition will extend beyond horizontal levels in the supply chain. For instance, we may no longer think of soft-drink giants like Coca-Cola and Pepsi competing against one another, but rather Coca-Cola's *supply chain* competing against Pepsi's *supply chain*. That

---

* For an excellent treatment of supply chain management, see Lambert, Douglas M., Ed., *Supply Chain Management: Processes, Partnerships, Performance*, Supply Chain Management Institute, Sarasota, FL, 2004.

proposition holds great bearing on the way in which companies structure relationships with suppliers and customers. While it is unlikely that suppliers serving both beverage makers would choose to serve only one at the loss of the other, there are clearly opportunities to structure a closer, more fruitful relationship with one. A supplier may choose to develop customer-specific ingredients or engage in cooperative promotional efforts with the preferred customer. Therefore, even while inputs might be gathered from the same source, the final product can be differentiated and so can the services provided to that favored customer. When advantage is gained based on the way in which the companies interact, supply chain management is at work.

What is also interesting is that while products can often be duplicated through reverse engineering, relationships are far more difficult to duplicate. Have you ever tried to reverse engineer a relationship? Once the bonds of collaborative effort and shared gains are formed, they can be very difficult to disrupt through simple interloping. So while the challenge is great to get one's own house in order and then extend the ropes of coordinated action to outside parties, the benefits can be even greater. Unfortunately, companies often find themselves tangled in their own ropes.

It is easy to say that a company must first get its own house in order, but, as suggested, this can be the most difficult aspect of supply chain integration. How can a company get on the same page without imploding? Not all companies are blessed with a culture that is driven from top to bottom and end to end by overall company performance. Rather, most companies are driven by functional performance — striving for excellence within each of the various functional areas, like manufacturing, procurement, customer service, finance, and logistics. Clearly, excellence must be achieved throughout the company in order to survive and thrive, but it is *coordinated action* toward a worthy objective that sets really great companies apart from everyone else.

As in life, business is about managing trade-offs. Trade-offs are found not only across the business functions but within each one. For instance, in manufacturing, it is commonly recognized that small batches provide greatest flexibility in accommodating customer demand, yet incur higher per-unit costs of production. So, there is a trade-off found among small and large batches in production. In marketing, small-budget promotions tend to enjoy lesser impact than big-budget promotions, but obviously cost less — another trade-off. Logistics is full of trade-offs. The most commonly held trade-off in logistics is the one between the level of service offered to customers and the cost incurred in providing that service. Occasionally, something comes along that can improve service and reduce costs. Technology advancements are often credited with the creation of these rare but beautiful moments when you can have your cake and eat it too. Lean Six Sigma Logistics can bring about these beautiful moments too, by maximizing the capabilities and balancing their contribution to logistics excellence, leading to overall enterprise success.

Lean Six Sigma Logistics is about capturing the trade-offs present within logistics and between logistics and other functions found in the company. Once you can manage these trade-offs effectively, you have the beginnings of integration at a higher level — supply chain management, where the levers at work in your company match up with the levers at work in trading partner companies. When you do this, you are essentially putting the environment to work in your favor rather than working against it. And it is through this level of coordination that your supply chain can outpace the supply chains of rivals.

In sum, logistics is a necessary function for all companies. No business can live without it. Companies that do not do it well, in fact, threaten their very survival. Companies that recognize and manage the trade-offs by measuring total cost can extend this "systems" thinking to the larger environment, the supply chain in which they operate. In the absence of integrated logistics and total cost perspective, the logistics wastes are inevitable. These wastes are overviewed next.

THE LOGISTICS WASTES

We have all heard the phrase "You can't make something out of nothing." Resources are necessary to accomplish anything great or small, but problems arise from using resources unproductively, applying the wrong resources, failing to tap into necessary resources, or directing resources toward the wrong outputs. In each of these instances, waste is created. Costs are incurred, people's time is consumed, opportunities for value creation and growth are lost, and customers are left less than satisfied.

While much has been said and written about the wastes found in a manufacturing environment, relatively little is mentioned about the wastes in logistics. The wastes in logistics are just as prevalent as in any other functional area of a firm, although they are not always as visible given the scope of logistics activity. In fact, it has been suggested that more than 80 percent of the work of logistics takes place outside the view of supervision, suggesting all the more that precise yet robust processes must be developed for logistics. The next section illustrates the potential wastes found in logistics. The sources of waste in logistics include:

- Inventory
- Transportation

- Space and facilities
- Time
- Packaging
- Administration
- Knowledge

We will discuss each of the wastes in the next section. As you read through each chapter, take personal account of how many of the wastes you recognize in your current business.

SECTION 2.
THE LOGISTICS WASTES

## 3

THE WASTE
OF INVENTORY

LOGISTICS AND INVENTORY MANAGEMENT

Logistics is all about managing inventory, whether the inventory is in motion or sitting, whether it is in a raw state, in process, or completed (finished goods). And true to the cliché noted in Chapter 2, which suggests that you cannot make something out of nothing, you must have inventory to sell anything. The promise to serve a customer cannot be extended assuredly unless the product is on hand or can be made available in a timely manner. The challenge comes when customers demand the product NOW and you have to speculate about what they will want, in what quantities, and where to position it. The imperative, therefore, becomes having inventory available when and where customers want it.

Logistics professionals often recite the "Bill of 'Rights'" when describing what it is that they do: delivering the *right* product to the *right* place at the *right* time in the *right* quantity and condition, and at the *right* cost. Having the *right* inventory on hand and near customers is the simplest way to ensure that they walk away happy. But like anything that is good for you and necessary for survival, it is possible to have too much of a good thing. We all need proper nutrition to survive, yet we also know what too many calories can do to the waistline. Unfortunately, as alluded to in Chapter 1, the strange truth of the matter is that many of us are addicted to inventory. How many plant managers do you know who stash an extra box of parts in their office like a forbidden pack of cigarettes to cover them when a craving becomes too strong? It is an obsession that afflicts more people and companies than you might imagine.

THE TEMPTATION OF INVENTORY

Inventory reduction is the driving force behind many a "Lean" initiative. It is one of the forms of "muda," or waste, originally identified by Taiichi Ohno in his list of seven. Inventory is also perhaps the most visible form of waste.* The fact that we have warehouses and distribution centers is a testament to the fact that we have inventory and, usually, lots of it. Inventory often represents somewhere between 5 and 30 percent of a manufacturer's total assets and may represent half of a retailer's total assets. These estimates are based on end-of-quarter or fiscal year-end observations, when inventories are at their most depleted state for the sake of periodic financial reporting. They may lurk considerably higher over the course of the period. And, like any asset, inventory has to be managed. It has to be acquired, received, housed, paid for, and insured — adding cost on top of the original purchase price for the goods or materials.

So why does it happen so often that we have more inventory than we really need? We hold inventory because in the absence of instantaneous manufacturing and delivery, we have to position inventory in the distribution channel in advance of demand to meet today's "I want it now!" society. Lofty expectations for in-stock availability drive the placement of these inventories not only in retail consumer channels but also in industrial (business-to-business) environments. Until we can achieve instantaneous mass-customized manufacturing and *Star Trek*–like beaming capabilities, the fact is that we must anticipate what customers want, the quantities they want, and where they want them when the expectation of perfect in-stock availability is in place. With this in mind, we make our best guess at demand (i.e., forecast) and acquire supplies in advance to support the expected demand.

The one thing that is absolute about a forecast is that it will be precisely *wrong*. The two important questions are "How wrong will we be?" and "In which direction will we be off — under or over forecast?" Some forces within a company make common practice of keeping the forecast (and ensuing expectations) low in order to beat the forecast, indicating perseverance and goal accomplishment. Others push the forecast higher to justify added capacity or to signal future sales to current and prospective investors. This inventory must

---

* Taiichi Ohno developed a list consisting of seven basic forms of muda: (1) defects in production, (2) overproduction, (3) inventories, (4) unnecessary processing, (5) unnecessary movement of people, (6) unnecessary transport of goods, and (7) waiting by employees. Womack and Jones added to this list with the muda of goods and services that fail to meet the needs of customers. (Sources: Ohno, Taiichi, *The Toyota Production System: Beyond Large-Scale Production,* Productivity Press, Portland, OR, 1988 and Womack, James P. and Jones, David T., *Lean Thinking,* Simon & Schuster, New York, 1996.)

often be sold off at discount, disposed of, or maintained until inventories eventually become depleted.

Many companies realize that working within a shorter planning horizon holds several important benefits. First, it allows a company to rely less on the long-range forecast, which we all know will inevitably be wrong. By relying less on the forecast and more on actual demand, we can reduce the risk of miscalculating the future and, in turn, hold less inventory. The shorter planning horizon also supports more frequent replenishment and smaller lot sizes, which should translate into fresher products available for customers and less risk of obsolescence.

When demand is highly seasonal, we often must engage in long-range planning, buying materials and producing products well in advance of the peak season, given an economic inability to make everything necessary to satisfy the seasonal spike in the immediate term. Still others concern themselves little with the fact that continuous, large-batch production leads to excess inventory. In many process industries like petroleum refining and paper milling, shutting down the machines is the equivalent of shutting down the ocean; you just cannot do it. Achieving the lowest per-unit production cost is still the single highest priority in many industries today. This mind-set also leads many companies and entire industries to seek offshore manufacturing activity to reduce production costs.

That speaks to the normal scope of business activity, but what about when something strange happens in supply or demand? Imagine an unplanned plant shutdown at a key supplier. Imagine all of the ports along the western coast of the United States being closed for an indefinite time period. Imagine the delivery truck that gets slowed by inclement weather or stuck in traffic or the driver who simply gets lost. Unfortunately, it does not take a wild imagination to conjure up these images; they can happen at any time to any company. And what about something positive like the new product that really soars into the marketplace, exceeding anyone's "realistic" sales expectations? Or what about the sales promotion that really had traction? Demand, too, can surprise us. And so we hold extra inventory to cover us in these situations when an unexpected hiccup occurs in a supply chain process or demand exceeds the forecast. What is interesting is that we NEVER expect to use the safety stock; if we did, it would be factored in the planned cycle stock.

These occurrences represent the many different ways in which variance manifests. It is the goal of Six Sigma to control the variation, to improve supply chain processes so that the job gets done better on a consistent basis. Six Sigma also captures the experience and expectations of the customer, reducing the likelihood of developing products and services that are inconsistent with market wants and needs, but also alleviating the risk of being caught off guard when a product tanks or skyrockets. Those companies that engage in offshore manu-facturing experience the brunt of these swings even more when they send their operations away from the home market, often moving operations away from not only the customer but also away from the predominant supply base. While production costs most definitely can be reduced through this action, most companies have learned that offshore manufacturing leads to an entirely differ-ent set of problems in the supply chain: variances. Variances in inbound and outbound logistics and variances in production control areas such as quality, quantity, and time make many question whether it was worth the leap. All these variances instill greater need for inventory.

Extra inventory is sometimes acquired for reasons other than protection from supply chain disruptions and demand spikes. Companies in many industries take on inventory for speculative purposes given the possibility that supplies might come into shortage or that price increases are on the horizon. Scrap recyclers, for instance, make a necessary habit of acquiring high-quality scrap materials whenever they become available. Dealers of limited-edition automobiles and other collectibles engage in similar *opportunistic* buying. Meanwhile, commod-ity dealers like those in the oil and gas industry, precious metals, and grain marketing keep close eyes on the futures market, with the prospect of arbitrage (buy low now, sell high later) driving their purchasing behavior.

THE COSTS OF HOLDING INVENTORY

Regardless of the reason, what companies have to realize is that there are very real costs associated with holding all inventory. The costs go well beyond the outlay of the inventory "investment." We will review the elements of inventory carrying cost that should be applied to the value of average inventory to de-termine the annual dollar cost of holding inventory (see Figure 3.1).

Inventory carrying costs serve up an interesting concept, representing both accounting costs and economic costs. An "accounting cost" is one that is ex-plicit and calls for a cash outlay and registers on the books of the company. An "economic cost" is implicit; it does not necessarily involve an outlay, but rather an opportunity cost. Most companies recognize that there is *some* cost associated with holding inventory and apply a round figure to the problem of determining carrying cost, but there is rarely any idea of where that figure originated. Too often, a company's inventory carrying cost percentage is deter-mined every great while and rarely understood, and even less commonly chal-lenged. This lack of understanding and reluctance to challenge the carrying cost percentage often results in gross miscalculation in determining annual inventory

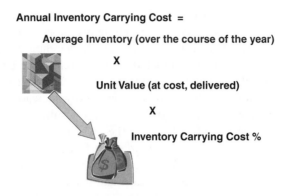

Annual Inventory Carrying Cost =

Average Inventory (over the course of the year)

X

Unit Value (at cost, delivered)

X

Inventory Carrying Cost %

Figure 3.1. Inventory Carrying Cost Calculation.

carrying costs, usually erring on the side of *underestimation*. Let's tackle the problem by examining the key components of the carrying cost percentage.

The single biggest factor is the opportunity cost of consuming capital on the hunch of future demand and supply events. So, aside from having $300,000, $3 million, or $300 million invested in inventory, what else could you do with that amount of capital if it were not tied up in inventory? This cost of capital component is the single largest piece of inventory carrying cost. Most companies simply apply the debt rate (cost of acquiring capital) for this component, but that implies that paying off debt is the best (and perhaps only) alternative for those funds. Keep in mind that inventory carrying cost should reflect the opportunity cost of the capital. The hurdle rate, or internal rate of return, at most companies easily exceeds the market-based cost of capital, and this hurdle rate (or weighted average cost of capital) should be the figure applied to the cost-of-capital component of the carrying cost percentage.*

The fact that inventory is viewed by the IRS and many state governments as taxable assets means that you must also apply the applicable property tax rates in the carrying cost percentage. And don't forget to tack on the insurance rate paid to provide coverage against loss or damage to the assets. Along the same lines, factor in the rates of product obsolescence, damage, and pilferage. Highly valuable products that seem to vanish more commonly than other goods will have a higher cost attached to them than lesser valued goods that are rarely pilfered — not that low-value goods are never picked over.

---

* For an excellent treatment of inventory carrying cost determination, see Stock, James R. and Lambert, Douglas M., *Strategic Logistics Management,* 4th ed., McGraw-Hill Higher Education, New York, 2001.

Finally, there is a component for the variable cost of storage. This component refers to the costs associated with handling inventory and variable storage costs such as those associated with hiring outside warehouses to hold excess inventory. The trick here is *not* to include fixed warehousing costs (costs that do not change with the volume of inventory maintained), but to include only those costs that increase as the volume of inventory increases. So, the fixed costs tied to the company-owned distribution center or the plant warehouse are not reflected here. These are fixed storage (i.e., warehousing) costs that should be determined in total logistics cost, but distinct from inventory carrying cost. In sum, the variable costs of warehousing belong in the inventory carrying cost component, while the fixed costs of storage and handling belong in the "warehousing" costs in a total cost analysis. The components of inventory carrying cost are summarized in Figure 3.2.

Along with challenging the carrying cost determination is the prospect of doing so frequently. Inventory carrying cost should be dynamic, as dynamic as a company's business opportunities. As a company's expected rate of return on new investments evolves, so too must the inventory carrying cost percentage. The percentage determined at one point in time should not be held in such

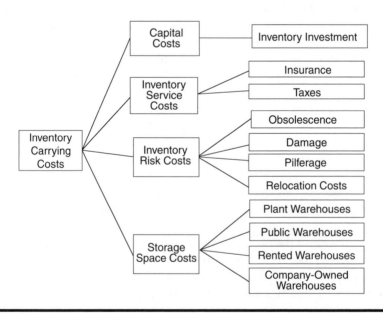

Figure 3.2.   What Costs Go into Inventory Carrying Cost? (Adapted from Lambert, Douglas M., *The Development of an Inventory Costing Methodology: A Study of the Costs Associated with Holding Inventory,* National Council of Physical Distribution Management, 1976, p. 68. Diagram courtesy of the Council of Supply Chain Management Professionals [CSCMP], Oak Brook, IL.)

regard that it cannot be questioned over time and revisited. Inventory carrying cost is not likely to change dramatically within the course of a year, but should always reflect the reality of the company's changing cost conditions and investment opportunities.

Once you have a better handle on what it is really costing you to hold inventory, interest should turn to how sales can be maximized with the least amount of inventory. All other things being equal, you should try to cover demand by ordering smaller quantities more frequently from your supply sources, thus achieving more inventory turns. "Inventory turns" refers to the number of times each year that average inventory sells. The number of turns is usually determined based on the value of average inventory and the sales volume at cost, expressed mathematically as:

Inventory turns = (Sales volume at cost)/(Value of average inventory)

Achieving more turns means that you are holding less inventory, on average, while presumably fulfilling demand (see Figure 3.3). Clearly, having no inventory on hand when demand surfaces is not a good situation, although it can make average inventory levels and inventory turns look appealing. Rather, the model for frequent, small-quantity replenishment that more closely matches demand is the method for keeping customers happy with less inventory: improving turns.

A key question is "How many turns are enough?" Many companies will benchmark their competitors and companies in similar industries to gauge how many turns they should achieve in their distribution network. But like inventory

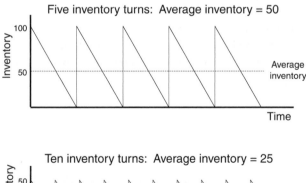

Figure 3.3. Inventory Turns and Average Inventory.

carrying cost percentages, the desired number of turns is unique to a company. In fact, a company's inventory carrying cost percentage and estimations of annual inventory carrying cost will factor into the decision. While achieving many turns suggests that average inventory is minimal and yet customers remain satisfied, the costs associated with shipping in smaller quantities and handling more orders (albeit smaller orders, on average) can offset the savings achieved in frequent, small-order replenishment and high inventory turns. So, again, there is a limit to a good thing. Finding this limit is the mandate of total cost analysis — understanding the trade-offs among logistics-related cost and service factors.

Companies can sometimes get carried away with pursuit of a singular objective that leads to suboptimal performance of the larger system, leading to dissatisfied customers, higher total cost, or both. A case in point was an aftermarket automotive supplier that devised the goal of replenishing its customers on a much more frequent basis than the typical once-a-week arrangement with which it had been conducting business for several years. The goal was established to provide daily replenishment to large customers and every-other-day service to smaller ones. While the customers were pleased with the prospect of more frequent deliveries and higher in-stock availability with less inventory, they were less enthusiastic about the mounting transportation costs required to support the frequent, small-quantity deliveries. In fact, it was determined that at the proposed level of delivery frequency, inventory savings and in-stock improvements would not offset the increase in transportation costs.

So while some level of inventory is necessary for meeting near-term demand and providing coverage for critical disruption or unforeseeable spikes, the focal problem becomes one of "right-sizing" the inventory. How much do we really need? Can we see through our addiction and hold only what is necessary? Recognizing the volume of inventory that supports customer requirements yet results in the lowest total cost represents the desired outcome. Putting an accurate price tag on the cost of carrying inventory is an important element of the solution.

## 4

THE WASTE OF TRANSPORTATION

LOGISTICS AND TRANSPORTATION MANAGEMENT

Transportation, like inventory, is a necessary activity within logistics. In fact, it is fundamental to allow us to make product in one place and consume it in another, closing the distance of geographic separation. Fast, efficient transportation explains a great deal about why cities develop where they do. See the U.S. western expansion for a history lesson on the pivotal role of transportation in economic development. Can you name the largest U.S. city *not* located along a river, lake, or ocean?*

Transportation represents the biggest single cost in logistics. About $600 billion is spent each year on transportation in the United States alone. That is just over 5 percent of U.S. gross domestic product or five cents out of every dollar spent in the United States. The vast majority (almost 83 percent) of those dollars spent on transportation are directed toward motor transportation (i.e., trucking) services.** The rest is consumed by rail, maritime, air, and pipeline services, with each mode catering to shipping customers' specific needs for speed, timeliness, reliability, flexibility, availability, safety, capacity, and cost efficiency. Companies dedicate about half of total logistics cost to transporting materials and goods in support of these objectives. Trucking excels relative to the other modes in flexibility, reliability, and availability, which explains why it represents the shippers' preferred mode.

---

 * Answer: Lexington, Kentucky (population: 260,512, according to 2000 U.S. Census).
 ** Wilson, Rosalyn, *15th Annual State of Logistics Report: Globalization,* Council of Logistics Management, Oak Brook, IL, 2004.

Not only is transportation a big cost consideration, but the time that goods find themselves in transit represents a big component of order lead time and can be a major contributor to variance in order cycle time. Again, in the absence of "teleportation" or the *Star Trek* beam, it takes time to move product from one place to another. And as alluded to in our discussion of why we hold buffer inventories, there is a host of reasons why shipments can be delayed: late pickups, equipment failure, driver failure, inclement weather, and traffic congestion, among endless possibilities. Despite these mounting challenges, there is decidedly less patience for failure and inability to meet on-time delivery commitments today.

The goal of a Six Sigma initiative in transportation might be to minimize the average time to move the goods and to minimize the variation around that average. Figure 4.1 shows that the *average time* should decrease, as should the *frequency* of occurrences around this new average. It should also be noted that the distribution curves in the figure are not perfectly normal, or bell-shaped, curves. Rather, they have a definite minimum (one day) and an open-ended right tail. In particular, we should concern ourselves with the right tail of the frequency distribution, or the events in which transit time exceeds the average. We should be particularly concerned about those observations that have very long transits in excess of the average (some apparently never reach the destination), as depicted by the first curve. It is in these instances that we miss delivery windows and cause our customers to lose faith in our ability to serve them, leading to more inventory to buffer against our unreliability.

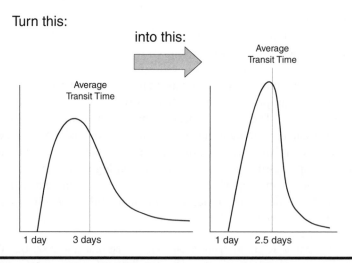

Figure 4.1.   Faster, More Reliable Transportation Is the Goal.

So while transportation is necessary to support our ability to make product in one place and sell it in another, there is inherent waste in the way most companies deploy and employ transportation assets. Waste is found in having many more assets required to cover transportation demand and in using the existing assets unproductively.

TRANSPORTATION AND LOGISTICS TRADE-OFFS

As indicated, transportation consumes well over half of a company's total logistics costs. Given that it is such a "big-ticket" cost, many companies try to minimize it with little or no regard to other related costs. This inclination is also pushed along by the fact that transportation cost is among the easier costs to tabulate, especially if a company hires out for most or all of its transportation services. One must only add up the freight bills over the course of the year to determine the annual freight expenditure. So, the cost is very big and very visible. In addition, transportation is often viewed as a nonvalue-added activity, a necessary evil associated with making here and selling there. And that is why so many companies place the mandate on the traffic manager to reduce the freight expense year after year.

Unfortunately, when the traffic manager is not accountable for other logistics-related costs, it is easy to cut costs in transportation only to see other expenses spring like leaks in a dam. Lower cost carriers might be lower cost carriers for good reason — outdated equipment, poorly trained drivers, underinsured provisions. And these reasons often lead to unreliable service and the late deliveries characteristic of transportation variance. In the wake of these issues, you have unsatisfied (if not irate) customers and cost recourses in inventory, warehousing, and administration as you try to correct all the ill will created by service failures and unfulfilled promises. Yet these costs are not as visible and, therefore, are less easily managed. So, the mandate comes down to the traffic manager yet again: Cut another 3 percent from last year's transportation expenditure. And the unfortunate cycle continues.

Along with understanding the "big picture" cost trade-offs is the systems approach to management, with recognition of total network optimization. A company's logistics network is composed of its inbound and outbound links. These links represent the company's connections with suppliers and customers (see Figure 4.2). Oftentimes, companies will only concern themselves with the outbound flow of materials, leaving inbound management in the hands of suppliers or production planners in the company. Suppliers are frequently glad to provide this service and will either: (1) embed the cost of freight in the cost of materials and refer to transportation as "free" (FOB destination), (2) include transporta-

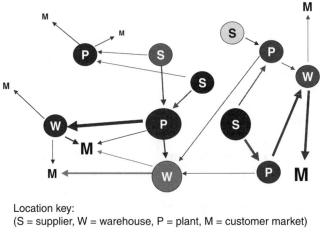

Location key:
(S = supplier, W = warehouse, P = plant, M = customer market)

Figure 4.2. Links and Nodes in a Network Map.

tion as a separate line item on the invoice (the supplier negotiates service and pays for it directly, or FOB destination paid and billed back), or (3) has the transportation service billed directly to the customer (FOB origin-collect).

Regardless of who pays the carrier, customers should rest assured that freight is *never* "free." In fact, it can be a convenient way to embed price increases, enhancing the supplier's margins. As a result, more companies are taking control of their inbound transportation flows and assuming the costs directly. However, the best solution is for the party that has the best contracts with carriers (probably based on volume) and the party that can best operate over a specific lane to negotiate the service. But freight should not be used as a means to cover inefficiencies in a supplier's operations.

Another temptation that many shippers face is the urge to locate the lowest spot-market price for each and every shipment. The Internet has fostered this temptation with the emergence of electronic transportation marketplaces (ETMs). These marketplaces were the darlings of many a venture capitalist in the early 2000s and promised that transportation capacity could be traded like a share on the commodities exchange. What the ETMs failed to realize, though, was that most shippers did not view transportation as a commodity service; it is too important and exposes the shipper to too many risks when service is negotiated in a faceless transaction.* Shippers wisely search for long-term relationships rather than flip though the matchmaking dating services that characterize most

---

* Goldsby, Thomas J. and Eckert, James A., Electronic transportation marketplaces: a transaction cost perspective, *Industrial Marketing Management*, 32(3), 187–198, 2003.

public transportation exchanges. Finding the lowest priced transportation service often leads to wastes in the form of inventory and extra action required to satisfy disappointed customers.

TRANSPORTATION CARRIER RELATIONSHIPS

Shippers are realizing that carriers should be part of the solution and not a source of problems. In order to make carriers part of the solution, you cannot afford to deal with literally hundreds or even thousands of carriers. Rather, shippers select a limited number of carriers to provide for all of the company's transportation needs. By putting the business in the hands of a few "core" carriers, the shipper earns volume discounts from the carriers. The shipper should also receive higher priority service in return for the commitment of higher volumes. It is like enjoying the benefits of frequent-flyer programs and other loyalty incentives. This concept of reduction in carrier base exemplifies the tenet of complexity reduction found in Six Sigma.*

Routing guides should be developed for all shipping locations so that shipping personnel understand the order in which they are to contact carriers in search of service. A well-monitored routing guide can minimize the misjudgment and "maverick" buying of transportation services that still exists in transportation, even today. So, not only is developing a routing guide important, but so is regular monitoring to ensure compliance.

Beyond relying on fewer carriers is the prospect of working closely with a very select few. Many shippers are finding value in partnering with carriers, identifying opportunities for mutual benefit and sharing the gains of the effort. Shippers that partner with a carrier become the preferred customer of the carrier and should receive highest priority when capacity is crunched. In addition, efforts to save the carrier money and the commitment of volume should result in favorable rate negotiations. In return, the carrier is better able to plan capacity, design efficient routes, and schedule assets and drivers more effectively. In the end, however, both parties must gain from the closer relationship. It is shortsighted for one party to win at the expense of the other and does not reflect true partnership.

Yet another possibility is to incorporate carriers into the collaborative relationship your company might have with a supplier or customer. Too often, trading partners work closely with one another only to leave the intermediaries

---

* For an excellent treatment of complexity reduction in services, see George, Michael L., *Lean Six Sigma: Combining Six Sigma Quality with Lean Production Speed*, McGraw-Hill, New York, 2002.

(like carriers and third-party logistics service providers) in the dark, forcing them to speculate about the business transpiring between the seller and buyer of the goods. A prime example comes to us from the relationships forged between consumer goods manufacturers and merchandisers in Collaborative Planning, Forecasting, and Replenishment (CPFR®) programs. CPFR® is a nine-step process that embodies several opportunities for the manufacturer and merchandiser to get on the same page — developing a common forecast for items of interest, scheduling promotions, and synchronizing operations.* At the end of the nine-step process, an order is generated. However, the process stops there. There is no before-the-fact coordination with the service provider. As a result, the service provider must continue to anticipate (i.e., guess) the demands of the manufacturer-merchandiser business and acquire capacity to cover the peaks of the anticipated volume, buying excess capacity — a critical waste. Collaborative transportation management promises to reduce this problem by bringing the service provider into the collaboration.**

MINIMIZING THE DAY-TO-DAY WASTES IN TRANSPORTATION

Once the logistics network and carrier arrangements are optimized, focus turns to managing the individual shipments. Inefficiencies and waste are rooted in the poor utilization of equipment, operators, and a host of other limited resources found in transportation operations. There is, in fact, a strong correlation between sound operations at the ground level and sound management of network-wide resources. Properly utilized assets will dampen the requirement for additional assets. However, many companies fail to recognize opportunities for load consolidation that can save money and improve service.

One prime example is found in shipping multiple less-than-truckload (LTL) shipments in the same direction at any point in time. Consider, for instance, the shipments shown in Figure 4.3. Let's assume that each shipment consists of a single pallet weighing 1,200 pounds. The natural decision might be to contact an LTL carrier to handle each of the single-pallet shipments. Each shipment would be charged separately and require multiple handlings as the loads are

---

* An overview of CPFR® can be found on-line at http://www.vics.org/committees/cpfr/ CPFR_Overview_US-A4.pdf.
** Sutherland, Joel, Goldsby, Thomas J., and Stank, Theodore P., Leveraging collaborative transportation management (CTM) principles to achieve superior supply chain performance, in *Achieving Supply Chain Excellence Through Technology*, Vol. 6, Montgomery Research, San Francisco, 2004, pp. 192–196.

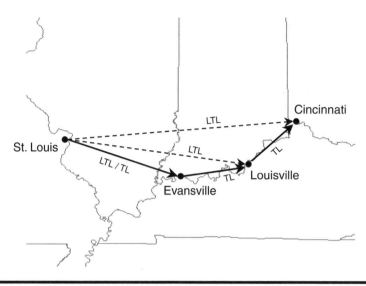

Figure 4.3. LTL Shipping Versus Consolidated Truckloads.

picked up and delivered to the St. Louis terminal for sorting. A line-haul vehicle might then transport each shipment to its respective destination terminal, where the shipment would be sorted yet again for local delivery. These sortings and resortings take time and introduce the potential for damage that comes with each handling of the freight.

In contrast, the three shipments could be combined and picked up by a truckload carrier. A single rate would be negotiated for line-haul service to Cincinnati (the final destination) with intermediate stops in Evansville and Louisville. Granted, stopoff charges will be allocated to the Evansville and Louisville stops and time will be consumed in getting off the interstate highway to complete these deliveries, but as long as the stops are not markedly out of route and the wait to unload is reasonable, it is likely that the Cincinnati delivery can take place sooner with the truckload carrier, with less potential for damage due to rehandling, and at a lower cost for the three combined shipments. The obvious challenge with load consolidations is the coordination of loads such that all three customers will be ready to accept the load as scheduled, and then to deliver consistent with schedule.

Transportation managers will take advantage of these opportunities for cost savings and service improvements if they are rewarded for identifying opportunities and acting on them. Unfortunately, many organizations continue to eye the big-dollar spend on transportation as an isolated entity without recognizing the trade-offs and service implications of reducing the spend. One must keep in mind that buying the cheapest freight service does not typically translate into lowest total cost; nor does reducing the total spend on transportation services necessarily lead to that outcome. For example, when lowest system cost is the metric, it may involve paying for premium service to reduce the sum of all related costs in logistics. The key is to "right-size" transportation resources for the needs of the organization. There is a whole host of *time-* and *administration-related* wastes found in transportation. These wastes will be described in subsequent chapters.

## 5

THE WASTE OF SPACE AND FACILITIES

LOGISTICS AND WAREHOUSING

Like transportation, warehousing has played a central part in the development of commerce and trade among distant locations. Given the interest and ability to acquire materials and build products in advance of demand, one understandably needs facilities to ensure the integrity and value of materials and goods. But today's warehouses are seemingly regarded as modern-day, high-tech temples. They are often located on prime real estate and positioned adjacent to infrastructure for multiple modes of transportation. They are loaded with automated storage and retrieval systems, literally miles of computer-controlled conveyors, reconfigurable walls for that impending expansion, and warehouse management systems to coordinate the activity within the walls of the facility. Have you ever met distribution center managers for these newfangled facilities? They describe the buildings and contents gushingly and beam like proud parents.

But all of the bragging rights come with a very real, significant cost. By the time you factor in the property, the infrastructure for roads and utilities, the high-tech equipment, and information systems, you are well into the tens of millions of dollars — if not over $100 million — all before moving a single box. Add the operating and maintenance costs to this sum and now you are looking at eye-popping figures. And that is for a single warehouse facility. What if you are running dozens of these facilities throughout your market?

Think back to why you have these facilities in the first place. They offer a place to store inventory, maybe months and months of inventory. Warehouses often serve as museums, housing collections of relics from bygone demand. If there is an addiction to inventory, then warehouses serve as the accomplice. They give us a place to stash the goods to cover our craving for inventory. And while each additional facility should reduce the average distance between ourselves and our customers, often little or no value is added to products while they are stored in a warehouse. In fact, products become susceptible to the losses and damage described in the discussion of inventory carrying costs (see Chapter 3). It has been estimated that half of all activities performed in the warehouse do not add value or lead to customer satisfaction while they all consume valuable resources. And more inventory does not necessarily translate into better service. As Taiichi Ohno once noted, the more inventory you have, the less likely you are to have what you need.

It is likely that you are stocking assortments that do not necessarily match the needs of customers. Even if you should have what you need, it can prove difficult to find it when the facility is brimming with inventory. In an extreme example, the U.S. Army has long sought passive radio frequency identification technology to resolve the challenges it faces in deploying assets and materiel, particularly in combat theaters. Imagine the challenge of finding critical supplies among the thousands of shipping containers that serve as mobile warehouses when the Army sets up shop in the desert. Product tracking information is either inaccurate or lacking entirely. Logistics personnel must literally pry open the containers to identify contents when trying to fulfill a "hot" requisition. All the while, field personnel file additional, redundant requisitions in an effort to ensure that the original need gets satisfied, creating even more inventory at the theater distribution center and more confusion.

The Army example speaks to yet another paradox in warehousing. If a warehouse runs inefficiently, what tends to be the result? More warehouses! Whether caused by confusion in the warehouse, poor picking practices, or damage-inducing storage and handling, warehouse activities that result in less than perfect execution will be covered by service recovery efforts and additional inventory — more work for the underperforming logistics network and the facilities that make it up. Though the root cause of these problems is found in poor process design and execution, the most common fix is the "inventory solution" and, hence, not only more inventory carrying cost but more warehousing space.

HOW MANY FACILITIES? HOW MUCH SPACE?

Most companies, however, could not imagine living without a safety blanket of one or more warehouses. The common conundrum faced by growing companies is to determine how many facilities and how much total square footage are needed to cover current and future demand volumes. This determination is further challenged by the erratic seasonality and cyclical nature of most businesses. Do we build enough space and enough facilities to cover all of the possible eventualities? Many companies rely on a mix of private and public facilities to cover their needs. Those companies that have private warehouses often operate under the misconception that storing product in a company-owned facility is "free." We know this is not true. While the fixed costs do not change regardless of volume stored, many costs of warehouse operations will vary with volume. Hence, the more product handled, the higher these variable costs mount. And, again, the fixed costs are incurred whether the facility is fully utilized, partially utilized, or not utilized at all.

A related misconception is that facility utilization is a good indicator of warehouse performance. Too often, metrics like utilization guide the wrong behavior. In other words, utilization is mistaken for efficiency. A warehouse filled with inventory that may or may not face any immediate demand can hardly be regarded as a success. Likewise, productivity alone is a poor indicator of efficiency. Measuring warehouse picker productivity with no check on quality, such as picker error or damage, is similarly shortsighted. Doing the wrong things very well or quickly will only prove wasteful and self-defeating.

To add insult to injury, many public and third-party warehouse companies charge their customers on the basis of not only how much square footage they "consume" in the warehouse, but also how many touches they place on the inventory. A "touch" might be defined as a value-added activity such as labeling, packaging, kitting, or something as innocuous (nonvalue adding) as repositioning inventory in the facility — all activities that consume resources and add costs but not necessarily any value.

ARE ADVANCED TECHNOLOGIES A CURE OR MERELY A CRUTCH?

Among those engaging in company-owned warehousing, many are calling on automated handling equipment to improve the speed, efficiency, and accuracy of warehouse picking and putaway activities. But automation must be entered into cautiously, for it only further cements the relationship between the company and the facility. Automated warehouses can be considerably more difficult to offload than basic storage facilities because of the many nuances presented by the automation. In fact, the automation tends to specialize the facility given that most automation is designed to accommodate product within a narrow band of shapes and sizes. Therefore, to enjoy a reasonable return on the investment, a company looking to offload an automated facility must find a prospective tenant with similar handling and storage needs.

Therefore, a company is forced to either ensure a quick payback on the investment or have a much longer outlook when adopting automation. Even if the company decides to keep the facility for an extended period of time and the product lines stored in the facility remain unchanged, it can still be difficult to assume that the technology will serve its prescribed purpose long enough for complete payback on the investment.

A case in point is sometimes found when companies invest in high-rise automated storage and retrieval system (AS/RS) technology. This equipment usually improves the speed and accuracy of putaway and picking operations dramatically, as long as the order profiles demanded by the customers are consistent with the technology's picking capabilities. For instance, consider the company that buys the pallet-load AS/RS given that retail customers order in full-pallet volumes. However, what happens when retailers decide to order in ways that require mixed-pallet assortments and place orders on a more frequent basis? Automation struggles to accommodate these configurations, forcing human labor to convert the full pallets to the mixed assortments consistent with the retailers' orders, thereby diminishing much of the efficiency advantage provided by the automated equipment.

The bottom line is that materials handling equipment used to facilitate warehousing operations must be viewed in the same light as the facility itself. If we do not need the inventory, then we do not need the warehouse and, in turn, do not need the warehouse equipment. We must question whether the facility is covering up inefficiencies in logistics operations or if it is providing false comfort to customers.

When and where warehouse functionality is needed, one must examine if a cross-dock facility can serve the purpose rather than a conventional storage facility. Regardless of the facility used, it must observe Lean Six Sigma Logistics principles to avoid the considerable waste that can be generated at any single location. When determining how many locations are needed, the decision should not be made on a location-by-location basis, but rather from a system-wide point of reference.

6

THE WASTE OF TIME

LOGISTICS AND TIME WASTES

Of all of the resources found in life and in logistics, none is more important than time. As in the adage, it is the only resource you can never reclaim. Time is also among the most important metrics found in logistics. We measure ourselves against order lead times and whether deliveries are ultimately "on time." Both aspects can support competitive advantage when provided on a faster, more reliable basis than competitors.

To understand how time can be wasted in logistics, we must examine the order cycle — the time that elapses from order transmission to order delivery. The five distinct steps of the order cycle are illustrated in Figure 6.1, including (1) order transmission, (2) order processing, (3) order filling, (4) order staging and verification, and (5) order shipping and delivery. Each step requires some allotment of time to complete, and each step experiences variance around the typical time allotment. When variance is found in the right tail of the frequency distribution (i.e., when it takes longer than the typical time to complete a task), then a waste of time is observed. The waste can be rooted in poor performance within the step or because of error/miscalculation in another step of the order cycle. A walk through these five steps outlines the many opportunities for waste of time found in the order cycle.

Order Transmission

Nothing happens in logistics until an order is received. While you can plan for anticipated business and position inventory, the actual order commences action. Most logistics thought and energy is centered on preparation for customer

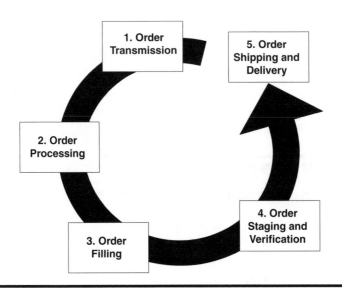

Figure 6.1. The Order Cycle.

orders and execution once received. Clearly, the quicker the supplier can receive the order from the customer, the sooner action can initiate and the sooner the order can be filled and delivered.

Conventional methods of communication can make order transmission a time-consuming stage in the order cycle. Take, for instance, an order transmitting over the phone between a customer's purchasing agent and a supplier's customer service representative. The purchasing agent must first find the opportunity to initiate the call at a time at which someone is likely to be at the other end to accept it. While most major companies provide 24/7/365 customer service availability, it remains far from universal. For that reason, the call might be confined to the overlap in the hours of operation for both the customer and supplier. A customer on the U.S. east coast may have to delay an early-morning call until the west-coast supplier is open for business. Likewise, a west-coast customer may have to wait until the following day if the late-afternoon order is after hours for an east-coast supplier. The problem can be even further exacerbated when international time zones and norms for doing business are involved.

Other conventional modes of communication suffer similar delays. Fax transmission remains a fairly common means for transmitting orders. This requires the customer to write up the purchase order, find an available fax machine, and transmit to an open fax line at the supplier. Technically, the order must then be printed at the supplier's location and delivered to the hands of a customer service representative who can act on it. Sounds simple enough, but have you ever waited for a fax that is ninth in the print queue? Have you ever failed to verify that there is actually paper in the fax machine? Some of the most basic forms of communication are prone to these disruptions, not to mention the inability to decipher somebody's handwriting, which calls for either guesswork or a follow-up phone call. While phone and fax communications can paint the picture of potential time lags, consider the fact that some companies still rely on conventional, postal mail ("snail mail") as the means for communicating orders. Little imagination is necessary to dream up the potential for long order transmission times and variability with this mode.

Electronic modes of communication have made order transmission virtually instantaneous. Electronic data interchange (EDI) has been hailed over the past few decades for its ability to facilitate communications between a customer's computer and a supplier's computer without human intervention and the error and variability inherent in human activity. However, many users of EDI rely on value-added networks (VANs) that charge a fee for each transmission. In order to economize the transmissions, VAN users often rely on batch processing of communications, where they send and receive information perhaps only once or twice a day. While batching provides transmission efficiencies, it clearly eliminates the advantage of timely delivery. Plus, EDI systems are not completely free from disruptions.

Many companies have sought on-line methods for communicating orders. The World Wide Web offers many of the same time advantages associated with EDI, but is a much more cost-effective means given that all you need is a personal computer and access to a shared public infrastructure (the so-called "information superhighway"). Most Web-based communications, however, serve effectively as automated phone conversations. Someone must key in the order and click "send," and someone must be at the other end to receive it. It is still relatively rare for a customer's inventory and purchasing system to communicate with a supplier's automatic order entry system. People generally remain involved in the process, hence leading to the same delays introduced in the human-performed methods above.

Order Processing

Once an order is received, it must undergo a screening process. The supplying company will concern itself with two things before agreeing to fill an order. First, is it *willing* to fill the order? That is, does the order come from a customer to which the company has provided service in the past? If so, was that experience good? Was payment received in full and on time? If the experience was not good, is the company willing to risk another potentially bad transaction? Are the terms of the transaction agreeable? The sales organization will typically provide answers to these questions, ultimately providing an assessment of willingness to serve the customer.

The second aspect the supplier will consider is its *ability* to fill the order: Does the company have the goods? If so, where? If not, how long will it take to fill the order and is the customer willing to wait? The logistics organization will interface with sales to determine whether or not the company can satisfy the order in a manner consistent with customer expectations of timely delivery and order completeness. Customer service policies should be established to provide a quick reference to customer expectations and the company's ability to serve.

While the determination of willingness and ability can be a rather involved process, many companies have automated these decisions with order management systems that can provide instantaneous consideration of all relevant factors and immediate order acceptance/rejection. However, where such technology does not exist, this process can take several days (even weeks) as the order information is shuffled among sales, customer service, logistics, and accounting, among other functional departments at the supplier company. It can prove impossible to follow the paper and phone trail that is left behind when order processing is organized haphazardly. And by the time such a process is finally completed, the customer may no longer have need for or interest in the order. Also, given the many opportunities for error in order processing, it is possible that the time and energy will be wasted when mistakes are made.

Order Filling

Assuming that a company finally determines a willingness and ability to serve, the order process finally moves into action when the order is communicated to the appropriate stockkeeping location and order filling commences. This is the step in which ordered items are gathered from the bins and shelves of the warehouse. As pointed out in the previous discussion of storage and facilities, these activities are sometimes laden with delay, disruption, and error — all of which leads to extended order lead times and prevents "perfect order" execution.

"Getting the job done right the first time" is the mantra of most warehouse operations, but it is much easier said than done. Poor organization of the warehouse, careless putaway and picking operations, poor training of warehouse employees, and inadequate information exchange are among the countless reasons why order fill operations can fall short of expectations. These problems result in increased order lead time, order variance, and growing frustration among customers, for in the customer's mind, the clock placed on the order does not stop ticking until complete satisfaction is ultimately rendered.

A lack of clear guidelines for dealing with problem situations can also prove costly. For instance, what is the rule for shipping an incomplete order (an order that is lacking some portion of the items requested by a customer)? Does the partial order get shipped and the remainder dismissed or backordered? Or does the order get held up until all items can be gathered? Perhaps the partial order is shipped separately from an order composed of the missing items from another facility. Is the same procedure used for all customers, or are you willing to jump a little higher and run a little faster for your "A" customers? This example simply points to the need to have a standard process for dealing with the inevitable events that impair "normal" warehouse operations. Knowing how to deal with these situations can be just as important as providing solid performance for ordinary business. Though customers might label all orders as "critical," some are clearly more critical than others, and these can be deal breakers in the modern competitive environment where the customer has alternatives from which to choose.

Order Staging and Verification

Once an order is gathered, responsibility often shifts from the order-picking crew to the shipping clerk. The shipping clerk will review the picked contents to ensure that they match with the order and prepare the bill of lading for shipping. Clearly, greater discrepancy between what is ordered and what is actually picked in the order fill activity will lead to greater effort and time expended to identify discrepancies and rectify them. In fact, when pickers are held fully accountable for what is picked and are given the ability to communicate discrepancies (e.g., shortages, substitutes), then the distinct step of verification can be eliminated.

Very few companies have the interest or wherewithal to place these responsibilities on the picking crew, however. The majority opinion is that pickers are meant to pick and fill as many order lines and complete orders as possible. Expanding the job scope to include aspects of accountability is viewed as a diversion. Warehouse management systems are helping to remedy discrepancies between what is ordered, what is picked, and what is shipped. However, even when a warehouse management system is employed in the facility, most warehouses will call on shipping clerks to verify the load, maintaining this step in the order cycle — a step that takes time and still cannot guarantee perfect service.

Order Shipping and Delivery

Once an order is picked and verified, it is loaded and shipped to the customer location. As you might expect, the time that a shipment spends in transit is usually the longest single component of order lead time for in-stock items. And, as noted, not only can the typical transit time be significant, but so can the variance around that typical time.

While it might be hard to argue that the time a shipment spends in motion destined for a customer is a "waste," there is a substantial amount of time in which an order is in this stage of the cycle but *not* moving. This would be the case with an order that is staged and ready to go but for which the transportation service is not available. Missed pickup appointments happen on occasion, of course. However, something that happens almost as often is the pickup appointment that is made in error. That is, a carrier is called, asked to show up at a shipping location at a specific time, and left to wait until finally summoned to a dock, wasting precious driver and equipment time.

Even more common, unfortunately, is the passing of delivery windows with a driver waiting for the opportunity to unload the shipment. U.S. long-haul truck drivers waste between thirty-three and forty-four hours each week *waiting* for invitations to load and unload their shipments.* Can anyone explain the value in that? Rather, the waiting only leads to increased costs. Frustrated drivers who typically earn the lion's share of their wage by actually covering miles quit the carrier in search of more lucrative opportunities with competing carriers, contributing to the driver turnover problem that consistently hovers at or above 100 percent for most long-haul operators. The turnover leads to additional costs in driver recruitment and training, unnecessary costs that become a burden on the entire economy.

Therefore, concern should be directed toward making not only efficient use of the time a shipment spends on the road, on the rails, in the air, or on the water, but also toward eliminating the waste-creating idle time, even if it is found beyond the scope of your direct responsibility and operations. Reducing time-constraining bottlenecks should be everyone's job because we all end up paying for these wastes.

As more and more companies operate on the basis of synchronized, just-in-time operations, the old expression that "time is money" becomes not an empty expression but a driving mantra. There are very real costs associated with wastes of time. It is not merely an inconvenience when a shipment arrives late or fails to arrive altogether. Simply saying "You'll get it when you get it" will not cut it in today's world. As we seek to minimize the wastes of buffer inventory and

---

* *Dry Van Drivers Survey*, Truckload Carriers Association, Alexandria, VA, 1999.

excess facilities, execution of the order cycle on a timely, accurate basis consistently must become not just the norm but the constant expectation. Subsequent sections will speak of the flexibility required in operations to accommodate timely, accurate execution in the face of uncertain circumstances. Designing robust processes that yield desired performance reliably at the lowest possible cost is not a simple luxury or even a competitive differentiator, but rather the requirement for sustainable growth and success into the indefinite future.

## 7

THE WASTE
OF PACKAGING

LOGISTICS AND PRODUCT PACKAGING

If you were to ask the average logistician the last time he or she had given any thought to product packaging, the answer would probably first be preceded by a long pause and would then result in a reply of "I don't know" or "I've never thought about it." Packaging is often considered a given in terms of quantity pack and design, and concern is usually only directed to the cost of the packaging. "Packaging" is a broad term that refers to all forms of containerization at the item and bundle levels. It includes outer packaging for an item as well as the dunnage that secures an item within a package. It applies to bundles of items in cartons and cases as well as the platforms used for shipping and conveyance, like conventional wood pallets, totes, and racks.

Packaging is an often overlooked resource in logistics. Its importance is eagerly recognized by marketers of consumer goods. The packaging must have appeal to attract potential buyers and contain necessary information to satisfy regulators. All you have to do is walk down any grocery store aisle to see the emphasis placed on packaging. Have you ever seen anything as colorful or splendid as the breakfast cereal aisle? But not all logisticians give packaging the same credence when it comes to product protection, handling and storage efficiency, handler safety and ergonomics, postuse disposal, and communication of necessary handling information. And the fact is that packaging is a critical part of any implementation of Lean operations.

Packaging is important to the logistician for several reasons. First, the package represents the fundamental physical unit of analysis within the logistics system.

In fact, logistics system design begins with the packaging file that documents the dimensions and capacity of all packages that flow through a company's facilities. Second, packaging is important for the many different ways in which it influences and is influenced by the logistics and manufacturing activities, not only within a company but also with suppliers and customers.

PACKAGING AS A SOURCE OF WASTE

Table 7.1 illustrates the relationship between product packaging and a host of operations activities. Perhaps the most obvious connection between product packaging and the creation of waste is found when packaging fails to protect its contents adequately, subjecting the goods to inordinate abuse and creating the waste of damaged goods. This tends to be a logistician's primary concern with packaging, along with the cost. When the acquisition cost of the packaging exceeds its demonstrated value, then waste also is found in such investment. However, buying cheap materials can fail to ensure the integrity of the goods and suggests that a delicate balance exists. Finding the right packaging design is critical. Some companies dedicate considerable resources in this search, but many others assume it away or conduct studies infrequently, failing to keep up with not only changing needs of products and their handling procedures, but also the innovation found in packaging design and engineering.

Consideration of the product packaging's dimensions and holding capacity is critical too. Packaging that can hold more contents safely within a smaller space (contained space) leads to improved material handling efficiency, gains in vehicle cube (weight and space utilization), and efficient warehouse space utilization. Clearly, the point here is that gains are not achieved when products are simply "stuffed" into a smaller box or great effort is required to fill and recover items from crammed boxes. Rather, the packaging design should con-

Table 7.1. The Impacts of Packaging on Operations.

Product protection
Line-side pack quantity
Trailer cube/weight utilization
Warehouse space utilization
Material handling efficiency
Product identity (visual control)
Ergonomics
    Suppliers' packaging process
    Your process
    Customers' unpacking process
Environmental concern
Total cost

sider the efficiencies that can be gained by better utilizing the space within the container to reserve handling effort and to save space in the transportation vehicle and warehouse.

Closely linked to the holding capacity of the container are the ergonomics involved with packing, handling, and unpacking the container. How difficult is it to pack, lift, carry, lower, unpack, and dispose of the container? This question should consider not only the ergonomic implications within your own operation but all parties that will come into contact with the container, including customers and logistics service providers. Can one person safely carry the container, does it require a duo, or is mechanized equipment required? Is the packaging safe and easy to open? Can the contents be removed from the container quickly or does the product or worker become subject to potential injury in the motion? These considerations point yet again to the need to find harmony and balance among many competing factors in determining proper packaging design. Stuffing many items into a box can improve the utilization of space but impair the ergonomics of using the container.

PACKAGING AS A WASTE

Clearly, poor or inappropriate packaging can lead to wastes in a wide variety of ways in an operation, yet we must recognize that the packaging itself can represent a huge source of waste. The fact is that whether you are talking about consumer packaging, corrugated boxes, or hardwood pallets, much (if not most) packaging is used only once and then disposed into the solid waste stream. Not only does this contribute to a negative environmental impact, but it also creates costs — costs that are often significant but viewed simply as necessary costs of doing business. Additional costs might be tacked on in the form of fines or penalties for excess packaging.

Careful review has led many companies and entire industries to adopt packaging that can be reused, returned, or recycled. Reusable packaging refers to containers and pallets that are intended for single use (i.e., viewed as expendable), but gathered and recirculated for additional uses with little or no repairs or reconditioning. Returnable packaging refers to containers, totes, racks, and pallets that are designed for long life and multiple uses. Recyclable packaging refers to materials that typically are used once but can be reconditioned or broken down and used as input for subsequent packaging material in place of virgin resources.*

---

* Goldsby, Thomas J. and Bullock, C. Jason, Returnable Packaging: A Must But at What Cost? presentation at the Council of Logistics Management Annual Conference, San Francisco, 2002.

PACKAGING AS A VISUAL CONTROL

A less obvious way that packaging can create waste is in failing to capitalize on its ability to convey what is happening in the supply chain. Packaging can be a critical source of visual control. Lean manufacturers revolutionized the use of returnable containers. These manufacturers have found that the use of returnable containers not only provides for improved product protection, improved environmental impact, and lower disposal costs over expendable packaging, but that the colorful returnable totes serve as an important signal of supply chain activity.

Today, many manufacturing operations in North America are virtually free of expendable packaging. However, the occasional shipment can show up at these plants in the old standard, corrugated box. The appearance of corrugated packaging serves as an important message that something is awry in the system. One of three possible things has happened: (1) the supplier has procured too few containers to handle the required volume at the plant, (2) the returnable containers have failed to make their way back to the rightful supplier that needs the totes for subsequent use, or (3) the supplier has built parts in advance of the need, outpacing the kanban demand for the parts.

In the first case, the manufacturer would run the numbers again and determine if additional containers were, in fact, justified. In the second instance, the flow of containers would be studied to determine if there was a bottleneck line side, in the so-called "returns land" where containers are temporarily gathered and sorted for return to the supplier, or if there was a misallocation problem in delivering the totes to the rightful supplier. Finally, in the third instance, the manufacturer would inquire as to why production of parts outpaced demand, pointing to the costs of holding the excess inventory and the risk of building in larger batches than called for in the final product. In any regard, the manufacturer knows that the system is failing when corrugated packaging touches the receiving dock.

So, while packaging may represent an afterthought in many operations, it can represent a considerable opportunity for damage prevention, improved flow and efficiency, material waste reduction, and cost savings and act as a critical eye on the operations of the supply chain. In most businesses, more focus can and should be directed to the packaging resource that is both necessary to support the business and also an opportunity to improve the business.

## 8

THE WASTE OF ADMINISTRATION

LOGISTICS AND ADMINISTRATION

Administration is a resource viewed by many people in business as a nonvalue-adding yet necessary evil within logistics or any other function. It is often perceived as a barrier to accomplishing great things, the force standing between you and the unattainable. However, administration is necessary to run a law-abiding, tax-paying, upstanding business, even if it means a departure from the most efficient organization and the optimal flow of work. The real question is not whether it is necessary, but how much administration do we really need?

Consider the order-processing activity previously highlighted in the discussion of the "time" resource. Recall that order processing involves the determination of willingness and ability to accommodate a customer order. From order placement and receipt to order release, there are virtually dozens of "touches" or interfaces with the order. From Stan in customer service to Kathie in accounting to Corrine in the warehouse, an order comes across the desks of many people in the supplier and customer organizations. Don't forget the invoice generation, freight bill auditing and payment, and a host of other paperwork that is created, reviewed, issued, reviewed again, acted on, and reviewed yet again with each and every order. And that is when everything goes according to plan!

What about the problem situations that generate volumes more in paperwork and unrecoverable time and energy? One might argue that none of these steps is value adding, yet they are necessary for getting the product out to the customer and getting paid in return. So while these steps may be necessary, they are probably laden with redundancy, confusion, and waste. Take, for instance, the number of people that touch the paper order associated with a requisition of supplies in the U.S. Army. It is estimated that *fifty* people touch the *paper order,* from the requisition officer to the accounts payable clerk. How many of these touches truly create value? Any? How many opportunities for error and delay are found with each of the fifty handoffs?

ADMINISTRATION AS HELP AND HINDRANCE

Following the trail of person-to-person communications often found in the order process can be like playing the campfire game "telephone." The game commences when a phrase or expression is whispered into the ear of the first person and then conveyed from one person to the next around the campfire. At the end of the chain of people, we find that the original message, say "Dog is man's best friend," is somehow transformed, into "My frog drinks only the best gin," after being received, processed, and forwarded by several people. How does this happen? Honest mistakes are often to blame. The unfortunate outcome is considerable waste in time and energy directed toward a failed outcome. It takes time for the message to make its way through the chain, and yet each person contributes to the mounting cost and risk for error. Clearly, communicative technologies like electronic data interchange and the Internet can minimize these costs and risks.

Administration tries to overcome these shortcomings, providing oversight of logistics activity and regulating the flows of physical product, information, and cash. Companies experience waste when they rely on administration to coordinate these flows in the absence of processes that allow the flows to proceed naturally in the desired, efficient manner. Oversight, for instance, is a redundant activity in its very essence. If people know what to do and act accordingly, there is absolutely no requirement for oversight. Where discipline is lacking, abuses that violate expectations inevitably will happen. In cultures where abuses are not tolerated, they are far less likely. Therefore, a culture that embraces discipline and accountability by all will naturally call for less administration, as expectations for all team members are set forth clearly, understood by all, and revered. In contrast, those cultures that lack discipline will need more oversight and administration.

TECHNOLOGY AND ADMINISTRATION

Many companies are turning to technological solutions to provide improved oversight and ease of administration. Take warehouse management systems

(WMS), for instance. A capable WMS can not only help the warehouse employee perform tasks more effectively, but also provide ready measure of that employee's performance by tracking productivity and accuracy in warehouse execution.

While information technology (IT) tools are often effective in gathering these measurements and providing a degree of oversight for operational activity, they sometimes create an entirely new layer of administrative responsibility: *maintaining* the system itself. And what is often found with technical administration such as that for IT systems, legal services, and international shipping, among others, is that in their uniqueness, bottlenecks are inherently created. For specialized services such as these, you cannot simply reallocate an untrained person who lacks the specialized skills and knowledge to critical tasks in these functional areas. For that reason, it seems as though you rarely (if ever) have the right number of people assigned to these administrative responsibilities. These departments are either idle and seemingly overstaffed or working feverishly to catch up to reduce organizational bottlenecks and free the constraints on productive work flow. Therefore, while many ITs provide much-needed reporting capabilities, they can also introduce new layers of technical support and administration. Most companies find that the administration or overhead lost through improved information exceeds the overhead gained in IT support. The key is to recognize the trade-off and to manage it accordingly.

IT offers the obvious benefits of better, faster, more accurate information capture and sharing, but there are benefits found also in what it avoids: the human element. As alluded to in the examples from throughout the order cycle, it is clear that we, as imperfect people, are prone to error and variance. IT can reduce the number of times that administration falls into the hands of managers. In addition, what many managers find when turning on a system is data overload, being overwhelmed by volumes of data that may or may not hold any significance for managing the business. To the extent that the data can be formatted to highlight exceptions (variances from the expected performance), the more meaningful and manager-friendly the system and its output will be.

In sum, inconsistent action breeds administration. The ability to engender confidence in the minds of customers that the "perfect order" will be delivered on a consistent basis reduces uncertainty and calms the customer. When customers know when they can expect a shipment with a high degree of reliability, the supplier is unlikely to receive the all-too-common "Where's my truck?" inquiries. In the absence of these calls, the supplier can focus almost exclusively on the value-added work that needs to get done. It can focus on the present and, more importantly, the future rather than the past. As a result, the company needs fewer people to provide the oversight and resolution to problems and inquiries.

## 9

THE WASTE OF KNOWLEDGE

LOGISTICS AND KNOWLEDGE

Knowledge is perhaps the least recognized and least understood resource in the management and success of any business. It cannot be seen, touched, or easily quantified, but is very much a resource. Knowledge is possibly the resource that is most often wasted in an organization. In the functions most commonly associated with business strategy, such as research and development, engineering, marketing, and finance, knowledge is at the very core of their existence — *knowing* what customers will buy, *knowing* how to build those products, *knowing* how to make customers aware of the offering. The operational areas, however, are often thought to be subordinates to the plans developed in the strategic areas.

The hierarchy of strategies in most businesses tends to look like Figure 9.1. While the strategies cascade from corporate strategy to product and marketing strategy to manufacturing strategy to, finally, logistics and procurement strategies, it does not mean that the functions lower in this hierarchy, the so-called "support areas," should be devoid of creativity and the search for new, better ways to conduct business. To the contrary, the innovative logistics organization can, in fact, influence (and even drive) corporate strategy. Think back to those pillars of excellence highlighted earlier in the book. Companies like Wal-Mart, Toyota, 3M, and Dell, among others, rely on distinct logistics capabilities to separate their businesses from the crowd.

Interestingly, when the operational areas of supply chain management (logistics, manufacturing, and procurement) are tapped for competitive advantage,

Figure 9.1. The Common Hierarchy of Strategies.

once achieved the advantage can prove not only significant but sustainable. Companies that achieve competitive advantage through these operations-oriented bastions of excellence do so by *thinking*, constantly challenging the status quo, by tapping internal bases of knowledge, by seeking new sources of potential advantage. This environment is in contrast to companies where strategies are set forth and handed down to operations as marching orders for execution. Creativity and challenging the status quo may not be rewarded, but instead actually discouraged and quelled in these settings. Going to work in places like this can resurrect images of those 1960s zombie movies where brain-dead figures show up on the scene and mindlessly pursue their own survival needs. Not only can workplaces that fail to nurture knowledge be miserable places to work, but they also consistently perform below par.

CULTIVATING KNOWLEDGE

Companies can call on both formal and informal means to avoid the waste of knowledge. Formal means include internal, company-sponsored training and educational opportunities at universities and professional associations through degree programs, certifications, seminars, and colloquia. Internal training is critical to building applied knowledge of company culture, values, and processes. However, the outside training is important as well, providing an "unbounded" normative influence on the way things *should* be, rather than the way things are. Unfortunately, outside training is often viewed as a luxury, reserved for those precious times when a company finds itself in a cash-rich position, with ample budgets for education. At all other times, training remains on hold, yet these are the times in which team member development is probably most critical!

Education in any form continues to offer the quickest, most solid return of any investment available. That much said, it must be recognized that not all knowledge gained through training exercises will translate into improved performance in the business. This is sometimes attributed to a lack of relevance or opportunity for application. In other instances, there is a simple "evaporation" of the knowledge when the material fails to be processed or "sink in." The student or instructor may be equally to blame for this outcome. For this reason, both students and trainers must be held accountable for the learning. These considerations help to minimize the wastes of knowledge sometimes found in formal educational venues.

Knowledge can also be developed by less formal means on the job by simply asking questions or seeking assignments in different areas of the business to broaden one's horizons. Nurturing cross-functional thinking among team members provides an appreciation for different problems, perspectives, and approaches. While it is hard to instill, individuals who demonstrate strong interest in what they do and an innate curiosity can go a long way toward solving the problems of the day and taking the business to uncharted, positive territory. These are truly rare individuals though. If you have made the effort to read this far into the book, you just might be among this rare set of motivated, deep thinkers.

MANAGING THE FLOW OF KNOWLEDGE

Once knowledge is gained, it often becomes captive to the individual. All organizations must have mechanisms in place to ensure that information and knowledge are shared to remedy the "islands of knowledge" phenomenon that plagues many companies. Sharing ideas and perspectives raises the general level of knowledge and understanding throughout the organization, across functions, raising the level of play for the company and building a sense of belonging to a team striving for a common objective. The sharing of knowledge is particularly important in those do-or-die situations, such as entering a new market, managing a critical start-up project, or introducing a new product line. Sadly, in the absence of established mechanisms for capturing knowledge gained by veterans of past endeavors, current managers are likely to repeat the mistakes made by their predecessors. Unfortunately, these mistakes can prove costly not only to the company but to the individual. Careers can be cut tragically short when mistakes are made and the manager "should have known better."

Similarly, best practices may be tucked away in one functional area or at a particular facility. Those practices should be communicated for application to other areas of the business, raising the company's overall level of play. Instilling a culture of continuous improvement throughout the company encourages best practices to be shared openly. The same may be true of sharing methods and tools that have proved valuable in one area or another. Too often, waste is created through duplicated effort in different parts of the company when a little collaboration might not only eliminate the redundancy but also lead to a more robust method, tool, or solution to a common problem. Companies that regard knowledge as a critical competitive resource by managing their knowledge effectively tend to enjoy greater ability to innovate and respond.

Just as individuals can serve as "islands of knowledge" in a company, so too can a company in the supply chain withhold critical knowledge that would benefit the whole. This is the case when companies practice an "information-is-power" approach to dealing with trading partners in the supply chain. The truth is that failing to share valuable information, knowledge, and skills only leads to suboptimal performance of the larger supply chain system, usually to the detriment of the very party holding the other supply chain members captive. Academics are now talking about concepts like the "knowledge chain"* and "knowledge supply chain," recognizing that imbalances (or "asymmetries") in information and knowledge serve the purpose of providing only short-term gains for the benefiting company, gains that often reverse into losses when disadvantaged trading partners elect to walk away from the relationship or simply become defunct as a function of the abuse.

So while knowledge is a less tangible resource, it is no less important than any of the more visible ones. An important take-away from this discussion is that complacency is the enemy of knowledge. As Confucius once said, "He who believes he knows everything, knows nothing." There is no bliss in ignorance. In the military, when strategists are aware of a problem or situation even though its gravity and causes are not fully understood, it is called a "known-unknown." This situation is far more preferred to the unknown-unknown, where one does not know what one does not know. To some extent, realizing what one does not know can be an epiphany that accompanies education and increased knowledge. Just as the unknown-unknown is feared in the military, so too should it be in business.

Equally important in our discussion of the wastes in knowledge is to recognize that nowhere is there mention of information technology (IT) as prerequisite for development and utilization of knowledge. Clearly, IT can support the exchange of information, but the application of technology provides no guarantee of gains in knowledge.

---

* See, for instance, Holsapple, Clyde W. and Jones, Kiku, Exploring primary activities of the knowledge chain, *Knowledge and Process Management*, 11(3), 155–174, 2004.

THE RIVER OF WASTES

Many of the wastes described in this section probably seem all too familiar to you. Anyone would be very fortunate (or untruthful) to say that they experience none or even few of these wastes. To sum up, these various inefficiencies and nonvalue-added consumptions of resources represent a river of wastes. Unfortunately, many of us are drowning in that river.

To take the "river of waste" analogy further, imagine two landmasses divided by a body of water. You are on land, blessed with certain resources and skills. Across the water on the distant shore reside your current and prospective customers. The key questions become "What do we have to offer them?" and "How do we reach them?" Recall that logistics provides that physical connection to your trading partners. Your first inclination might be to build a boat to traverse the water.

Let's think of the boat as a ferry. No question, in the absence of a better way to cross the water, the ferry can provide a valuable, if not necessary, function. Yet, it is not the easiest to use, the most enjoyable, or the most certain of all services. Despite the best efforts of the company, the service is only available when the ferry is at dock and in service, with everything and everyone fully functional. Until these factors are completely aligned, there is no action and you wait. If the line is particularly long, you might have to wait through several shuttles before you have the opportunity to cross. Yet even when aboard the ferry, the speed of service is not particularly swift, perhaps working against a strong current. The service is also prone to any one of several possible disruptions: inclement weather, low water, high water, waterborne obstacles, ferry operator strike, etc. You get the idea. And in the event you encounter rough waters, you could become seasick! Oh, and don't forget the various forms of pollution created with each crossing. If the ferry is part of a pleasure trip, the novelty of its quirks and inefficiencies may not bother you but rather may, in fact, be charming. But if you have business to tend to or find yourself in an emergency situation, it can be an unsatisfying or even loathsome experience.

Logistics in most companies looks and acts something like the ferry. As illustrated in Figure 9.2, the ferry is immersed in the water, the very "river of waste" that the service is trying to overcome. Service is hit or miss in its inconsistency. It is prone to disruption. It is dependent on a few key individuals. And, unfortunately, the experience leaves customers wishing for a better way.

Now let's assume that you are enlightened enough to replace the ferry service with a bridge, a beautiful suspension bridge that spans the distance between the two landmasses, say you and your customers, like that in Figure 9.3. The bridge rises high above the water, free from the river of waste, providing an efficient connection between the landmasses. It offers a robust solu-

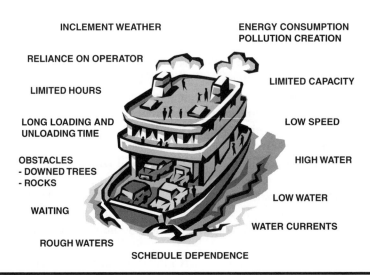

INCLEMENT WEATHER

ENERGY CONSUMPTION
POLLUTION CREATION

RELIANCE ON OPERATOR

LIMITED CAPACITY

LIMITED HOURS

LONG LOADING AND
UNLOADING TIME

LOW SPEED

OBSTACLES
- DOWNED TREES
- ROCKS

HIGH WATER

LOW WATER

WAITING

WATER CURRENTS

ROUGH WATERS

SCHEDULE DEPENDENCE

Figure 9.2.   The Many Ills of a Ferry Service.

tion to the basic need of crossing the water. Only the most extreme conditions
will ever cause it to close, so flow is constant and smooth. Speed, safety, and
variability are controlled by the individual experiencing the service and are
dependent on the need, not the whims of a disenfranchised operator. This is
exactly what Lean Six Sigma Logistics promises the enlightened manager —
an opportunity to provide the greatest value to customers free from the disruptions and wastes found in the conventional means of connecting a company to
its trading partners in the supply chain.

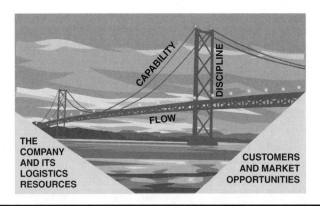

CAPABILITY

DISCIPLINE

FLOW

THE
COMPANY
AND ITS
LOGISTICS
RESOURCES

CUSTOMERS
AND MARKET
OPPORTUNITIES

Figure 9.3.   The Logistics Bridge.

Unlike the bridge, Lean Six Sigma Logistics does not call for the huge investment, bands of specialized experts, or years to take the concept from the drawing board to completion. What is required to build the Logistics Bridge are three critical understandings:

1. Logistics Flow
2. Logistics Capability
3. Logistics Discipline

These principles of the Logistics Bridge Model are described in the next section along with their supporting tenets.

This book has free materials available for download from the
Web Added Value™ Resource Center at www.jrosspub.com.

SECTION 3.
THE LOGISTICS
BRIDGE MODEL

## 10

A TOUR OF
THE BRIDGE

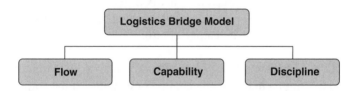

There is no question that Lean and Six Sigma principles will contribute positively to logistics and supply chain activities. The challenge is to understand *how* to leverage the value of Lean and Six Sigma in logistics. Lean principles can sometimes be counterintuitive, making it difficult for operations people to embrace the value proposition. For example, a transportation manager will struggle with the concept of increasing frequency of deliveries if personal performance is measured on transportation costs. Hence, for Lean Six Sigma Logistics to be implemented successfully, it must be a corporate initiative. This is not to say that a company must be a Lean organization prior to implementing Lean in the logistics function. Of course, it is ideal if the organization has embraced Lean holistically, but Lean and Six Sigma bring many applications that can be applied to logistics in the absence of a corporate Lean initiative. What does this tell us? The important lesson is that Lean and Six Sigma teach us sound business principles. Lean and Six Sigma are not a trend, fad, or "flavor of the month." They are a well-packaged set of business excellence principles and tools. The trick is to unwrap the package and choose the principles and tools that are needed and best suit your particular situation. By using those principles and tools, an organization can design a business excellence model that will fit the culture and goals of the company.

HISTORY OF LEAN SIX SIGMA LOGISTICS

Lean logistics started as the inbound logistics function supporting Lean manufacturing. Therefore, if you mentioned Lean logistics, you were talking exclusively about the inbound process connecting suppliers to a manufacturing facility practicing Lean. Typically, this meant that the inbound function was focused on increasing frequency of delivery, leveling flow, and reducing inventories. Fortunately though, Lean and Six Sigma started to be implemented in nonmanufacturing environments where the principles and tools could still be applied. This acted as a catalyst for Lean and Six Sigma to be embedded in logistics in a more general sense. To this end, we now have two focuses relative to Lean Six Sigma Logistics. These are:

> **Lean Six Sigma Logistics #1**: The inbound logistics function supporting a Lean manufacturing facility.

> **Lean Six Sigma Logistics #2**: Logistics activities where the overall operational strategy is based on Lean Six Sigma principles and tools. This can include transportation, warehousing, order management, material handling, and inventory control.

This distinction is very important, especially if you plan to go to training courses for Lean and Six Sigma in the supply chain. For example, if the corporate focus is to reduce waste inside the warehousing operations, you will want to ensure that your education focuses on Lean and Six Sigma principles in warehousing.

With these two definitions in mind, it becomes apparent that Lean Six Sigma Logistics has the potential to become a confusing and complicated model. The goal then is to simplify the complicated. That is what we have attempted to accomplish in this book. Reviewing and analyzing all Lean and Six Sigma principles, we have put together a model that bridges Lean and Six Sigma with the logistics function. Our goal is to arm the logistics professional with the knowledge required to reduce waste, manage inventories, and create more effective processes.

THE IMPORTANCE OF THE LOGISTICS BRIDGE MODEL

Implied in Lean and Six Sigma theory (but rarely discussed) is the importance of having a model to act as a compass, to set direction. Standardized work, the DMAIC (Define-Measure-Analyze-Improve-Control) process, and hoshin planning are examples of Lean and Six Sigma principles that describe and promote a standard model for improvement initiatives. The use of a model allows an organization to talk a common language, the first step to any significant initiative. We all need to be on the same page! This is especially true for the logistics function, where a corporate global logistics strategy may not exist.

Logistics needs to be a priority in the boardrooms of our companies. To get there, logistics professionals need to articulate the value of logistics. The value proposition of Lean Six Sigma Logistics includes cost reduction, increased competitive advantage, and market growth. These topics should certainly attract the attention of any CEO! As logistics professionals, we need to be talking to our CEOs, and we need to talk to them in "CEO language." The framework of the following Logistics Bridge Model will allow us to have these conversations armed with knowledge, vision, and direction for the future.

Any model that focuses on results will be multidimensional. With the Logistics Bridge Model, the dimensions are based on the management hierarchy of a typical organization. The model looks at logistics from the point of view of the CEO first and then drills down to the strategic level and lastly describes the tactical areas for successful implementation. This approach follows Lean doctrine by creating a model that can be understood by all levels of the organization. By following the model, the CEO will know what will be accomplished, as will the senior management and front-line managers. The Logistics Bridge Model provides a corporate strategy that can be used to implement a world-class Lean Six Sigma Logistics system.

The CEO's Perspective

The job of a CEO is certainly not easy. The CEO is the one person who is ultimately responsible for company performance, the one person who needs to balance the needs of the customer, the employees, and the shareholders. The CEO's job may depend on increasing shareholder value, but what does this have to do with logistics? In a word, everything! In fact, logistics may be the single most overlooked area for opportunities in business today. This is very surprising when one considers that the world's most successful companies today credit their logistics and supply chain activities as the secret of their success.

Once a commitment is made to embrace logistics from a strategic point of view, the focus turns to how best to engage the logistics function. Where does a CEO start? The Logistics Bridge Model answers this question. We suggest that the CEO be concerned with the three key principles:

1. **Logistics Flow**: Flow is a crucial aspect of any corporate logistics strategy. The CEO recognizes that elements of flow are inherent in every business function. Understanding flow inside the organization allows a firm to understand its strengths, weaknesses, opportunities, and con-

straints. Flow describes the operational effectiveness of the company. The CEO will be most interested in three types of flow: asset flow, information flow, and financial flow. How productive are the assets, how do we manage information, and how do we generate a return on our investment? These three key elements of flow must be closely tied to logistics activity, creating awareness of the importance of flow and strategic logistics management.

2. **Logistics Capability**: Capability is the second priority for the CEO. Once the organization understands how assets and information are flowing, the question of whether or not the firm is capable will arise. Capability is very interesting because an organizational infrastructure is only as capable as the system is at any particular point in time. In other words, a CEO can mandate cost reduction, better service, and reduced lead times, but the mandate does nothing to change the capability of the organization. An organization is a complex series of functions and processes that act interdependently as a global system. Therefore, the system has a finite capability, by conscious or unconscious design. Uncovering, defining, and articulating this capability is at the heart of Six Sigma. Improving on this capability is at the heart of Lean. The Logistics Bridge Model shows us that a capable system enjoys predictability, stability, and visibility. These are the three tenets that are fundamental to logistics capability. Progressive CEOs know and understand this fact. Successful CEOs will drive capability to exceed customer expectations. Leading CEOs know that Lean Six Sigma Logistics is required to improve the capability of the organization.

3. **Logistics Discipline**: Maintaining flow and capability requires discipline. Discipline is the third key focus area for CEOs as they develop a logistics strategy. Enlightened CEOs recognize that logistics and supply chain management are not about technology, but rather about people and process. For people and processes to be effective, there must be discipline to the principles and strategies being used. Lean is a quintessential example of the importance of discipline. Many executive managers review the principles of Lean and recognize them as nothing more than common sense. Yet their attempts to implement Lean fail miserably! Why? The number one cause of failure is lack of discipline. Lean Six Sigma and eliminating waste are not difficult conceptually. At the end of the day, they are nothing more than a lot of hard work. And hard work requires discipline. To work hard and to work smart require a commitment to the principles and consistent application of the tools. Relative to logistics, discipline is extremely important. The Logistics Bridge Model describes logistics discipline as focusing on three main

aspects: collaboration, systems optimization, and waste elimination. These three tenets will drive discipline and success and are necessary to support any corporate Lean Six Sigma initiative.

In summary, the Logistics Bridge Model starts with higher order principles that will be the focus of the top executive of the organization: Logistics Flow, Logistics Capability, and Logistics Discipline. Once the CEO believes this is the proper strategic approach to logistics, he or she can pass the strategic focus areas to the next level of management.

Senior management will be tasked with implementing the three key Lean Six Sigma Logistics principles. This takes us to the next level of tenets in the model. Logistics Flow will focus on asset flow, information flow, and financial flow. Logistics Capability will focus on the logistics system's predictability, stability, and visibility. Logistics Discipline requires strategies focused on collaboration, systems optimization, and waste elimination.

In the end, the senior executive will embrace these nine second-order tenets and will develop an execution plan to implement the strategies, engaging the next management level of the organization. This takes us to the level of the doers, the people who have to implement the strategy. Fortunately, the Logistics Bridge Model has developed third-order qualities. These are the tactical areas that the implementers need to focus on, twenty-seven tactics that represent the best of what Lean and Six Sigma have to offer the logistics organization and processes.

The Implementer's Perspective

The implementer will receive a vision of strategy from the executive level. The CEO has asked that strategy be developed around Logistics Flow, Capability, and Discipline. The executive management team has extrapolated the CEO's vision to focus on asset flow, information flow, financial flow, logistics predictability, stability, visibility, collaboration, systems optimization, and waste elimination — nine strategies for the management team to implement. Where do we start? The Logistics Bridge Model can help.

1. **Logistics Flow**: The first order of business for the implementer is to get an understanding of flow inside the organization. The three key areas of flow are asset flow, information flow, and financial flow. Within each of these key focus areas are three tactical areas that need to be fully dissected to gain a full appreciation of flow.
2. **Logistics Capability**: To serve customers effectively, our logistics systems need to be capable. Our overall systems have a finite capability,

with variability providing for *ups and downs* in the customer service experience. What is the customer expecting? What is the capability of the logistics system? What is the gap between customer expectations and system capability? These are questions that need answers. To gather these answers, we need to recognize customer expectations and define a capable system. The Logistics Bridge Model defines a capable logistics system as having predictability, stability, and visibility.

3. **Logistics Discipline**: Logistics is driven by people and process. Lean and Six Sigma teach us that we need to have standards, meet those standards each day, and continuously strive for improvement while eliminating waste from the logistics system. Discipline is required in the planning and implementation stages of any Lean Six Sigma initiative. More importantly, it is required to sustain any significant improvement. Yet, how do we define and introduce discipline in our logistics processes? The Logistics Bridge Model describes logistics discipline as requiring collaboration, systems optimization, and waste elimination.

THE LOGISTICS BRIDGE MODEL: GETTING STARTED

The following chapters outline the main concepts described in the Logistics Bridge Model. We hope you can use these ideas as your model to drive logistics excellence. Beware though: You will at first end up with more questions than answers. It is virtually impossible for one book to provide solutions to every conceivable problem in logistics. However, embedded in the Logistics Bridge Model is the answer. Although perhaps implied and not obvious at first, the answer can be developed by using the model described in the following pages.

## 11

LOGISTICS FLOW: ASSET FLOW

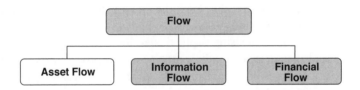

Assets represent the resources that companies use in order to generate revenue. How well we manage these resources can mean the difference between profitability and bankruptcy. Lean and Six Sigma drive out waste, and many forms of waste involve the inefficient use of resources. Yet, to understand how assets flow, we need to categorize the types of assets that support the operations. Categorizing assets and determining flow for each asset type will ultimately lead to a greater understanding of how hard the assets work to produce returns for the shareholders. The three strategic focus areas for Asset Flow are:

1. People Flow
2. Inventory Flow
3. Fixed Resources Flow

These three areas will be discussed in this chapter.

PEOPLE FLOW

> **Truism**: Excellence in logistics depends on having a team of well-trained and highly skilled people in the right places.

It is often said that people are a company's most important asset. Yet, how many companies pay homage to that belief? Not many. Excellence in logistics depends on companies recognizing workers as an extremely valuable piece of the corporate puzzle. After all, logistics processes are labor intensive and hence the importance of people.

Logistics processes not only are but will continue to be complex and people driven. The complexity is not necessarily conceptual; rather, it is due to the number of opportunities for error given the large number of steps and the amount of paperwork involved. Although many companies are looking for the logistics "magic bullet" from technology, the fact remains that logistics is about processes, and *people* execute processes. Whether we are unloading trailers, filling out bills of lading, or using sophisticated tools to design milk runs, it is the human mind that determines the outcome. As a process-driven function, logistics is a service-based practice. Unlike manufacturing, logistics is not "ground beef in–hamburger patty out." Rather, it is a service that is offered to internal and external customers. Similar to any other service, the quality and consistency are limited to and constrained by the efficiency of the people providing the service.

One example of variance in service is familiar to everyone who travels. When we travel (for example, when checking into a hotel), our experience varies depending on the attitude and abilities of the individual providing the service. Among the greatest challenges that organizations face are recruiting, training, developing, and retaining teams of competent workers. This challenge increases as customers become more knowledgeable and, consequently, more demanding. The role of logistics is under pressure. Logistics managers have internal demands to reduce inventories, lead times, and waste. At the same time, they are being pressured to increase services to both internal and external customers. How is this done? Each part of the process requires people with the skills to do the work. We acknowledge that it is complex and difficult work. Consequently, we need to organize, manage, develop, and control the flow of human capital inside the organization.

The People "Perfect Order"

Human capital management in logistics is no different than *perfect order* management. That is, we need to have the *right* number of the *right* people in the *right* place, and all that at the *right* cost. Definitely easier said than done! It is well known that most organizations have significant room for improvement. Progressive companies are recognizing that logistics and supply chain activities require educated, trained, and experienced professionals. American universities have certainly recognized this issue as more and more schools are offering undergraduate and graduate degrees in logistics. We need to embrace these new professionals, our salaried human resources, and make a place for them within our organizations. Next, we need to consider the nonsalaried side of our human capital. These are the hard-working team members who drive trucks, run material, handle equipment, pick up orders, and interface directly with our customers.

In many cases, nonsalaried employees are the core of the organization. They are also the personnel whose functions contain a large number of process steps. Most often these processes are procedural driven. Sadly, these employees are often eliminated from roles in leadership. For many companies, corporate vision and customer expectations rarely reach the floor where the work gets done. Consequently, some team members do not perform their jobs accurately or consistently. Invariably, they do not understand how their part of the task fits into the master plan.

Questions to be discussed with these workers are:

1. What is the purpose of the work or task being done?
2. How does each participant know when the job is done successfully?
3. What is the best way to perform this work?
4. What is the role of the individual's task in the overall success of the company?

Successful organizations that embrace logistics as a core competency will create, develop, and nurture an environment with the following attributes:

1. Human resource management based on human capital flow and the *people perfect order*
2. Formally educated, experienced, and disciplined logistics professionals
3. Trained, informed, and engaged nonsalaried team members

Organizing People

In most cases, the logistics function evolves as the company grows or declines. Logistics departments are organized in a variety of ways, such as centralized, decentralized, reporting to sales and marketing, or reporting to purchasing. The list of potential variations in logistics and internal infrastructure is a long one. To reach our vision of excellence, the *people perfect order*, we need to ensure that the logistics function is organized and structured appropriately within the firm. To do this, we need to understand fully the *current condition* relative to human resource management and the logistics function. To understand the current condition means to answer the following questions.

1. *What* are the logistics-related processes inside the company?
2. *Who* performs the logistics activities?
3. *Where* in the organization are the activities performed?
4. *What* does it mean to be qualified to perform the activity?
5. *How* are we training and developing logistics team members?

At a glance, these questions seem elementary; however, experience shows that finding the answers can be a major challenge. Accurately understanding the current condition of human capital and becoming knowledgeable about the skills and talents of employees are daunting tasks. Not only must the tasks be accomplished, but they also must be sustained and updated over time. Logistics is about complex, multiple-step processes, and processes are about people. Logistics is people! Figure 11.1 shows how we can prioritize the skills required for logistics professionals.

Bridging the People Gap

Once we have determined our firm's current condition relative to *human capital flow*, we need to analyze the situation juxtaposed to our vision of excellence. What we need to ask ourselves is how to bridge the gap between where we are now and where we want to be. With most initiatives, this is a case of brainstorming the required tasks and then putting together a disciplined project time line to be followed and executed. However, when it comes to people, getting to where we want to be is intricate, complex, and can be very difficult. Building a team with the right players at all levels in the organizational chart is the most important job for any leader. To do this, we need to understand fully what logistics is trying to accomplish for the company — what it is that we are trying to do. After we determine what we are trying to accomplish, we need to carry out the following key project steps:

1. Commit to human capital flow and the people perfect order.
2. Collaborate and engage with universities teaching logistics as a formal discipline.
3. Train and develop all team members in excellent logistics practices.

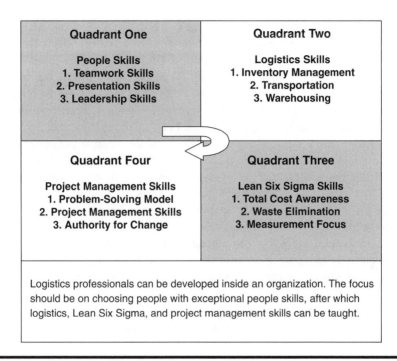

Quadrant One **People Skills** **1. Teamwork Skills** **2. Presentation Skills** **3. Leadership Skills**	**Quadrant Two** **Logistics Skills** **1. Inventory Management** **2. Transportation** **3. Warehousing**
Quadrant Four **Project Management Skills** **1. Problem-Solving Model** **2. Project Management Skills** **3. Authority for Change**	**Quadrant Three** **Lean Six Sigma Skills** **1. Total Cost Awareness** **2. Waste Elimination** **3. Measurement Focus**

Logistics professionals can be developed inside an organization. The focus should be on choosing people with exceptional people skills, after which logistics, Lean Six Sigma, and project management skills can be taught.

Figure 11.1. Logistics Professionals: Prioritization of Skills Set.

INVENTORY FLOW

Flow → Asset Flow → Inventory

Truism: Once you have eliminated industry's acronyms and jargon, logistics is about managing inventory.

Best practice on how to manage inventories is rare and elusive. How do we measure inventory turns? How do we calculate average on-hand inventory levels or required safety stock levels? Experts agree that inventory needs to be managed proactively; that is, inventory flow needs to be examined, planned, measured, and improved on a regular basis. We will explore the question "What is inventory management?" as well as the question "Why does it seem to be so complicated?"

As illustrated in the description of wastes in Section 2, there are many labels placed on inventory. Some are cycle stock, seasonal stock, speculative stock, safety stock, opportunistic stock, and dead stock — the list is long. After close scrutiny, however, there are really only two types of inventory: cycle stock and a combination of all of the other categories. Cycle stock is the inventory we expect to use to meet customer demand. Other inventory types (we will call them all "safety stock") represent reactive efforts to identify and manage differences or variations. This means that cycle stock is about flow and safety stock is about variation management. Likewise, Lean is about flow and Six Sigma is about variation. Thus, we recognize another crucial example of how Lean and Six Sigma make up a key element of the logistician's tool kit. When we understand this connection, we are ready to plan an implementation.

The first step, to understand and manage the flow of cycle stock, calls for the analysis of demand for raw materials, work-in-process inventories, and finished goods. Far too many organizations believe that demand is nonmeasurable and unmanageable. Managers often believe that Lean theory will not work in their business because their demand is unknown. In fact, all material demand follows some sort of pattern. This pattern may not be level or predictable, but it is a pattern, and any pattern can be documented, described, and understood. Understanding the pattern allows us to observe the flow of material and then determine accurate order cycle times, reorder points, effective stocking locations, and effective transportation systems.

Understanding Safety Stock

Unnecessary safety stock (the aggregate of everything other than cycle stock) is among the biggest wastes faced by most companies. Although there are reasons to hold safety stock, one must understand these reasons and then carry *just-in-case* stock levels that minimize the amount of inventory. To be sure, the reasons for safety stock will hinge on variation in the logistics systems. For example:

1. Uncertainty (variation) in supplier order-to-ship lead time will result in safety stock of raw materials.
2. Variation in transportation lead time (due to carrier performance) will lead to safety stocks of raw materials or finished goods.
3. Variation in customer demand will lead to forecasting models that will result in safety stock requirements to meet unexpected spikes in demand.

Consequently, the trick to inventory management lies in determining the safety stock necessary to hedge against the uncertainties inherent in any business system.

Inventory Management

Lean principles focus on eliminating waste from business processes. Inventory is not isolated to raw materials and finished goods. Companies will carry inventory masquerading as service parts, repair items, administrative suppliers, automobile fleets, and a host of other types of assets that are managed by setting and maintaining certain levels. The problem is that almost every function inside an organization can affect inventory levels. Whenever decisions are made in purchasing, marketing, manufacturing, or customer service, inventory levels across these asset types will be impacted. Unfortunately, all too often, these decisions are made in a vacuum and, consequently, inventory management becomes very difficult. For example, it is extremely hard for an inventory analyst to attempt to reduce inventories when the manufacturing area is frequently changing production schedules without informing the inventory analyst of the changes.

Therefore, inventory management is not just about managing inventory levels; more often, it is about recognizing the complex workings of the entire organization. This complexity is embedded in the system of the organization, and it is this system that produces surplus inventory. Taking a systems approach to inventory management is crucial when we begin our journey toward Lean.

Starting with the Systems Approach

Value stream mapping is a powerful technique that we find in the Lean toolbox. Typically, we do not think of inventory and value stream mapping in the same light. This is because we reserve value stream mapping for processes and we do not think of inventory as a process. However, there is merit to managing inventory as a process throughout an organization, making it difficult to understand the total process or the larger picture. For example, in a manufacturing environment, many departments (many that do not talk to each other) are involved in the complexity of setting a production schedule, ordering raw materials, and managing inventory levels of finished goods. Although these functions may appear to be isolated, independent activities, the reality is that they are interdependent parts of a system. The laws of *cause and effect* are active among the activities. This means that a decision in one area will impact other areas. Unfortunately, few managers understand or are encouraged to understand how their decisions affect other areas and vice versa. Refer to Figure 11.2 to see a high-level approach to understanding inventory from a systems approach.

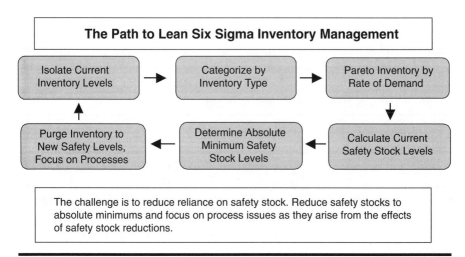

Figure 11.2. Inventory Flow: The Beginning.

Inventory and Cause and Effect

Similar to all living things, organizations are impacted by natural laws. Among natural laws are growth, variation, change, balance, and cause and effect. Although no law is more or less important, the law of cause and effect is of interest to the supply chain professional. In essence, cause and effect relates to three critical points:

1. An action today will create one or more effects in the future.
2. The future effect caused by an action today will generally be felt and managed by someone other than the creator of the action.
3. The future effect caused by an action today could be felt tomorrow or years later, depending on the significance of the action.

A closer look at these points shows that quality decisions (actions) cannot be made without considering their short- and long-term impacts (effects). In other words, we need to stop making decisions *in a vacuum*. Decision making in a vacuum is a sign of well-entrenched, functional barriers. It is vital that professionals take into consideration how the organization works as a system. Each decision will impact the future and will reach across functional divides. This demonstrates the need to be proactive and to manage decisions that impact the system. As well, we need to ensure that measurement systems describe the global impact of prior decisions and guide decision making. The quintessential example of systems thinking is, in fact, an integrated supply chain. The much talked about, but rarely managed, concept of *total cost* has its roots in systems thinking. For example, ill-conceived purchasing decisions today result in increased warehousing costs six months from now and inventory obsolescence two years from the original purchase. Unfortunately, because the ultimate effects take two years to be realized, the root cause will go unseen and unmanaged.

Inventory Management Fundamentals

We can focus on the intricacies of inventory management once we understand how decisions and processes work inside the organization relative to inventory management. However, it is crucial to remember that inventory management fundamentals cannot be implemented effectively without a rigorous understanding of the inventory cause and effect and processes within the organization and spanning with supply chain trading partners. After this is accomplished, the logistician can focus on fundamental inventory management processes that would include:

1. Inventory and ordering strategy of raw materials
2. Inventory strategy of finished goods
3. Inventory strategy of work-in-process inventories
4. Inventory placement and location strategy
5. Transportation strategy

In summary, the basic premise of inventory management is: How much inventory should we have, where should we keep it, and how will we transport it? Yes, this may seem elementary to most logisticians, but many organizations cannot produce documented strategies to manage these three basic aspects. The successful organization will have a formal plan surrounding these basics, and this plan will be integrated into the sales, operational, and financial strategies of the company. Lean organizations focus on these three items from a different point of view.

When inventory strategies do not exist, the three principles described above will be managed reactively. For example, in the absence of a planned inventory strategy, warehousing and transportation functions will simply react to the daily operational situation. In this case, inventory will be transported and warehouses will be filled, yet nobody really knows whether the operation is running effectively or not. Whereas this approach illustrates *reactive* management, the Lean system is managed proactively. Logistics systems that are managed proactively have two distinct characteristics:

1. Ordering, inventory control, transportation, and warehousing functions are planned and synchronized to the customer's demand, getting to the heart of *pull* systems.
2. The real focus is not on managing day-to-day activities of the logistics function, but on reducing the need for the logistics activities in the first place.

As indicated, a significant difference is that Lean systems question the need for logistics activities. Likewise, the goal is not to develop a fleet of trucks and trailers, but to reduce the need for trucks and trailers. In a Lean logistics environment, the goal is not to build a network of warehouses, but to eliminate the need for warehousing altogether. In a Lean logistics environment, the goal is not to build up inventories, but to reduce the reliance on inventory completely. Lean is about the elimination of waste. Lean is about flow and pull. Six Sigma is about understanding and reducing variation. When we allow Lean and Six Sigma to create synergies in operations, inventories will be reduced, transportation strategies will become more effective, and warehouses will be few in number or nonexistent.

FIXED RESOURCES FLOW

Truism: Managing fixed resources is hard work. For this reason, many organizations either do it poorly or do not do it at all. The management of fixed resources presents an opportunity to reduce costs and improve operating efficiency.

Fixed resources surround us in our professional lives. Computers, office furniture, warehouses, and material handling equipment are all examples of fixed resources. Generally speaking, fixed resources are assets that show up on all three financial statements (the income statement, balance sheet, and statement of cash flows):

1. **Purchased assets**: These assets, or fixed resources, sit on the balance sheet. Their cost to the organization generally shows up in the depreciation line on the income statement and cash out (on statement of cash flows) on purchase.

2. **Leased or rented assets**: These fixed resources show up as an operating expense on the income statement. Consequently, their cost is generally more visible to management.

Regardless of whether an organization prefers to buy or lease, the fact remains that these resources command significant money and energy to maintain.

Logistics activities are major users of fixed resources. For example, warehouse facilities and transportation equipment represent two heavy commodities. Therefore, it is imperative that we micromanage the procurement and use of all logistics assets.

Lean is about the elimination of waste. First we need to uncover the waste where it sits. To accomplish this, all fixed resources need to be identified, analyzed, and justified. For example, facility leases should not be renewed as a matter of course, but should be scrutinized carefully each and every time the lease is up for renewal. The lease should be analyzed with the following questions in mind:

1. How can we eliminate the need for this space entirely?
2. If it is not possible to eliminate the need, how much space is actually required?
3. How does the need of this space correlate with the need for space at other facilities?

These three questions are critical because fixed resources are governed by natural laws. These natural laws teach us that fixed resources will be justified to the extent that you have them. In other words, if you have a million-square-foot facility, you will likely convince yourself that it is needed. The final question brings the total logistics network to light, recognizing the interaction among facilities in the network.

In a Lean environment, one is pressured to do more with less, literally challenging the organization to be less reliant on fixed resources and more focused on speed and flow. As you reduce your need for fixed resources, speed and flow will develop naturally due to the fact that inventory and process have fewer places to stop or to accumulate. In other words, reducing warehousing will force inventory to flow.

Identifying and Mapping Fixed Resources

Although identifying and mapping fixed resources sounds like common sense, it can be quite difficult, so much so that in the last decade *asset management* has become a hot topic, gaining the interest and energy of many software developers. As painful as it may be, it is imperative that we identify all fixed resources involved in the logistics activities. When you begin to identify fixed resources, do not justify their use; just itemize the "what" and "where" of each fixed resource. Justification comes later.

After itemizing fixed resources, map them relative to use and flow. This is often an eye-opening experience for companies. Using a white board or mapping software (Microsoft® Excel works fine too), map the fixed resources in the order that they are used in a logistics-related process. Map resources and then itemize quantities used. At this point, it will be clear that certain questions need to be asked. In most cases, these questions will sound something like:

1. Why are the warehouses placed where they are?
2. Why do we have twice as many lift trucks in our smallest facility?
3. Why are there so many trailers in the yard?
4. Why do we have tractors sitting at all locations?

This is hardly an exhaustive list; the point is that only through mapping out our fixed resources will we be able to visualize and question the use of these assets. For large organizations, this exercise can be difficult due to complexity, and that is precisely why it needs to be done. For example, if we cannot map out where all our warehouses or pieces of transportation equipment are, how can we manage these assets? One approach for large organizations is to map one resource category at a time. Start with facilities and then move to transportation equipment, then to material handling equipment, and then down the list in order of value of the asset. Once you have mapped the fixed resources independently, you can overlay each map in order to get a feel for the bigger picture.

Questioning the Need

Work begins in earnest when you question the need for fixed resources. At best, this is a rigorous analytical exercise, and at worst, it is enormously disrupting and disturbing. Even so, it is well worth the effort. If we look closely, we will see that the reason for the complexity of the task is that people are attached to these fixed resources, and jobs go with fixed resources. It is likely that an individual, a worker in the company, fought hard to acquire the asset. Someone who fought to acquire an asset will surely fight to save it.

Change management aside, there are harsh realties that need to be recognized. Fixed resources are an immense drain on cash, and companies will not survive unless they get this drain under control. Consequently, the value of all

Priority for Elimination	Fixed Resources: Interrogation Questions
Priority #1: Warehouses and Space Priority #2: Transportation Equipment Priority #3: Material Handling Equipment Priority #4: Racking – Storage Equipment Priority #5: Computers – Software	1. What is this resource costing us? 2. Why do we need this resource? 3. How could we operate if we were forced to do without this resource?

When dealing with fixed resources, we must first identify the resource and seriously question the need and value of the resource. Although we may not eliminate the resource immediately, brainstorming how we would operate without the resource is a critical exercise.

Figure 11.3.   Logistics Fixed Resources: Prioritization of Waste Elimination.

current fixed resources needs to be justified. A rigorous approval process needs to be in place surrounding requests for acquisition of fixed resources. Two basic questions need to be asked for each fixed resource:

1. Why do we have this resource?
2. How would we run the operation if this resource was eliminated?

Notice that the second question does *not* ask "Can you do without the resource?" Asked that way, the answer will invariably be "No, we cannot do without the resource." The question is not whether you think you need the asset; the question is about how to run the operation without the resource. Such questioning promotes innovative thinking, thereby uncovering assumptions and *sacred cows* that could be standing in the way of success. Figure 11.3 shows a typical prioritization path to help identify which fixed resources to reduce first.

Vision of Excellence and Fixed Resource Flow

Fixed resources flow through an organization. Although this flow may be counterintuitive, successful organizations will recognize this asset flow and will develop an infrastructure to manage it. We should never be proud of fixed resources. State-of-the-art warehouses may seem glamorous, but excellence occurs when we eliminate the *need* for the warehouse. Similar to all Lean initiatives, this drive for waste elimination takes commitment, discipline, and organization.

Commitment is required to deal with the current condition. Only through unwavering commitment will we conquer the disturbing side of reducing reliance on fixed resources. Discipline is required to ensure that from this day forward we embark on an unrelenting quest to run the operation with a minimum of fixed resources. Companies need a rigorous approach to the accomplishment of goals without adding fixed resources. This will require organization, which facilitates the following items:

1. Communication and decision-making channels for fixed resources
2. Analytical and problem-solving models that demonstrate a reduced reliance on fixed assets

Fortunately, the tools of Lean and Six Sigma will help the logistician to accomplish these goals.

## 12

FLOW:
INFORMATION FLOW

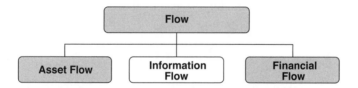

Of all functions inside any organization, logistics invariably deals with the most information. All of this information flows through a company in many different formats, at different speeds, and for many different reasons. Information is used to manage the present, plan for the future, and reflect on the past. This information originates from the supply base, internal employees, service providers, and the customer. Managing all of the information can be a daunting and overwhelming task, yet it must be accomplished for effective logistics management. The three strategic focus areas for Information Flow are:

1. Data Flow
2. Knowledge Flow
3. Communication Flow

These three areas will be discussed in this chapter.

DATA FLOW

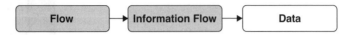

Truism: Logistics activities generate more data than any other business function, yet logisticians continue to search for the best way to use data effectively.

We need to turn data into information and information into knowledge, but the bridge from data to information and then to knowledge remains an elusive one. What is preventing us from extracting the knowledge buried in our data? There should be no shortage of information since logistics activities produce and process a plethora of data.

The task is to extract useful meaning from our data. The first thing to do is to stratify the data into meaningful data groups, after which we need to determine how the data flow through the organization. Data management works well when grouped into three families: historical, event or real time, and future or deterministic.

Historical Data

Historical data are the kind most available to organizations. They are accessible from monthly financial statements, past shipping volumes, and carrier on-time performance reports. The challenge with historical data is that they do not allow us to manage in a timely manner. That is, managing by historical data is like driving a car by looking through the rearview mirror.

Historical data can be manipulated to suit the needs of a particular analysis. It is simply too easy to take historical data, crunch the numbers, and then produce the answers that we need or want. This is because we tend to normalize the data by rationalizing data points, discarding data that we deem unnecessary or threatening to the message we intend to convey. A prime example of this phenomenon exists with carrier on-time performance. It appears that *everybody's* on-time performance for transportation is 98 percent! Yet we know this cannot be true.

Nevertheless, the story of using historical data is not all bad news. Historical data provide us with an ability to understand patterns and trends in our operations. They allow us to determine sigma levels and performance metrics. These patterns and trends are crucial in order to develop models that can show us the ways of the future. This is where the data turn into knowledge. We need the ability to use historical data to develop meaningful trend analysis that can be used for decision making now and in the future.

Event and Real-Time Data

Event data (or real-time data) are the voice of the process as the process is in operation. In other words, event data are the feedback from our processes at the exact time they are being executed. These data are powerful, but hard to gather. Although advanced technologies have helped to gather event data, the fact remains that most organizations do not have real-time feedback mechanisms. Without event data, we continue to manage with information derived from historical data and, consequently, expose our decisions to the evils described earlier. When we do capture event data, they enable us to make sound business decisions in real time. The ability to make real-time decisions is crucial to waste elimination and Lean implementation.

Some simple examples of event data include daily revenue generation, inventory availability, and transportation asset utilization. These are valuable, but we need to strive for real-time knowledge on all crucial processes. Essentially, having event data at our fingertips allows us to make meaningful decisions precisely when we need a correction or to address an abnormal condition.

The Lean concept of *poka-yoke* describes the importance of event feedback. A poka-yoke is a mistake-proofing tool that creates visibility in an abnormal or unplanned condition. For example, ordering raw materials using a pull replenishment system means that we order and replenish material in the exact quantities that we have consumed. With event data and a simple poka-yoke, we will be notified if an order goes to a supplier that is incongruent with what was used on the shop floor. This means we can correct the order immediately before transmitting it to the supplier.

Future and Deterministic Data

The one thing we all know about forecasts is that they can and do go wrong. Yet, we cannot run a business without forecasting since planning ahead is necessary if we want to become Lean and eliminate waste. There is much that can be done to mitigate the impact of meager planning of future events. We need to use the historical and event data to understand fully the variability caused by the system. It is the variability that we need to plan for. In other words, forecasts should not just plan for future demand, but should also plan for future demand variation. It is the *variation* of demand that creates unnecessary inventories and excessive waste in any logistics system.

Managing deterministic data is crucial to the concept of true supply chain management. The theory of supply chain management is that we will eliminate the *bullwhip effect,* or the perception of exaggerated demand, by sharing data within the entire supply chain. This data sharing is absolutely necessary, and all Lean initiatives need to include a practical plan to share demand data with internal parties and external supply chain partners. This key point cannot be overlooked and must be embraced at all levels of the organization. Why is this crucial? The answer rests in the *law of large numbers.*

As a simplified explanation, the law of large numbers shows us that the more data points we have, the better our understanding of the information will be. From a statistical point of view, the more data samples we have, the more confident we can be in our predictions. If we take this concept and apply it to supply chain management, we conclude that the more data and information we have from each partner in the supply chain, the closer we are to predicting future needs. In the end, this will result in more "nearly" accurate forecasts and less overall systems waste for all supply chain partners. Figure 12.1 shows us that an intersection of all data types will result in the most effective decisions.

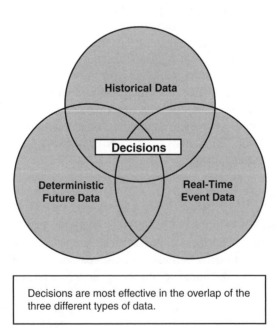

Decisions are most effective in the overlap of the three different types of data.

Figure 12.1.   The Data Balancing Act.

Data Excellence

Excellence will come to organizations and logisticians that embrace all of the available data. In some respect, the logistician is the professional who needs to champion the available data and ensure that the data flow unencumbered through the supply chain. This can only be accomplished by creating a culture of discipline where data are captured accurately and in real time. This means focusing less on historical data and managing more often with event and real-time data. When we learn to manage in real time, we will be more inclined to share information with supply chain partners. Then and only then will our data collection efforts yield information that create corporate knowledge.

To accomplish this, successful organizations need people who understand gathering and analyzing data. It is imperative that we use our ability to recognize critical data and create organizational knowledge. Analyzing data relative to variation is the heart of the challenge. To restate, an ongoing premise of this book is that having the right people in the management of data flow is crucial. In the future, organizations that can successfully transform data into knowledge will:

1. Develop a culture where management decisions are based on fact rather than opinion or intuition.
2. Reduce inventory and waste due to supply chain information sharing.
3. Understand, articulate, and develop strategies to manage variation in the business system.

KNOWLEDGE FLOW

Truism: Allowing corporate knowledge to go to waste is a crime. Capturing and sharing knowledge should be priority one at all levels of an organization.

As noted in our discussion of the "people perfect order," logistics processes are heavily reliant on people, and this makes consistency in quality of process difficult to achieve. Unlike a manufacturing process completed by calibrated machines, logistics processes are completed by people. Consequently, there is high variability in the way processes are managed. The level of training, commitment of employees, and clarity of work procedures can all create negative or positive variability in the effectiveness of processes. The work will be done differently depending on the person assigned to the task. For the logistician, this indicates a need to focus on best practices.

We have all heard the phrase "sharing best practices," but very few organizations are able to harness the power of this concept, creating undue waste in knowledge. Unfortunately, knowledge too often flows out of the organization, creating critical voids. This seems particularly true in small- and medium-sized organizations, where there is high variability in the way processes are completed. It seems that a small organization should be able to complete tasks in a consistent way, but this is not the case. This variability of process in any size organization produces poor quality, waste, increased costs, and customer confusion. We must ask "What are best practices and how can we share them throughout the organization?"

A "best practice" is a relative term. It is relative because it is the best way that a firm completes a task or process at a particular point in time within the organization. This does not necessarily mean that the task is being done the right way or the best way possible. It simply means that at this point in time, this is the best that can be done. This should not be seen as discouraging, but rather as a starting place from which to strive for improvement.

Continuous improvement and standardized work are two very powerful tools of Lean manufacturing. These two concepts are linked to our need to share best practices and ensure that knowledge flows through the organization without springing leaks.

Continuous Improvement and Knowledge Flow

Knowledge is gathered when we work to improve a process or situation. If we do not attempt to improve, we do not critically examine what we are doing. Knowledge is gained through critical analysis. For example, significant corporate awareness and knowledge are exposed when workers are busy "putting out fires" and coping with service failures. This is because serious service failures will engage the attention of senior management, who will no doubt try to uncover the cause of the problem. Senior management will ask questions about process such as "Why are we doing what we are doing?" At this point, the process will be examined, and if all goes well, the need for change will be recognized and the process will be improved. When we embark on improving the process, we are looking for knowledge in the form of best practices. It is hoped that these best practices exist internally or can be borrowed externally. If they are not available, then the continuous improvement process will result

1. No formal knowledge-sharing infrastructure
2. No incentives for individuals to share knowledge
3. No accountability for individuals to share knowledge
4. No time to share knowledge
5. No awareness on what knowledge should be shared
6. No training on how to share knowledge
7. No departmental or interdivisional communication
8. Defensiveness resulting in knowledge "hoarding"
9. No tools in place for sharing knowledge
10. No commitment to "get it done"

Similar to all processes, knowledge sharing requires people, process, and commitment.

Figure 12.2. Top Ten List: Why Knowledge Does Not Flow.

in design and development of a best practice. In this case, tools from *Design for Six Sigma* can be used.* However, the challenge is not to wait for service failures to occur, but to examine processes continuously, to isolate best practices, and to share this knowledge throughout the organization. This is where standardization of work procedures comes into the equation. Figure 12.2 outlines possible reasons why knowledge is not shared properly inside many organizations.

Standardized Work and Knowledge Sharing

People are hesitant to associate standardization with the more glamorous concepts of knowledge acquisition and sharing. How could something as boring as standardized work procedures have anything to do with best practices? Standardized work is one of the simplest, yet most misunderstood, tools in the Lean lexicon.

Standardized work is not intended to turn people into mindless robots, carrying out a repetitive task. The heart of standardized work is to determine the best way to complete a task, share the knowledge, and continuously improve

---

* Design for Six Sigma is a holistic methodology for incorporating customer specifications into the new product development process to support defect-free product performance in the eyes of the customers.

the standard. That is, change the standard as often as you need to in order to improve it. This is one of the many Lean paradoxes. For standards to change, we need to ensure that we have rigorous procedures for sharing knowledge gained while improving the process. For example, if we improve and change a process on first shift, there needs to be a way to ensure that second-shift employees gain the knowledge of the improvement through instruction. This requires commitment and discipline on the part of all employees. Indeed, the transfer of knowledge can be so daunting that companies, consciously or unconsciously, often do not have a vehicle for improvement. Consequently, their processes are seldom improved, mainly because they do not know how to share what they know and what they are learning.

In the end, the ability to share knowledge may be the determining factor that differentiates corporate success from failure in the new age of technology and unmatched customer awareness.

Getting Knowledge to Flow

The first order of business is for companies to recognize that knowledge flows in the same way as cash and inventory. Consequently, we must develop infrastructure that is designed for knowledge sharing. As knowledge flows through the organization, best practices can be recognized and embedded in the process as standardized work. This standardized work will become a benchmark, creating a positive cycle of continuous improvement. The infrastructure required will depend on the size, depth, and vigor of the organization, but the discipline required is the same for all companies. Sharing best practices requires nothing more than a communication or delivery system and commitment. Commitment represents a sizable portion of the equation.

Global companies will need a way to share best practices through the use of technology. Intranets are effective, as are face-to-face meetings. Too often, when trying to share knowledge, we get trapped in the process of sharing and lose our focus on the knowledge itself. In other words, we focus too much on the delivery system and not enough on the content.

Regardless of the delivery system, excellence requires a commitment to sharing knowledge — providing time in our day for knowledge sharing and possibly providing a formal infrastructure to facilitate the flow of information. The cost associated with knowledge sharing needs to be acknowledged as an investment and not as an incremental overhead cost. It is difficult to calculate the cost of lost knowledge, but the future may prove that commitment to knowledge sharing ensures sustained corporate success.

COMMUNICATION FLOW

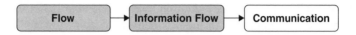

> **Truism**: Communication is like any other function inside the organization. If it is deemed important, then it should have a formal structure.

Organizational communication is complex and troublesome. Most organizations experience communication as the primary area of disappointment among their employees. Communication problems are more prominent as you work your way down the organizational ladder. It seems the lower you are on the organizational chart, the more you feel left out of the loop. Employees often complain that they do not understand the vision or strategy of the company. Note, however, that communication flow involves more than just strategic issues.

Most service failures in logistics can be attributed to breakdowns in communication. Given the complexity of some supply chains, it is a miracle that product ever gets delivered to customers correctly. The complexity does not stop with the logistics activities themselves, as the communication channels are complicated as well. If Lean and Six Sigma are to have the expected impact, then effective communication flows are a requirement. Recognizing the potential power of communication, progressive organizations design and implement formal processes. Effective communication makes the difference between reaching and not reaching organizational goals. Two key communication infrastructures needed are those for strategic communication and operational communication.

Strategic Communication

Those of us who study communication are surprised that organizations continue to succeed given how little their employees know about what is going on. Employees often do not have a clear understanding of either their firm's vision or their goals for the short and long term. While some companies succeed in spite of this lack of communication, it is unacceptable in a Lean environment.

Lean approaches the business from a systems point of view. To begin, Lean organizations recognize that each function in the company is part of the entire system, and consequently, we need to have an understanding of how the system works as a whole. Second, Lean focuses on total cost, which necessarily means that all functional areas of the organization need to be synchronized. Third, in a Lean environment, the customer is crucial, which means all employees in a Lean company need to understand the company's overall business strategy. Bringing the excluded people into the communication loop is not easy, but it is necessary if every employee in the company is to work toward a common goal. To accomplish this, Lean enterprises embrace a technique called hoshin planning, described next.

Hoshin Planning

Hoshin is a planning technique used to make certain that strategies are communicated throughout the entire organization.* It is a communication vehicle for managers to collaborate with their superiors concerning the achievement of goals. In essence, it works as follows:

1. Senior executives develop a high-level vision of strategy and goals for the company. They pass these down to the next level of management in a process called "catch ball," referring to the top-down handling and communication of ideas.
2. The second level of management reviews the goals and sends the executive managers a list of the steps required to meet the goals. This back-and-forth discussion may transpire several times until both levels of management are satisfied with both the goals and the steps to achieve them. When it is completed, the tactical plan from senior managers will be sent down to another management level, where a plan will be developed to meet the goals.
3. This conversation continues until the goals, steps required to achieve them, and a plan to carry out the steps have reached the bottom level of the organization.

Clearly, this process covers several important issues. Not only does it communicate the overall vision and strategy of the company, but it also sets out individual objectives for each employee. This is accomplished through the process iterations, where each person sends the manager a list of tactical steps to complement the senior manager's goals. This approach will achieve the firm's overall goals due to the fact that all employees are working toward the same goals. Most importantly, the strategic vision of the organization is communicated to everyone inside the company. Once the strategic communication infrastructure is in place, we need to develop the operational infrastructure.

---

* For a more in-depth discussion of hoshin planning, see Dennis, Pascal, *Lean Production Simplified*, Productivity Press, New York, 2002.

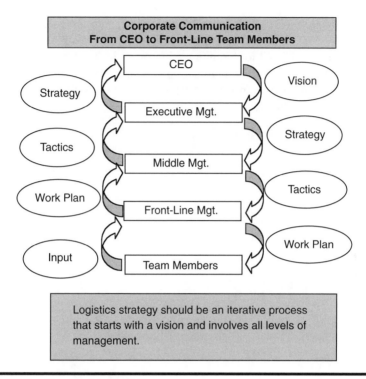

Figure 12.3. The "Catch Ball" Process.

Figure 12.3 illustrates how communication can flow up and down inside an organization effectively.

Operational Communication

Lean Six Sigma Logistics concentrates on eliminating waste by focusing on total cost. Once we begin to focus on total cost, we realize the need to synchronize for operational success. For example, we cannot reduce raw material inventories to a minimum without discussing the implication of this move with production planning. Production may be expecting high variability in schedule changes, which would cause a reduction in raw material, a high-risk situation. As we can see, communication is critical to successful operational implementation of Lean initiatives.

For effective communication, everyone needs to understand how the system works (this will be discussed more later). Excellent communication within the organization requires a formal infrastructure. This infrastructure can be a standard report, a regular meeting, or a conference call. The challenge is to make the communication method effective by addressing both issues and opportunities. As you most likely have experienced, many meetings are updates on current affairs as opposed to communication on serious issues. In the end, the organization needs to view communication similar to the way it views all other important functions. It requires a process for itself that will guarantee responsibility and accountability.

## 13

FLOW:
FINANCIAL FLOW

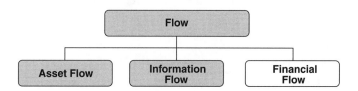

A company must be profitable to survive. Profits reward shareholders, provide growth opportunities for suppliers, and result in increased products and services for the customer. Any form of waste will drain financial resources, a runoff that may be either visible or invisible. Every dollar spent and earned should be treated with disciplined respect. What would our organizations look like if every dollar were treated as if it were our own personal money? The logistics function touches every aspect of financial flow in and out of the organization, from supplier to customer and all operations in between. The three strategic focus areas of Financial Flow are:

1. Income Statement
2. Balance Sheet
3. Cash Flow

These three areas will be discussed in this chapter.

INCOME STATEMENT FLOW

> **Truism**: The income statement paints a mixed picture. On one hand, it shows us the direction we are headed; on the other hand, it fails to uncover significant waste.

Books on Lean and Six Sigma seldom focus on the income statement. They would argue that if you focus on physical inventory flow and the elimination of waste, the results will appear in the income statement eventually. Seemingly, the income statement is a report that outlines the effect of decisions made during the previous accounting period. Managing through your income statement is a *rearview mirror* approach. A disciplined organization will focus on strategic and operational issues as opposed to the income statement. Even so, in reality, the income statement cannot be ignored. Logistics professionals need to be aware of the income statement and the system feedback that it provides on the following items:

1. Revenue
2. Cost of goods sold
3. Gross margin
4. Operating expenses
5. Interest and tax expense
6. Net earnings

Three key features of the income statement are:

1. Logistics operating costs may be hidden throughout the income statement.
2. Logistics processes flow across the entire document.
3. Inventory carrying costs are not clearly identified in the income statement.

Once again, we stress, Lean is about flow and the elimination of waste. Without argument, reliance on excessive inventory represents the root of many wastes. In other words, a significant majority of the waste that exists in an organization is a result of building and managing unnecessary inventories. Unfortunately, the income statement does not identify the kind or extent of the waste effectively, nor does it tell us what we can do about the waste. In fact, the income statement can actually drive decisions that may have a negative effect on the organization. Figure 13.1 shows a typical income statement and indicates where logistics processes are represented on the income statement.

Income Statement Line	Logistics Drivers
Revenues	Customer Satisfaction
	Order Fill Rate
	Order Cycle Time
Goal: ⬆	On-Time Delivery
	Pipeline Visibility
Less Cost of Goods Sold	Inbound Transportation
	Lot Size
	Frequency
Goal: ⬇	Inventory Carrying Costs
	Lead Time
Equals Gross Margin	***XXXX***
Less Operating Expenses	Warehousing Costs
	Shuttle Transportation Costs
	Outbound Transportation Costs
Goal: ⬇	Inventory Carrying Costs
	Logistics Administrative
	Technology Costs
	Lead Time
Equals Operating Profit	***XXXXX***
Less Interest and Taxes	Inventory Financing
	Fleet and Equipment Financing
	Facility Financing
Goal: ⬇	Technology Financing
Equals Net Income	***XXXXXX***

Figure 13.1.   The Income Statement and Logistics Drivers.

Logistics Activities and Hidden Operating Costs

There is no question that logistics is getting more attention in boardrooms these days. Operational costs in logistics can exceed 15 percent of revenue without taking inventory carrying costs into consideration. When inventory carrying costs are considered, total logistics cost can climb substantially higher. Considering the financial impact of total logistics cost, one might think we would manage the income statement and the logistics function from a holistic point of view.

When we say "holistic," we mean a corporate and perhaps global perspective. To reach this goal, the first step is to examine the income statement and understand where the logistics function is impacting the performance of the organization. The second step is to create a vision of how logistic activities flow across the income statement. From this, we will generate important insights about waste and its financial impact.

To begin, put the income statement into perspective from a logistics point of view. This requires identifying the *buckets* that make up total logistics costs. Typically, these buckets will be:

1. Transportation
2. Warehousing
3. Material handling
4. Ordering costs
5. Inventory carrying costs

We soon find that these key cost buckets are not visible in a neat and tidy manner. For example, transportation costs for inbound raw materials may be hidden in cost of goods sold, whereas transportation costs for outbound finished products may be in the operating expense line. Complicating the situation even further, some transportation costs may be paid by suppliers or customers and factored into piece or finished goods price. This lack of visibility is one reason why logistics and supply chain activities frustrate financial managers. For this reason, logistics has the reputation of being an "evil cost of doing business." Yet, effective logistics processes are not simply a cost of doing business, but rather a significant point of competitive advantage. Consequently, we need to embrace the fact that logistics costs should be visible and understandable on the income statement.

Logistics Costs Flow Across the Organization

One will inevitably find logistics costs scattered across the entire organization. No particular manager or department is wholly responsible for the impact of logistics on the income statement. The absence of responsibility contributes to the absence of accountability, which contributes to logistics decisions that suboptimize the organization. When we say "suboptimize," we mean the local decisions made may be optimal, but the overall impact on the firm is not optimal. For example, a purchasing coordinator may get a 10 percent reduction in piece price by buying a full year's worth of product. In this case, the piece price has been minimized, but the overall total logistics cost will most likely be suboptimized due to the cost of carrying a year's worth of inventory.

This dynamic of costs flowing across functional boundaries creates a need for collaborative management of the income statement. In other words, the income statement cannot be managed in a vacuum. When this occurs, poor management decisions are made and impenetrable functional silos develop. More importantly, without collaborative management of the income statement, it will be virtually impossible for an organization to execute the Lean task at hand successfully. This is the task of uncovering, articulating, managing, and eliminating inventory carrying costs.

Inventory Carrying Costs and the Income Statement

Most companies struggle to capture inventory carrying costs on the income statement. To understand why, it is necessary to review the DNA of inventory carrying costs. As discussed in Chapter 3, the key inventory carrying costs are:

1. **Capital costs**: Represent the cash cost or opportunity cost of inventory investment
2. **Inventory service costs**: Include insurance and taxes relative to inventory investment
3. **Storage space costs**: Include internal space costs as well as any third-party space in use to store inventories
4. **Inventory risk costs**: Include obsolescence, damage, shrinkage, and relocation costs

We are on familiar terms with the all-too-obvious fact that inventory carrying cost items are not plainly represented on an income statement. Case in point: an income statement will not have a placeholder for *opportunity cost* of capital, cost of space being used specifically for safety stock, or relocation costs of inventory that is obsolete. The income statement does not give us a clear representation of inventory carrying costs that can be used to make effective management decisions. The good news is that Lean and Six Sigma teach us principles that can be used to guide our decisions.

One of these principles is the *inventory carrying cost principle*:

All inventory carrying costs move in a positive direction with the level of inventory.

This principle states that each and every inventory cost moves up and down with the inventory level. Therefore, if inventory levels go up, so do all inventory carrying cost components. Similarly, if inventory levels go down, so will each inventory carrying cost component (over time, of course, with fixed costs). This principle is good news for us relative to the income statement: Even though inventory carrying costs may not be visible on the income statement, we know intuitively that they will go down as inventory levels go down. As inventory carrying costs go down, positive results will be evident in the bottom line. This is an extremely important learning point because it influences decisions in organizations about whether or not to pursue Lean.

Vision of Excellence and the Income Statement

The income statement attempts to draw a picture of corporate performance over a period of time. Having a time-lapse dimension makes the income statement valuable for understanding flow. As flow happens over time, it is good to be able to see how revenues and costs flow over a specific period. However, as discussed previously, the income statement does effectively identify the costs associated with carrying inventory. Inventory is waste. Lean is about eliminating waste. As a result, we are reminded that inventory carrying costs will go down as inventory levels go down. The job at hand is not to manage the income statement, but rather to focus attention on the elimination of inventory. Excellence will follow when the organization works collaboratively to eliminate unneeded inventories at all levels.

Progressive companies that embrace Lean will reduce their focus on the income statement during the implementation phase of the Lean initiative. If you make decisions based on short-term, quarterly profit goals, then you will never realize the true benefits of Lean or Six Sigma. For Lean to be effective, decisions need to be driven by total cost, and therefore, these decisions may have counterintuitive impact on the income statement. These counterintuitive effects need to be recognized, embraced, and applied so that Lean can achieve success.

Recall that transportation cost is the largest and most visible cost of the logistics activities. It generally has a budget line, which means that it can be managed to a plan versus actual expense from the income statement. Typically, if a large expense line can be measured from a planned number to an actual number, then some employee will no doubt have compensation tied to the actual number in some fashion. The result is a logistics manager who has personal motivation and incentive to keep transportation costs below plan.

In the event that the company in this example embarks on a Lean initiative, the logistics manager will eventually be involved in conversations about increasing frequency of deliveries to the plant in order to reduce inventories. If we are embracing Lean in totality, then this is a given, as delivery frequency is the most powerful Lean tool to reduce raw material level at a plant. To be sure, the results take time, and overall financial benefits may not be realized immediately. That is, the income statement may not show positive results right away. Compounding the issue is that transportation costs may, in fact, go up in the short term to facilitate the increase of delivery frequency, although they will eventually be stabilized with sound logistics design processes. This short-term increase in transportation costs creates a serious problem. First, because transportation cost is visible on the income statement, any trend upward will receive attention and concern. Second, the logistics manager will now look at how personal compensation potentially may be impacted as a result of transportation costs perhaps exceeding a planned budget. What motivation will exist to implement Lean principles if compensation is reduced?

Lean implementation will flourish in an environment where Lean principles are understood and embraced. Of course, we need to manage the income statement responsibly; however, it is important to know that Lean has income statement dynamics that are counterintuitive. In order to realize the benefits of Lean fully, we need to focus on eliminating inventory and the negative effect of inventory carrying costs. To accomplish this requires faith that single line items on the income statement may trend upward, but overall corporate performance over the long term will be improved dramatically.

BALANCE SHEET FLOW

> **Truism**: Warehouses and inventory show up on the balance sheet as assets, yet a Lean practitioner knows they are, in reality, liabilities.

As discussed previously, the income statement provides feedback about organizational performance over a period of time. This may be a month, a financial quarter, or a full year. Similarly, the statement of cash flow shows the aggregate of actual events where cash is being paid out or taken in by the company over a period of time.

The balance sheet, on the other hand, represents a different view of organizational health. The balance sheet shows the current condition of financial and operational dynamics at a particular point in time. This allows us to compare current and past balance sheets in order to understand how managerial decisions impact items such as assets, liabilities, and owners' equity. The challenge with the balance sheet is that it can create false perceptions of what is good or bad for the organization. For example, two balance sheet paradoxes are:

1. Inventory sits on the balance sheet as an asset, which implies that inventory is liquid and as flexible as cash.
2. Inventory turns are calculated by comparing inventory levels from one period to another from the balance sheet.

In addition to these two paradoxes, it is important for the logistician to understand that the overall goals of the firm typically can be described by the balance sheet. Rarely should the goal be to accumulate assets on the balance sheet. Instead, the goal of any organization should be to increase the return on shareholder equity. The balance sheet provides us with a snapshot view that helps to complete the picture and to improve our understanding of these concepts.

Inventory as a Current Asset

A current asset is loosely defined as an asset that can be turned into cash with reasonable ease. This is extremely important to the organization as current assets are used to pay employees, pay suppliers, and fund growth. To look at it from this perspective might suggest that inventory is a good thing. This sounds logical — inventory produces sales, sales produce revenue, and revenue produces profits. The Lean logistician knows that nothing could be further from the truth.

Perhaps the most significant waste outlined in the Lean concept is the waste of overproduction. In fact, other wastes are created because of overproduction. For example, when a company builds finished products for which there is no demand, the next thing it does is to store them. This need for storage creates warehousing expense, another waste caused by overproduction. The overall impact of overproduction is major, but a balance sheet point of view is confusing as it implies that inventory that has no immediate demand is an asset.

Inventory cannot be perceived as cash! If inventory were equated to real dollars, then the automobile industry would not need to discount vehicles in its desperation to sell and retailers would not be so obsessed with sales promotions. Companies have sales to move inventory and to generate cash. Organizations need cash to pay expenses such as employee payroll, suppliers, and overhead. These expenses are the cost of manufacturing a product that is in demand in the marketplace. In other words, if we consume cash by building products that are not required in the marketplace, we force the organization to sell these products at a heavy discount in order to cover the costs of production. This sounds absurd, yet it happens on a regular basis.

Consequently, when managing the balance sheet, Lean Six Sigma logisticians need to have an objective view of inventory. They need to understand inventory levels and whether or not the inventory holdings actually represent

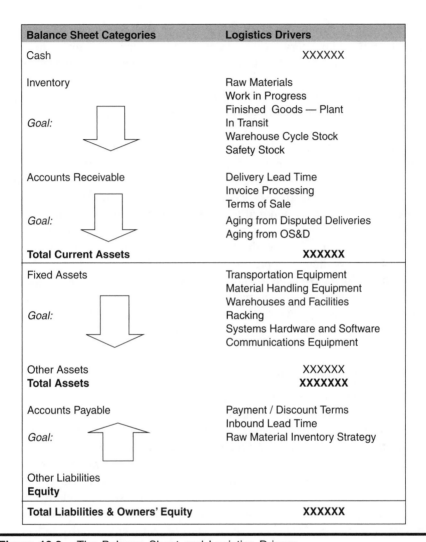

Balance Sheet Categories	Logistics Drivers
Cash	XXXXXX
Inventory	Raw Materials
	Work in Progress
	Finished Goods — Plant
Goal:	In Transit
	Warehouse Cycle Stock
	Safety Stock
Accounts Receivable	Delivery Lead Time
	Invoice Processing
	Terms of Sale
Goal:	Aging from Disputed Deliveries
	Aging from OS&D
Total Current Assets	**XXXXXX**
Fixed Assets	Transportation Equipment
	Material Handling Equipment
	Warehouses and Facilities
Goal:	Racking
	Systems Hardware and Software
	Communications Equipment
Other Assets	XXXXXX
Total Assets	**XXXXXXX**
Accounts Payable	Payment / Discount Terms
	Inbound Lead Time
Goal:	Raw Material Inventory Strategy
Other Liabilities	
Equity	
Total Liabilities & Owners' Equity	**XXXXXX**

Figure 13.2. The Balance Sheet and Logistics Drivers.

an asset. Figure 13.2 shows a typical balance sheet and where logistics processes are represented on the balance sheet.

Inventory Turns and the Balance Sheet

Inventory turns are an extremely important metric. In a Lean environment, we want inventories to be at a minimum. Therefore, we need to be able to measure our operational initiatives relative to their impact on inventory levels. Typically, this is done by dividing sales (at cost) by the average of on-hand inventories. Average on-hand inventory levels are derived by averaging inventory levels as reported on the balance sheet. The challenge is to ensure that the balance sheet reports an accurate representation of what inventory is actually on hand. Creating false images of inventory levels is all too common and, in the end, accomplishes less than nothing for the organization. We need to ask why this happens.

Lean practitioners know that systems thinking is an important part of Lean. As we have examined, systems thinking leads to systems optimization, which means that we are focused on the overall system rather than individual functional output. Consequently, we want the balance sheet to draw an accurate picture of the system, as opposed to a purposely manipulated picture. To accomplish this, logistics managers must not fear having inventory on the docks at the end of the period or month. If inventory levels are high, they should be reported and a continuous improvement team should be created to understand and fix the problem. We need to know that inventory level reporting is accurate and that the balance sheet is, in reality, a view of the normal system at work. This course of action prevents the distortion of the facts, which can lead to unwarranted, reactionary tampering with the system.

The Balance Sheet and Business Strategy

It is difficult to draw conclusions relative to an organization from a balance sheet. Organizations have differing strategies, and that will be evident on the balance sheet. For example, one organization may buy assets whereas another firm may lease assets. Another firm may prefer centralized, privately owned warehouses when its competitors use decentralized, public warehouses. All of these strategies will appear on the balance sheet in one form or another.

It is hard to say whether or not Lean has a specific strategy relative to the balance sheet. Nowhere is it written that assets should be owned or leased. However, a couple of Lean principles need to be considered relative to balance sheet management. These are flexibility and visibility.

Flexibility

Lean systems need to be flexible. In a Lean environment of pull replenishment and continuous improvement, assets need to be flexible. Pull replenishment means that we replenish inventory as the internal or external customer consumes it. By definition, if demands change, so does the replenishment cycle. To accomplish this, assets need to be flexible in order to accommodate the variation in demand. For example, transportation and warehousing assets should have some flexibility in their procurement. Even if the organization's balance sheet strategy is to own real estate and warehouses, it should keep flexible a minimum of 20 percent of forecasted space requirements. This will allow continuous improvement initiatives to have a better chance of being implemented as opposed to being caught in the middle of internal politics and functional barriers that typically result when assets are owned.

One Lean paradox is that Lean strives for perfection even though perfection is not attainable. Striving for perfection means to improve processes continuously. This is the spirit of *kaizen*. Kaizen means slow, incremental improvements instead of drastic re-engineering. However, our systems and asset base need to be flexible in order for improvements to take place. Although it may not seem obvious, this flexibility is part of the balance sheet strategy of the organization.

Visibility

The second Lean principle, visibility, is another concept that is not normally associated with the balance sheet. Yet, the balance sheet provides people with a "picture" of the organization, so assets should be visible to the reader. As Lean Six Sigma logisticians, we need to focus on asset productivity and eliminating waste in the form of underutilized assets. How can we do this if assets are not visible to our managers? By reading the balance sheet, it is crucial that we are able to dig down into the organization and determine where assets are used, where assets can be redeployed, and where assets can be eliminated.

The balance sheet is one of the three main financial statements used to manage an organization. Consequently, the Lean Six Sigma logistician needs to understand the strategy used by the company from a balance sheet perspective. Inventory should not be considered an asset; inventory turns need to be reported accurately, and the organization needs to develop a balance sheet strategy based on flexibility and visibility. With this systems approach, decision making will be easier, better, and more effective management decisions will result.

CASH FLOW

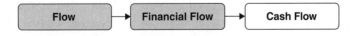

Truism: If cash is king, then logistics represents all the king's horses and all the king's men.

If you think of a company as a human body, cash would be the blood. Positive cash flow permits a company to operate, grow, invest, and work toward organizational potential. Without sufficient cash flow, a company is unable to meet payroll, will default on payments to suppliers, and operations will cease. Cash is necessary to sustain the life of an organization.

So what does this have to do with logistics? Once again, the answer is "everything." To survive, organizations must focus on cash management, which means (yet again) understanding the business from a *systems* point of view. That is, we need to understand in totality the cash implications of decisions across functional areas. This means understanding the drivers that affect cash flows inside our companies. We need to manage and to control these key cash drivers. When we begin to do so, we will soon recognize that we are managing the supply chain. To manage the supply chain successfully, we need a commitment to sound and disciplined logistics processes.

Cash Flow Drivers

There are seven main business activities that affect cash flow. These are:

1. Accounts Payable
2. Accounts Receivable
3. Revenue Growth
4. Gross Margin
5. Selling, General, and Administrative Expense
6. Capital Expenditure
7. Inventory

To understand the impact of logistics on these key cash drivers fully, it is important to study them individually. Next we fuse them, creating a picture of the system that describes how these seven drivers work together inside the organization. Figure 13.3 outlines the seven key cash flow drivers and how logistics processes interact with these seven drivers.

Accounts Payable and Cash

No business is an island; we rely on suppliers and trading partners to supply us with goods and services, without which we could not serve our customers. When we purchase goods and services from our supply base, we typically buy on account with a predetermined payment agreement. When payment is due, we use cash to settle our debts. Consequently, the faster we can receive and

Cash Flow Drivers and Implications	Logistics and Supply Chain Value
Accounts Payable	
1. Payables = Cash Out	1. Increase working capital
2. Timing between receipt, payment, and use of goods	2. Reduce order-to-build lead time
3. Timing between receipt, payment, and use of services	3. Reduce service-to-build lead time
Accounts Receivable	
1. Receivables = Cash In (waiting for cash)	1. Increase working capital
2. Timing between customer receipt and payment	2. Reduce order-to-delivery-to-invoice lead time
3. Accuracy of order and invoice	3. Increase perfect order rate and invoice accuracy
Capital Expenditure (CapEx)	
1. Capital Expenditure = Cash Out	1. Conserve cash
2. Must relate CapEx with strategy	2. Focus attention on core competencies
3. Strategic use of outsourcing	3. Invest cash in core competencies
Revenue Growth	
1. Increased Revenue = Cash In	1. Increase sales
2. New markets determine growth	2. Create/supply new markets
3. Current customer satisfaction drives growth	3. Meet critical-to-quality measures
Gross Margin	
1. Sales – COGS = Gross Margin = Cash In	1. Increase bottom-line impact
2. Reduce COGS = Cash In	2. Reduce operating expenses
3. Focus on reduced COGS	3. Develop optimized logistics infrastructure
Sales-General-Administrative	
1. SGA = Cash Out	1. Increase bottom-line impact
2. SGA must be value added	2. Reduce operating expenses
3. Need to focus on waste reduction	3. Develop optimized logistics infrastructure
Inventory	
1. Opportunity cost of holding inventories = Cash Out	1. Increase working capital
2. Services Costs = Space, Insurance, Taxes, Transportation	2. Reduce inventory service costs
3. Risk Costs = Obsolescence, Shrinkage, Pilferage = Cash Out	3. Reduce inventory risk costs
4. Overproduction = Cash Out	4. Reduce overproduction

Figure 13.3. Cash Flow Drivers and the Logistics Function.

transform purchases into our own products, the faster we will have product to sell to our customers, which ultimately means cash in our till.

Note to the logistician regarding Accounts Payable:

1. Reduce supplier order-to-consumption lead time.
2. Reduce work-in-process inventories and focus on inbound logistics in order to optimize use of credit terms with suppliers.

Accounts Receivable and Cash

Accounts receivable is a significant driver of cash flow. In fact, your outstanding days receivables can often be the differentiating factor of the company's fiscal viability. Remember, cash is the life force of your organization. Employees cannot pay their mortgages with receivables from customers. This is so important that it is tempting to make all salespeople responsible for collections as well as for selling their product. To be sure, an order is not complete until the payment has been received.

For this reason, the Dell model is enviable. Dell receives its cash payment for its product before it must pay for raw materials. Unfortunately, unlike Dell, most of us have to accept the existence of cash receivables. Yet, our ultimate goal can be to receive payment as quickly as possible after we make a sale. This means we need to focus on the perfect order. The perfect order will provide the customer with the right product to the right place at the right time and in the right quantity and condition, thereby alleviating customers withholding payment.

Note to the logistician regarding Accounts Receivable:

1. Deliver the *perfect order* every time.
2. Reduce order-to-delivery lead times so payment is received quickly.

Revenue Growth and Cash

Many management gurus have argued that the only purpose of any business is to develop a customer. The logic here is that without a customer, there is no business proposition. However, some customers are better than others. Therefore, it is important to understand that cash is generated from *good* customers. A good customer can be defined as one that has a genuine need for our service and allows us to generate a competitive rate of return on our investment.

Increased revenue from "good customers" will result in increased cash flow. So how do we secure additional customers? The most effective way is to retain current customers and to be cost and quality leaders in our industry as we solicit new business. These goals require a strategic focus on logistics and supply chain issues.

Note to the logistician regarding Revenue Growth:

1. Be able to identify "good" and "bad" customers based on the profitability of individual accounts.
2. Retain current customers and develop new, profitable customers to generate increased cash flow.
3. Reduce inventories to become more cost competitive and increase visibility on product and process quality.

Gross Margin and Cash Flow

Gross margin is generally defined as net revenues less cost of goods sold. Gross margin is the first line of profit contribution that a firm will see from operations. It plays a significant role in cash flow. Logically, the larger the gross margin, the more gross income we will have to contribute to corporate overhead burdens and net profit. This will result in cash generation (after dealing with receivable issues described earlier). To increase gross margins, we need to ensure that our cost curves do not grow linearly with our revenue curves. That is, we need to be able to generate increased revenues without a proportional increase in cost of goods sold. This is the quintessential example of doing more with less. To reach this goal, we need to focus on the activity drivers of cost of goods sold. As capable logisticians, we must recognize that many of these drivers are logistics related.

Note to the logistician regarding Gross Margin:

1. Manage inbound logistics and reduce overall supply chain and manufacturing lead times.
2. Reduce work-in-process and raw material inventories in order to reduce inventory carrying costs and, therefore, reduce overall cost of goods sold.

Selling, General, and Administrative Expense and Cash Flow

Although not all companies call it the same thing, selling, general, and administrative (SG&A) expense is the most common term used for corporate overheads. Reducing the corporate overhead burden will result in increased cash to the bottom line. Many companies have outbound logistics rolled up into SG&A.

Some companies believe that outbound logistics is purely a necessary evil, a cost of doing business. It may come as a surprise to some C-level officers that logistics costs could exceed 12 percent of their revenue. In today's business climate, where 1 percent of sales can mean the difference between viability and bankruptcy, logistics needs to be an area of concentration. The logistics function can, in fact, become a strategic area for differentiation. There are definitely opportunities for cost reduction with respect to logistics; there are also remarkable opportunities to create a strategic advantage over the competition.

Note to the logistician regarding SG&A:

1. Improve internal processes and reduce SG&A expenses ultimately to increase cash flow.
2. Reduce customer order-to-delivery lead time and reduce finished goods inventory to yield competitive advantage.

Capital Expenditure and Cash Flow

Capital expenditures are the best example of how cash flow and accounting income diverge. For example, if you purchase a building for $1 million, you may decide to outlay $1 million in cash to close the purchase, yet the cost of the building will show up on the income statement as depreciation expense over the useful life of the building. The consequence in the first month will show $5,000 depreciation expense, yet a full million disappeared from the cash drawer. Capital expenditures are an immense drain on cash and possibly an area where ineffective decisions are being made. If so, these ineffective decisions may be due to ill-conceived logistics strategies.

Private fleets, warehouses, and advanced supply chain software are three examples of capital expenditures that require significant amounts of cash to finance. How do we know if we are making the right decision? Why would we invest in a private fleet when our for-hire trucking companies have all the latest technology and years of experience in the trucking industry? Why do we continue to build warehouses when we should be focusing on eliminating the inventories that we store in them? When will we learn that there is no magic software pill to cure our supply chain woes? Capital expenditures drain our companies of cash that can be better used in revenue-generating activities. Therefore, we need to focus attention on logistics strategies that take advantage of existing infrastructure, and we need to focus on effective supply chain processes and the people who will fulfill them.

Note to the logistician regarding Capital Expenditures:

1. Reduce reliance on fixed assets and allow cash to be used on revenue-generating activities.
2. Focus on reducing inventories as opposed to building more warehouses for inventory you do not need.

Inventory and Cash Flow

Inventory is the most elusive of all the cash bandits. The reason is that everything about inventory is counterproductive. For example, inventory sits on the balance sheet as a current asset. Inventory sitting in our warehouse consumes cash and can be difficult to liquidate (a prerequisite to being a current asset). We have already argued that inventory is, in fact, a liability.

Another counterproductive aspect of inventory is that the more inventory you have, the less likely you are to have what you need when you need it. In other words, too much inventory means inventory that is not needed and may never be needed. To store and move surplus inventory drains cash from our organization.

The third and arguably most significant point about inventory is that inventory itself is visible, yet its costs and cash impact are not. Although we can walk the floors of our facilities and see inventory, we cannot easily go to our financial statements and determine how much cash is being consumed by this inventory. Risk costs such as obsolescence and shrinkage drain cash. Service costs such as taxes, material handling, and interest drain cash. In addition, there is an implicit cost of lost opportunity when money is tied up in inventory, as well as the value of space being used to store that inventory. Any way you slice it, inventory consumes cash.

Note to the logistician regarding Inventory:

1. Eliminate inventories and conserve cash.
2. Have the courage to gather the data required to calculate and articulate the cost of carrying inventories.

Vision of Excellence and Cash Flow

To be competitive in today's market, we need to manage cash like the life force of the organization that it is. Logistics and supply chain activities all affect the seven key cash flow drivers within a firm. Accounts payable, accounts receivable, revenue growth, gross margin, SG&A, and capital expenditures can all be managed more effectively by focusing on logistics issues strategically. The reduction of the seventh cash flow driver, inventory, should become the relent-less pursuit of all logisticians.

Alone, each of these seven cash drivers acts independently. Together, they form the organization's *cash-to-cash cycle*. This cycle must be understood, measured, and managed in order for an organization to reach its potential. As a logistician, you can learn about cash flow function. Support the placement of a skilled logistician at a C-level position within your firm and as part of board-room discussions within your organization.

## 14

CAPABILITY: PREDICTABILITY

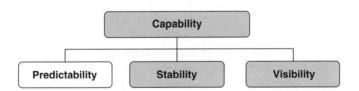

Capable logistics networks have minimal variation. Minimizing variation results in a predictable operation. Predictable operations improve customer service as delivery commitments are kept and customers do not feel the negative effects from out-of-control processes. Predictable processes are the foundation for continuous improvement because predictability is preceded by standard operations. The three strategic focus areas for Predictability are:

1. Organization
2. Coordination
3. Complexity

These three areas will be discussed in this chapter.

ORGANIZATION

Truism: Being organized is a prerequisite to any major accomplishment.

Walk through any Lean plant and the first thing you will notice is that the workplace is organized. Yellow tape on floors, signage everywhere, labels and instructions on every post — that is the Lean norm. As we know, any Lean training curriculum will have a significant component allocated to the "5S" method of organization, and its importance cannot be overstated (a full description of 5S is given in Chapter 22). Why, you might ask, does something as simple as being organized get so much attention? Organization is so important, but we seldom attain and sustain an organized workplace. Recall that Lean is about the elimination of waste. The organized workplace facilitates waste elimination. To begin, it is important to discuss the concept of workplace.

Asked to picture a workplace, many people visualize a manufacturing facility and, likely, the specific area of the facility in which they work. For logisticians, the workplace requires a much broader definition. Their workplace starts at the supplier's facility, which leads to transportation equipment, then on to their own facilities, back to transportation equipment, and ultimately to the customer's facilities. Consider the complexity of the supply chain and the parts of the workplace as one complete entity.

Given the defined span of the logistics workplace, it can be an overwhelming task to comprehend the many activities as one complete operation. Our goal is to know and understand exactly what is happening in the supply chain at any given time. A predictable supply chain is one that allows for this. A capable supply chain is one that has a plan measured against an actual condition. This comparison of plan versus actual condition will only be accomplished if we maintain the discipline necessary for an organized workplace. Overall, the organized workplace contributes to Lean logistics in the following ways:

1. Highlighting waste and clarifying the root causes of waste
2. Supporting standardized operations and orchestrating priorities
3. Reducing clutter and complexity that lead to quality issues in products and processes
4. Supporting measurement
5. Promoting safety in all operations

Highlighting Waste and Creating Visibility

Waste is everywhere. In fact, if we think of our work processes, one could argue that the process itself is alive and its goal is to create waste. That is, organizational processes have inherent forces that create waste. Indeed, there are days when it seems the system is happiest when waste is being created. Our job is to fight the natural tendencies toward waste creation by designing, implementing, and sustaining an organized workplace.

Waste happens! Once we face this brutal fact, we can begin to eliminate it. The first step in waste elimination is to locate the problem. Although this sounds easy and intuitive, it is much easier said than done. Many of our organizations are so inundated with inventory, equipment, and facilities that it is virtually impossible to differentiate what is required and what is waste. Organizing the workplace is a necessary step. Figure 14.1 shows us how being organized helps one to understand any situation.

Box A: What Number Is Missing?						
2	5	12	23	1	15	25
3	9	18	24	8	7	22
4	13	17	14	6	10	20
21	11		16			

Box B: What Number Is Missing?						
1	2	3	4	5	6	7
8	9	10	11	12	13	14
15	16	■	18	19	20	21
22	23	24	25			

The top box is indicative of many workplace conditions. Clearly, the organized manner of the bottom box allows for more effective visual control. These numbers can represent inventory, fixed resources, or even customer expectations.

Figure 14.1. The Organized Workplace. (Adapted from material by Art Smalley, Lean Enterprise Institute.)

The organized workplace can be defined as a place for everything and everything in its place, a concept most of us were taught in kindergarten. This definition leads to disciplined predictability. The goal is to plan (anticipate needs of the operation) and then organize the workplace according to the plan. When the operation is in motion, any deviation from the plan will make waste *visible*.

A logistics example that highlights the importance of the concept of an organized workplace is inventory. Inventory levels should be planned. We should know exactly how much of what inventory we want in the system at any given time. This inventory will, in turn, take up a certain amount of space or tracking. The organized workplace will anticipate this need and allocate exactly that amount of space for the inventory. The space will be labeled and identified in order to understand visibly what the space is for. With this type of organization in place, during the course of the day a manager can easily identify an abnormal condition by looking at the allocated space and labeling. For example, if too much inventory was received, the inventory will be using more than its allocated space, or perhaps no inventory was received, which means that the space will be empty when the labeling clearly shows there should be inventory in the space at that time. There must be a place for everything and everything in its place.

Standardized Operations and Setting Priorities

Standardized operations are a significant part of the Lean lexicon. A standard operation is one where we know the input requirements, the procedure of the process, the time for each step in the procedure, and the expected output of the operation. To have these standards firmly in place requires an organized workplace. For example, let's review the process of filling out bills of lading for daily outbound shipments to customers. An organized workplace would have a place for all bills of lading. In the morning, required bills of lading would be in a tray, visible and well labeled. Throughout that day, the bills of lading would be completed and the container would be replenished with the work for the next day. Yes, this sounds obvious and simple, but many traffic functions in reality are disorganized, and the disorganization causes mistakes and creates waste. To be sure, mistakes happen; the goal is to have the workplace organized so that mistakes are found and corrected before they produce a defective product or service. To succeed and sustain its success, a standard operation requires an organized workplace.

Once standard operations are firmly in place within an organized workplace, priorities can be set. Let's go back to our bills of lading example. The visible inbox can now provide valuable information about the operation. In the morning, we would fill the container with the required bills of lading for the day.

As the day progresses, we can monitor the processing of the bills of lading. If processing is inadequate or problematic for any reason, this will be a signal to go to the shipping area and check schedules. This *go see* technique may result in a correction, but if that is not possible, at least there will be an opportunity to notify the customer as quickly as we can. The corollary of this example is perhaps all bills of lading are used by noon, and traffic coordinators are now filling in bills that were not planned for that day. This should result in questions that may highlight that we are pulling shipments ahead or shipping product that has no firm order. Once again, this will highlight priorities and events that need immediate attention.

The Organized Workplace: Clutter, Complexity, and Quality

Clutter creates complexity, and complexity creates waste. This is the most intuitive yet least managed element of 5S and the organized workplace. The intuitive part is that clutter is a form of waste, and it is the first waste that needs to be eliminated. This is because the clutter is hiding the real and significant waste that is our target of elimination. This clutter may be paperwork, boxes of old files, or obsolete inventory and equipment. Waste could be processes that do not add value to the operation. Accepting clutter means accepting complexity.

For example, when we stock obsolete inventory, the inventory is physically in our facility and the information for the inventory is in our systems (or so it should be). When new and required inventory comes into the facility, we may not have a place to put it because the facility is full of other inventory, some of which may be clutter. We can move the clutter around to make room for the new inventory, and that requires handling material and updating management systems. These movements are wastes and exist because we have not organized the workplace by eliminating all clutter in the facility.

Complexity will, in turn, affect quality. Certainly, the process described above (moving obsolete inventory around) does not represent a quality process. Quality processes are described as processes that create value for the customer. Clutter and a disorganized workplace will eventually cause product quality issues. Excessive material handling, errors in product identification, and misshipments can all cause damage to product. Products can be rendered useless and returns cause waste.

Measurement and the Organized Workplace

We will discuss measurement at length in this chapter, but it is important to highlight the relationship between measurement and the organized workplace.

Measurement is crucial for success. Whether or not you embrace Lean or Six Sigma initiatives, survival in the future depends on having effective measurement systems. Before we can eliminate waste, we need an effective measurement system.

Prior to putting a measurement system in place, we must organize the workplace. How can we have effective measurement if we have a disorganized workplace? For example, before you can measure a trailer yard, any broken-down trailers sitting in the yard need to be cleared. Before we determine our optimal office space, we need to confirm that each person working in this area is adding value. In other words, how can we know our current condition (the first step in measurement) if the business is inundated with clutter? How do we begin to organize the workplace?

One Lean tool that is useful in highlighting waste in the workplace is the *red tag* initiative. Effective and fun for all employees, a red tag initiative is a blitz technique to rid the business of clutter. Simple in concept and application, all employees are given the opportunity to eliminate clutter in the workplace. This is accomplished by creating a *red tag* that can be placed on paper, boxes, inventory, equipment, and anything that does not have value in the workplace. For instance, you can red tag the box of old paperwork that you have been "walking around" for the last few years. The red tag will indicate clutter. The tag will give all employees forty-eight hours to justify keeping the box. Unclaimed boxes go into the garbage. The red tag initiative is simple, fun, and effective.

COORDINATION

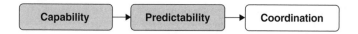

> **Truism**: Logistics is grounded in the coordination of multiple processes across multiple stakeholders.

Lean is about the elimination of waste through flow and reducing reliance on inventories. Six Sigma focuses on understanding and eliminating variation in processes and systems that create waste and inventory. Both Lean and Six Sigma bring power to the logistics function as operations and inventory management have significant variation and multiple sources for the creation of waste. One fundamental characteristic of a Lean logistics system is that each detail is planned. Lean's microplanning creates a logistics system that can monitor deviations from the plan in real time. The result is a system that is understood, visible, and coordinated.

Coordination is the primary mechanism by which supply chain management is achieved. Coordination means that all process owners in the chain have full understanding of their roles and all functions are linked through an operational plan. The plan is what creates the coordination. Planning requires proactive design and execution of processes as opposed to reactive management of processes. Another Lean goal is visibility of the logistics processes. Visibility relies on predictability, which in turn relies on coordination.

Coordination of a logistics system requires three elements:

1. Value stream mapping of the processes requiring coordination
2. Detailed planning around the "moment of truth" of the logistics processes
3. Measurement of key metrics to drive continuous improvement initiatives

Coordination and Value Stream Mapping

One of the most powerful tools in the Lean tool kit is the value stream map. Although the mapping of all processes would seem like basic management protocol, many organizations are operating without it since most start as small businesses and their processes have evolved over time. This incremental evolution of process is what creates confusion and redundancy within the processes of companies. In contrast, a coordinated and planned environment can easily be documented and mapped to identify process owners and critical touch points of the processes. These critical touch points can be called the "moments of truth" for the particular process. Moments of truth are extremely important and need to be coordinated, managed, and measured. One example is the process of moving raw materials into a production facility.

In the absence of coordination, processes are not mapped or documented and, consequently, are not understood by all logistics partners. When we order raw materials in this environment, we cannot be sure of what will arrive at our manufacturing facility. Quite literally, when we open the doors of an inbound trailer, it is like opening a surprise package. Why is this and how can it be managed?

Lean systems are coordinated. Coordinated systems are value stream mapped and documented. In our example, the Lean inbound system value stream map will identify critical moments of truth:

1. Did the supplier receive the order and can the supplier support the request?

2. Did the order get shipped in full and on time?
3. Did the order arrive in full and on time?

An infrastructure must be created to manage these three events. It is foolish to think that critical processes will manage themselves. A well-thought-out plan is needed to manage the moments of truth throughout each step of the process.

Coordination and Detailed Planning

Even though business seems to be moving at the speed of light, we should never lose sight of the intrinsic value of effective planning. Effective planning focuses on coordinating processes; each step of the process itself must be efficient and effective. Efficiency is doing things *right* and effectiveness is *doing the right things*; both are required to coordinate logistics activities. Drawing from the previous example, how can we plan to ensure coordination of the process?

After looking at the value stream map, we quickly recognize that a critical moment of truth occurs when the supplier actually ships the product from its facility. In other words, once the supplier has loaded the truck and shipped from its facility, the process is at the mercy of what was shipped. Recognizing this, we understand that coordination of the process relies on ensuring that what is shipped is what was ordered. The traditional Advanced Shipping Notice (ASN) attempts to manage this; however, the fact is that the ASN is generally nothing more than an electronic reply to the original order. Consequently, even though an ASN is sent saying an order was shipped in full, we are still not sure that what was loaded is what was ordered.

Clearly, the solution to successful coordination is a planned process around the moment of truth. In this case, the answer is to coordinate with the carrier and connect the carrier with the pickup procedure at the supplier. Known in the Lean environment as *point of pickup verification*, this is a process where the drivers on the pickup routes are trained and equipped with the tools to verify what suppliers are to ship. When the driver shows up at a supplier, the driver will have a pickup manifest that details what the supplier is to ship on that order. Part number, part description, part quantity, packaging, and labeling requirements will all be verified by the driver prior to the parts being loaded on the truck. This process coordinates the moment of truth with the value stream map of the order process. Continuing this example, if the driver identifies a discrepancy between what is being shipped and what was ordered, the driver will stop the process and immediately call a dispatcher to report the noncompliant condition. The manufacturer will receive this information while the driver waits at the supplier for further direction. The manufacturer will call the supplier and sort out the confusion immediately, and the supplier can then correct the order and load the truck in compliance with the original agreement.

In contrast, in an uncoordinated environment, the supplier will load the truck, and the shipment may or may not reflect what was ordered. If there are discrepancies, they will not be caught until the trailer is unloaded at the manufacturing facility, which is too late.

In summary, the key aspects leading to the successful design of the process are:

1. Documenting and mapping the process
2. Isolating the moment of truth
3. Coordinating logistics partners to ensure that there is quality built into the process at the exact point of the moment of truth

Once we understand the moments of truth and coordinate around them, measurement systems become the next step to ensure that coordination is effective and that continuous improvement is happening. Figure 14.2 supports the concept of managing the moment of truth.

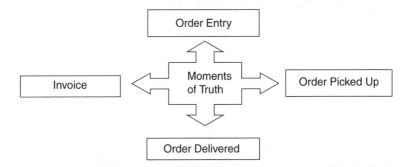

Common Carriers and the Moment of Truth

Although transportation carriers have a multitude of processes to manage, only a chosen few mean anything to the shipper. For example, in a typical shipment, the moments of truth for the shipper/customer look like:

Order Entry

Invoice   Moments of Truth   Order Picked Up

Order Delivered

As we can see from this example, the customer has very few moments of truth in the shipper/carrier experience. Although many carriers focus on other processes, the priority should be on activities that directly affect the moments of truth.

Figure 14.2.   Coordination: Detailed Planning on the Moments of Truth.

Coordination and Measurement

Ultimately, we want logistics processes to be capable. For a process to be capable, it must be predictable. As discussed, for a process to be predictable, it must be coordinated. Coordination relies on managing the moments of truth, and therefore, it is only logical that measurement systems should start by measuring the moments of truth in any process.

Coordination is critical in all business processes, but in particular it is a major component of the logistics process. Logistics processes have a high level of complexity relative to process steps, handoffs, information requirements, and opportunities for process defects. This is not to say that logistics processes are complex conceptually, but rather that the sheer number of steps in logistics processes creates significant opportunities for a process to break down.

This concept of *opportunities for defects* is embedded in Six Sigma principles. When combined with the Lean tool of value stream mapping, we find the path to creating coordinated processes. Why is this? Value stream mapping identifies the process moments of truth, and the Six Sigma processes allow us to measure the opportunities for process defects, which, when accomplished, allows us to initiate improvement in the process. True coordination of process will develop and be sustained once this cycle of renewal is established.

COMPLEXITY

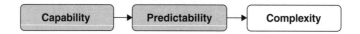

> **Truism**: Progressive and successful companies know that reduction in complexity is a priority.

Have you ever been to a restaurant where the variety on the menu made it difficult to decide what to order? Too many choices make it difficult for the customer and create a burden for the restaurant that must fill the orders. First, each menu item requires raw material, and this requires inventory. Second, each menu item requires knowledge to prepare the dish, and this requires trained personnel. In truth, the menu does not need to offer so many items. People tend to create complexity of product and process that is unnecessary and only serves to increase costs and destroy value inside the organization. Complexity increases each time we add a dynamic or variable to the product or process. When this happens, opportunities for defects and increased inventory result. This combination is dangerous and is likely to be detrimental to your organization.

A famous quote is often attributed to Henry Ford and the production of his Model T: "You can paint it any color, so long as it's black." Although this quote is generally used to produce a smile, Henry Ford knew that building cars in a variety of colors was no laughing matter; he recognized that a variety of colors meant complexity that would have a ripple effect throughout his entire manufacturing process. As an engineer committed to the elimination of waste, Mr. Ford could not understand why a company would add this burden of complexity, cost, and inventory to the process. Unfortunately for Henry Ford, the market demanded multiple colors from which to choose, and this opened the door for General Motors to take the lead in the automobile industry.

Logisticians need to understand and manage complexity by:

1. Identifying and differentiating complexity relative to products and processes
2. Measuring and quantitatively articulating the cost of complexity

Complexity exists in products and processes. Although complexity is detrimental in both areas, the effect of complexity differs for products and for processes.

Complexity of Products

Products can represent any inventory stockkeeping unit (SKU), which may be finished goods, subassemblies, or raw materials. Products can also include fixed assets, packaging materials, or repair items. In fact, products that have complex dynamics surround us. For example, let's look at a manufacturer of everyday batteries. Not only are there different sizes (D cell, C cell, AA, AAA, etc.), but there are multiple packages available as well. You can get 2-packs, 4-packs, 8-packs, 16-packs, bonus packs, and the list goes on. The packaging can be so complex that it takes a frugal consumer many minutes to figure out which package is the most economical. Significant cost is created by the complexity.

Complexity of products and packaging configurations increases the number of finished goods SKUs. With the addition of each SKU, the manufacturer is forced to forecast sales at the SKU level. Each forecast introduces a margin of error because demand and forecast will never quite match. The variability between demand and forecast increases inventories, and these inventories cost the organization real dollars. Not only is there a real cost to SKU proliferation complexity, but it also creates an environment where Lean and Six Sigma disciplines are difficult to initiate and sustain.

Lean is about flow and the elimination of waste through the reduction of inventories. Six Sigma is about reducing defects by understanding, eliminating, and controlling variation. Consequently, product and SKU proliferation goes against all disciplines within Lean and Six Sigma. This is precisely the reason why successful manufacturers manage products very consciously and deliberately, rigorously scrutinizing attempts at SKU proliferation and ensuring that the increased complexity is absolutely necessary.

Complexity of Processes

Complexity has significant impact on processes. The implications of this impact are waste of energy, waste of resources, and increased opportunities for errors that may result in process and product defects. Complexity in process results from the number of steps that it takes for processes to be completed properly. This is especially important in logistics as not only will processes have multiple steps, but often they will have many elements of paperwork as well. Each process step and paperwork requirement creates complexity that, in turn, creates an opportunity for defect. This is based on the mathematical principle of cumulative probabilities.

Cumulative probabilities show us that overall performance of a process is equal to the multiplied performance of each process step. In other words, overall performance is at the mercy of each step in the process. This relates to the concept of *throughput yield*, or defect-free processed volume, which is used to measure "effective efficiency" in many manufacturing settings.

Consider a logistics process such as shipping a pallet to a customer. This process may have twenty steps and five pieces of paper involved with the entire process. These steps may include building the pallet, staging the pallet for shipping, loading the carrier, completing a packing slip, completing a bill of lading, and other steps associated with shipping a pallet. Consequently, the overall performance of the process is a function of the success of each step. For instance, if each step has a performance level of 99.5 percent, then a process with twenty steps would have an overall performance of 90 percent. This describes the power of the multiplying effect of process performance. The key is to eliminate process steps and paperwork requirements in order to reduce the number of opportunities for defects. Figure 14.3 outlines the power of the multiplier effect.

Complexity of process is becoming even more critical as we globalize our supply chains. Importing and exporting material requires multiple process steps and a large amount of paperwork. In addition to all this complexity of process, logistics security issues create another dynamic that adds to complexity. Con-

The more steps or complexity in any process, the more opportunities for defects. Consider if the "perfect order" components were all running at 99 percent performance levels. What would be the yield performance of the entire process to the customer?

Perfect Order	Performance
Right Part	99 percent
Right Place	99 percent
Right Time	99 percent
Right Quantity	99 percent
Right Quality	99 percent
Right Cost	99 percent

Overall Logistics Performance = 94 percent

Figure 14.3. Complexity and Perfect Order Completion.

sequently, it is imperative that we value stream map processes to isolate the process and paperwork requirements in order to measure each leg of the process. Organizations must have a full appreciation of the importance of process to their organization.

## 15

CAPABILITY: STABILITY

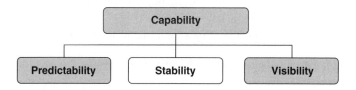

Capable processes and systems are stable. Stability requires reduction of variation; stable processes can be trusted and relied on. Stability is one of the pillars of the Lean enterprise as all significant Lean principles require stability in order to be implemented successfully. Integrated logistics networks must also be stable. However, creating stability in logistics is no easy task, as logistics activities rely on multiple channel partners, significant administrative burdens, and global rules and regulations. The goal of the logistics professional must be to create a stable logistics network in spite of the challenges. The three strategic focus areas for logistics Stability are:

1. Standardization
2. Flexibility
3. Control

These three areas will be discussed in this chapter.

STANDARDIZATION

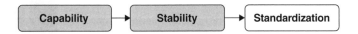

> **Truism**: Standardization is necessary for a multitude of reasons; however, standards need to change as often as is required for success.

Standardization is not just part of the Lean lexicon; it is a brick in the Lean foundation. Yet, standardization does not begin and end with Lean; Six Sigma and logistics also rely on the concept of standardization. In fact, standardization is a concept that can be used effectively in many aspects of our lives, both personal and professional.

In the previous chapter, we discussed the importance of complexity relative to performance of processes. We recognize that we need to reduce complexity; the next question is how. How do we reduce complexity inside our organizations? Standardization plays a key role.

To understand the importance of standardization, consider the following:

1. Without standards, we cannot effectively determine the current *condition of process*.
2. Without standards, we cannot execute sustainable continuous improvement initiatives.
3. Without standards, operational measurements have little meaning, bearing, or *benchmark*.

Our goal is to create a logistics system that is stable. Stability means that the logistics network must be predictable. Consequently, we need standards that are trustworthy and reliable. That is, our operations must have predictable standards that behave in a predictable way given certain parameters. For example, when we route a shipment with a trusted transportation provider, we do so with the knowledge that standards are in place. These standards will result in the carrier managing our shipment using a particular set of procedures that we know and trust. Without standards, we do not know what to expect and every shipment will be an operational roll of the dice.

The Key Aspects of Standardization

As individuals, we tend to develop our own standards as they are needed to complete our work. We do things the same way each time we complete a task, and sometimes we improve the process as we work. Similarly, attempts to standardize processes are evident in all organizations, even when the company is not making a conscious effort to do so. The challenge is to isolate the best practice and implement it throughout the organization. The SIMPOC (Supplier-Inputs-Measurement-Procedure-Outputs-Customers) model can help by providing a framework for documenting standardized processes such that best practices might find application throughout the organization. The SIMPOC model is described in detail in Chapter 22.

Standardization and Continuous Improvement

Standardization plays a critical role in many aspects of Lean logistics, but the highest impact is relative to continuous improvement. Although we discuss continuous improvement at length, it is important to highlight the relationship between standardization and continuous improvement.

Regardless of what model we use to drive continuous improvement, the initiative will start with understanding the current condition of the process. Clarifying one's view of the current condition is only possible if standards are in place. For instance, you cannot know what the transportation lead time is from Chicago to Atlanta if you use different carriers each time and the carriers have no standards. In one case, it may take one day, while in another case, it may take two or three days. How do we know what it should be? Starting with a standard or benchmark is essential to having a focal point for improvement.

Using an analogy, there are many people in the world who want to improve their golf game. Occasionally, an amateur golfer hits a shot as well as a professional. The golfer's challenge now is to understand how this remarkable shot was created so that it can be repeated. The golfer might ask questions such as "How did I hold the golf club? How were my feet planted? How hard did I swing the club?" If we do not have standards relative to these variables, we will never know how a good shot was made. In other words, each time the golfer walks up to the tee, standards must be used. From that point on, minor modifications can bring about continuous improvement. Figure 15.1 shows the different elements used to break down standardized work.

Logistics is similar to golf. How we load trucks, how we track and trace shipments, and how we determine inventory levels are all variables in the overall process. To succeed, we need standards in place for each process. Standards allow us to set expectations and assess current processes.

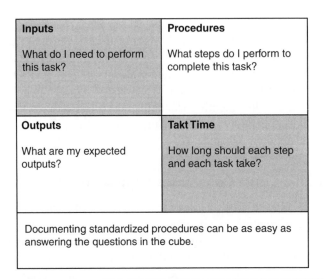

Figure 15.1. Standardized Procedures: Cube Checklist.

FLEXIBILITY

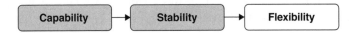

Truism: Flexibility in the supply chain is not about technology or the Internet. Flexibility is about planning and resource management.

Flexibility is a popular word in the logistics vocabulary. All service providers will claim the ability to deliver flexibility to the logistical activities. To understand what this means we ask "What exactly does a *flexible supply chain* look like?" This is a question that needs to be answered prior to designing flexibility into the logistics function.

The goal is to build a logistics system that is capable and stable. When we think stable, we assume "firm," something that cannot be moved. In logistics, stability means there are standards in place and processes in control. Yet, we need these systems to be flexible. Once again, we recognize that Lean Six Sigma Logistics has many paradoxes. The paradox here is that we want stability, standards, and control, but we also want to retain flexibility. We need standards with the flexibility to change in an instant when it is required.

Inbound logistics supporting manufacturing facilities is a perfect example of required flexibility. Raw material might be ordered based on a pull or material requirements planning (MRP) replenishment system. Parts will normally flow into the plant without issue as long as the plant is building according to schedule without interruptions. When the plant is running according to plan, the logistics system will take on the design of a pipeline with material flowing in perfect balance to the beat (or takt time) of the plant. In this situation, the supplier is in tune with the trucking company, the trucking company is in tune with the manufacturer, and the logistics system is stable and in control. However, in real life, stability does not last. Manufacturing lines go down, parts shortages occur, and production schedules are changed in midstream to meet customer demands. Typically, when these happen, we cannot shut off the pipeline, and the plant will receive material it no longer requires and will expedite material that is not needed. All of these activities will result in significant cost to each organization, perhaps overburdening the suppliers and carriers involved. Consequently, the challenge is for the logistics system to build in the kind of flexibility that can respond to changing requirements. How do we build flexibility into the logistics system?

Developing Flexibility and Back to Basics

There are people who will argue that flexibility is a technological issue, but Lean and Six Sigma principles tell an entirely different story. A flexible logistics system is a system that can change as required to produce an essential service at the least total cost. First, we need to ensure that we only manage material that needs to be managed. Second, we need the ability to transport and store product for the least possible total cost. This means that our systems, processes, and infrastructure must be flexible in order to change proportionally with shifting demands on the logistics network. To build this flexibility into the logistics network, we need to focus on the following areas:

1. Reduction of inventories
2. Reduction in lead times
3. Maintenance of a scalable and flexible infrastructure
4. Sustained planned network design and visibility

Every concept in this book advocates the reduction of waste, most notably inventories. Lean and the elimination of waste seemingly begin and end with inventory. Excess inventories create the evils within our organization that result in nonvalue-added activities, increased costs, and the *hidden factory*. The hidden factory includes people, equipment, and processes that exist for no other reason than coping with inventory activities. For example, when obsolete inventory is moved around the warehouse to make room for active inventory, the cost is the "hidden factory."

Examples of the hidden factory are evident if not abundant in most organizations. This hidden factory, along with excess inventory, reduces our flexibility. To be flexible is to be Lean in all respects. If we are inundated with inventories and warehouses, it is difficult to know what we have on hand; therefore, our flexibility is reduced. This may seem counterintuitive, but flexibility will occur when the system is purged of all inventory but that which is required at any given time and business condition. Freed of nonessential inventories, we can identify variations in demand on the system. Then we have the ability to plan accordingly, allowing the infrastructure to support only what is required. Before we do this, however, we need to ensure that lead times are reduced to absolute minimums.

Flexibility and Lead Time

Lead time is important relative to logistics flexibility. Certainly, longer lead times result in increased safety stocks to hedge against uncertainties in the logistics pipeline. These uncertainties may be supplier quality issues, transportation lead-time variability, or customer demand fluctuation. These forms of variability increase as lead times increase, and this reduces flexibility. Reduction in flexibility results in an increase in safety stocks. This is certainly one of the negative aspects of the recent move to outsource raw materials to offshore locations. Significant increases in lead time will result in substantially less flexibility and significantly more inventory buildup.

For example, in a situation where a manufacturer currently has a supplier a few hundred miles from the manufacturing facility, total order-to-delivery lead time may take less than twenty-four hours. That is, we place an order one day, it is shipped perhaps the same day, and it arrives the next day. This lead time results in significant flexibility. For instance, if we change the production schedule later on one day, we can cancel the order with the supplier and avoid shipping the order to the plant. In this way, we avoid receiving product that is not required. In essence, shorter lead times give us the flexibility to make day-to-day adjustments without building up inventories. This makes us less reliant on forecasts and more successful in implementing pull systems. The possibility of implementing pull systems reduces proportionally as lead times increase.

To examine the relationship between likelihood of implementing pull systems and lead times, we can examine the recent push for overseas sourcing from China, in particular. Order-to-delivery lead times may be as high as forty-five days. That is, we order material today and we receive the container at the plant in forty-five days. This means we need to forecast what we will be building forty-five days from now. Currently, we are forecasting anticipated customer demand, and this demand can change considerably in forty-five days. Consequently, if all parts arrive as scheduled in forty-five days, we may be building product that has no demand in the market. Essentially, we are building a product because we have the raw material. Our production schedule is now being driven by the location of this raw material as opposed to the customer's requirements! This situation is neither Lean nor clever. Increased lead times reduce flexibility, which will result in significant inventory buildup. Again, if we maintain reduced lead times, we will more likely recognize the variation in the demands on the logistics system. Only then can we plan accordingly, allowing the infrastructure to support just what is required. This is known as flexibility of the logistics infrastructure.

Logistics Infrastructure Flexibility

By definition, a flexible logistics system should bend with the demands of the system. In theory, if we want to reduce costs to the daily minimum requirement, we would pay for exactly what we use. For example, if we are using 35,000 square feet of warehouse space, we want to pay for that amount of space on that day. This is impossible because warehouses and transportation equipment are fixed costs. For instance, if we have 100,000 square feet under one roof, we are paying for the entire space regardless of our usage. Truckloads are similar in that we pay full truckload rates even when shipping three-quarters of a full truckload. Incredible savings can be made when assets used are congruent with assets required. This is logistics flexibility. To accomplish this, we need to design flexibility into the system from the beginning.

From a logistics infrastructure point of view, flexibility means utilizing and paying only for infrastructure that is required at that time even though logistics infrastructure items are often fixed assets with fixed costs. The question is "Does it need to be this way?" One Lean Six Sigma technique is to build your infrastructure to support the average demand of the network and not the peak demand. Suppose we own 80,000 square feet of warehouse space, but have another 20,000 square feet available from a local third-party warehouse. The terms on the third-party agreement should be flexible so that we pay for what we use. This logic applies to transportation equipment, space, material handling equipment, and human resources. The logic of Lean is to smooth and level operations over all available work time. Consequently, we want to have the infrastructure designed to handle average demand and not peak demand. When operational needs arise, we will require additional resources. These added resources should be temporary so they do not become part of the fixed cost of the operation. To do this requires a commitment to planning.

Planned Network Design and Visibility

For a competent logistics network, you need visibility. Visibility must be planned. One of the least understood concepts in Lean logistics, visibility is more than knowing what is in the pipeline. We may accomplish this kind of visibility with systems and Web-enabled technology, but it tells us very little without a plan for comparison, a plan to compare with the actual condition. Flexibility and logistics management rely on our being able to change a situation instantaneously. To do this, we need to ask the following:

1. What is supposed to be happening today? What product inventory should be flowing through the system?
2. What inventory is actually flowing through the system and how does it compare to the plan?

This concept of *plan versus actual* is at the heart of Lean Six Sigma and answers the questions "What are we expecting the system to do?" and "What is it actually doing?" In addition to allowing the flexibility to make changes and fully utilize resources, managing planned versus actual is the basis for effective measurement systems. Consequently, the opportunity exists for most organizations to develop planning capability in the logistics function. Figure 15.2 describes how visibility and flexibility work together to achieve results.

Logistics planning capability does not need to be elaborate or technologically sophisticated. All that is required is a commitment from the organization to allocate a small team of logistics engineers to plan resource requirements and to have visibility on the actual condition. This minimal investment can result in significant cost savings and improved operations. For example, for the cost of three salaries and a few simple tools (spreadsheets, database, etc.), an organization can have a continuous view of what is moving and what needs to move in the logistics network. Having these three analysts will result in increased transportation equipment utilization, space reduction, and inventory optimization. How does this happen? An analyst will be looking at all opportunities to do more with less. For instance, it is a certainty that the easiest way to reduce transportation cost is to move more products with the same resources. An analyst's focus on this will result in consolidations, multistop loads, and opportunities to create full truckloads. It is imperative for organizations to recognize that logistics is a planning, as opposed to a reactive, function. Organizations that do not have logistics planning capability are paying too much for the operation of their network. In summary, planning capability provides visibility on the day-to-day operations, and this visibility results in flexibility to make instant changes, utilize resources, reduce inventories, and cut costs.

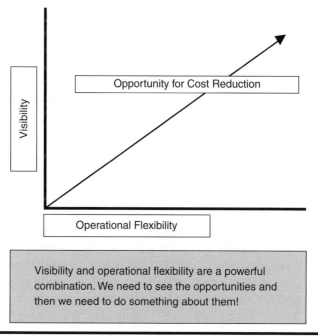

Figure 15.2.   Flexibility + Visibility = Cost Reduction.

CONTROL

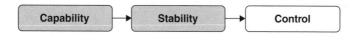

Truism: A controlled logistics network does not mean that it is without variation. What matters is that we recognize what part of the system is out of control.

A logistics network is a living system with many variables and dynamics that affect the entire system. For example, ordering strategies impact transportation strategies, which impact warehousing strategies, which impact inventory strategies. The key is that none of these variables acts independently. As part of a system, they are interdependent. Consequently, variability in each step of the system will result in operational issues in other parts of the system. This variability and its resultant impact need to be in control, even though being in control does not necessarily mean the performance of the system is acceptable to the customer. Being "in control" simply means that the system is behaving as it should relative to the operational capabilities of the system. Stable logistics systems are systems that are in control. To gain an understanding of logistics and controlled systems, we need to appreciate the following:

1. A logistics system is only capable of performing at its capability today.
2. There is a significant difference between common cause and special cause variation.

Today's Capability Is the System's Capability

When a shipment arrives late to a customer, as it often does, the customer complains vociferously and executives demand answers and countermeasures. They want proof that this will not happen again. It would certainly be a career-limiting move for a logistician to tell the executives the truth: "The system behaved exactly as it was designed." In other words, the shipment arrived late, right on schedule! What we fail to recognize is that systems have a set capability. This capability will have average performance levels with variation on both sides of the average performance. This natural variation is what describes the capability of the system.

For example, order-to-delivery lead time for a particular customer may average seven days, although the natural variation will result in some deliveries making it in five days and others making it in nine. Problems are realized when a shipment is delivered in nine days; the customer is upset and we believe the system failed. The system did not fail; the system responded exactly to its capability. Indeed, the particular shipment had no way of making it in anything other than nine days. If the customer was expecting less than nine days, then the order was doomed for failure from the beginning. The system will behave to its capabilities at any point in time.

Throwing tantrums and issuing executive edicts do nothing to change the capability of a system. It is a mathematical certainty that the system will perform to its capabilities. Therefore, it is time to start working on the logistics system itself. It is easier said than done when it comes to implementing changes for sustainable reductions in lead time. One more time: system capability only changes when changes are made to the system. This is at the heart of Six Sigma. Six Sigma demands an understanding of the system, especially the inherent variation in the system as well as how to reduce the variation to meet the customer's requirements every time. To begin this journey, we need to explore the difference between common and special cause variation.

Common and Special Cause Variation

A controlled logistics system can still experience variation in the performance level. The goal is to reduce and manage that variation. The goal is also to make sure that the natural variation is always contained within the specifications and expectations of the customer. To accomplish this, we need to isolate and understand *common cause* and *special cause variation.*

Common cause variation is simply the variation that is inherent in the system, and it describes the current capabilities of the system. For example, transportation networks have a capability of approximately 98.5 percent on-time performance. This means that the system is designed to produce on-time performance of 98.5 percent. Therefore, we should not be angry or surprised when 1.5 of every 100 shipments is late. These late shipments are simply the result of natural variation in the system. This natural variation is a result of everyday factors outside our control. These items may be natural traffic patterns and delays or on-the-road issues such as equipment breakdowns. The point is that these events will happen and therefore are a common cause for natural variation in the system. The less-than-truckload (LTL) industry is an example of a system that has a determined and well-recognized common cause variation. In doing so, the LTL industry recognizes that it can only guarantee 98 percent on-time performance levels. You can get a 100 percent on-time performance level for a premium price. Yet, does this premium freight run through a different operational infrastructure? Absolutely not! The premium freight is flagged as premium, and special attention is given to the particular piece of freight. In other words, the LTL carrier manually manages the common cause variation. Special attention is paid to the points where the common cause variation tends to happen. This situation begs the question "Why can't they do this with every shipment?" The key point is that variation happens. Figure 15.3 provides questions we can ask when processes are out of control.

As discussed, common cause variation exists in systems that are in control. However, not all variation is common, as some is caused by special circumstances. These events are described as special cause and should not reflect badly on the process itself. For example, a port strike or temporary closing of a border point would be considered a special cause and should not result in adjustments to the process. That is, if there are multiple late loads because of a closed border crossing, we should not fire the carrier or redesign the logistics network. This is a special cause circumstance and should be treated as such. How do we know the difference? This is where we rely on tools from Lean and Six Sigma. Specifically, we need to ensure that we have control charts and running values that describe the important processes in our organizations.

Processes will not go out of control randomly. Some event has happened that resulted in the process going out of control. If a process seems to be out of control, ask yourself:

1. Have we changed the way we measure this process?
2. Has there been an environmental change (weather, supplier location)?
3. Have we changed the people that manage this process?
4. Has there been a change in the procedures of the process?
5. Have we changed suppliers to the process?

Figure 15.3. Questions for Out-of-Control Processes.

Control charts are not widely used even though they are the most effective way to display information about a process graphically. When we plot running averages and ranges, we soon see how the process behaves in a natural setting. As well, plotting values will allow us to differentiate between common and special cause variation. Once we have control charts in place, we will see how the process acts in normal and abnormal conditions, which will allow us to focus on continuous improvement initiatives. These initiatives will focus on centering the process and reducing common cause variation to within customer specification limits.

## 16

CAPABILITY: VISIBILITY

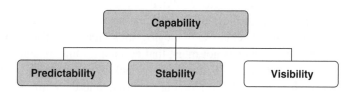

Capable systems are visible. In fact, logistics visibility is now on the priority list of all logistics professionals. Yet, what exactly is logistics visibility? Is visibility only realized with massive investments in technology? Lean Six Sigma Logistics drives inventory reduction, a process that requires visibility: What inventory do we continue to hold in the pipeline? In fact, organizations that do not have logistics visibility are managing in the dark, not a sustainable proposition. The three strategic focus areas for logistics Visibility are:

1. Understandability
2. Measurability
3. Actionability

These three areas will be discussed in this chapter.

UNDERSTANDABILITY

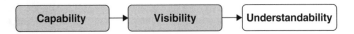

Truism: Most logistics processes are hidden from plain view. This means that we need to understand intuitively how the system works.

It is alarming how little some managers know about their logistics and supply chain processes. Although the system produces results in the end, its workings can be puzzling to the typical executive. Traditionally, logistics has not been a boardroom topic, in many cases considered an evil cost of doing business and one that simply needs to be minimized. However, the tides are turning and logistics is beginning to gain momentum in corporate boardrooms. Some of this change is proactive and some is reactive. The proactive change is driven by organizations that recognize that improved logistics functions can provide a competitive advantage. Reactive organizations are being forced to study their supply chain due to changing global dynamics and increased supply chain security requirements. Regardless of the motivating factor, organizations need to understand their supply chain and the logistics function. The fact that it sounds like common sense does not mean that companies understand how their logistics network operates. This is not due to a lack of commitment, but to the complexity of the logistics network. Trying to understand the entire system can be an overwhelming task. Figure 16.1 shows us that visibility begins with understanding who the channel partners are in the logistics system.

Capable logistics networks are visible, and visible systems are more easily understood. Understanding a system is vital for improvement. Unlike a manufacturing process, a logistics process is not under one roof. Unlike other business processes, logistics processes involve multiple channel partners, often companies physically separate from the organization. For example, some managers would be shocked to learn that truck drivers from their outsourced carriers have more face-to-face contact with their customers than their own employees do! The logistics function spreads across multiple geographic boundaries as well as multiple channel partners. This supports the need for a better understanding of how it works in order to manage it effectively. The value of understanding our logistics system cannot be overstated. From a Lean point of view, we want to eliminate waste in logistics. From a Six Sigma point of view, we want to reduce variation in the logistics processes. To accomplish this, we must first learn how the system works.

Channel Partners	Moments of Truth
What role do channel partners play?	What are the critical touch points with channel partners?
Continuous Improvement	**Measurement**
How do we know we are improving?	How do we know if we are succeeding or not?

Understanding the logistics network starts with understanding all the stakeholders and determining what role each plays.

Figure 16.1.   Understanding the Logistics Network.

Beginning to Understand

We have already discussed value stream mapping and standardized work. These two concepts are instrumental in order to understand a logistics system as well as to make the entire network visible to the organization. Understanding starts with mapping the logistics network. First, plot suppliers and customers; now you will begin to see how the logistics network takes shape. Second, understand how the processes work in the network itself. To do this, we rely on the SIMPOC tool (described in detail in Chapter 22). In brief, the SIMPOC outlines a process from the point of view of process suppliers, inputs, measurement, procedures, outputs, and customers. Once the mapping and SIMPOC are complete, you will be able to answer the following questions:

1. Where are our facilities as well as those for suppliers and customers?
2. Who are the channel partners involved with the network? What role do they play? How intensely do we rely on them?
3. What are the moments of truth and what opportunities exist?

Channel Partners and Their Important Role

Understanding the role that logistics channel partners play further illuminates how the system works. This understanding creates the visibility that we require to manage and improve the system. For example, it is estimated that more than two hundred documents are completed for the delivery of a single global shipment. Try to answer the following questions:

1. Who is completing these documents?
2. What is our liability?
3. Is there duplication of effort?
4. Can we streamline the process?

These are questions that most of us cannot answer because we blindly delegate process activity, relying on channel partners to get the job done. Channel partners include customs brokers, freight forwarders, transportation providers, and third-party logistics providers. We need to understand what these providers do and how they do it.

Understanding the role played by our channel partners is not to suggest that we micromanage the services they provide. They are the professionals, and we need to trust their part in the logistics system. However, Lean teaches us that it is a system and that all systems are alive; each node in the system is interdependent on the other nodes in the system. To understand the system in its entirety is to understand each component of the system. To understand each component requires an understanding of how each partner contributes to overall system performance.

Once the map of the logistics network is completed, bring channel partners together for a meeting to develop a complete value stream map. Ask each partner to discuss its role in the process as well as the following aspects:

1. Describe your impressions of how well the process works.
2. Explain the challenges you have with this process.
3. Discuss how costs could be reduced if a collaborative effort was made.

After answering these questions, we will gather information relevant to potential opportunities and moments of truth.

Opportunities and the Moment of Truth

As distressing as it may seem, our channel partners know our logistics processes just as well as, if not better than, we do. Consequently, we can call on them to help us isolate areas for improvement. Customs brokers, carriers, and third-party logistics providers all have sophisticated information technologies that store data and information about our logistics system. We need to take advantage of the availability of this information and urge the service providers to generate opportunities for improvement. These channel partners not only know where the system can be improved but also know where we, the customer, are adding costs to the channel partner's system. In other words, as the customer, we are adding costs to our suppliers that will eventually be passed back to us for payment. These costs may include excessive waiting time to be unloaded, extra trailers in a pool, or manual paperwork processes that could be automated. The list of opportunities and possibilities is endless, some of which are relatively easy to implement. Trust and collaboration with logistics channel partners are significant and necessary requirements.

Gaining an understanding of the system brings visibility to the moment of truth in a logistics process. Moments of truth are the critical points in the customer relationship where everything matters. The exact moment of truth is when plans come together and the customer has a positive experience. This is analogous to the cell phone. The average cell phone user neither has any idea what technology is used for cellular communication nor cares. It does not matter where the company's cell tower is or whether or not the company has a partnership with yet another cell company. What matters is that when the user wants to make a call, the phone works. The moment of truth for the cell phone provider is when the customer flips open the phone to make a call. This is the critical point in the customer-supplier relationship.

Similarly, we need to isolate and understand the moments of truth with our customers and channel partners. To increase our understanding of the system we need to ask:

1. What are the contact points between the customer and our logistics system?
2. How well are we performing at these specific times?
3. What can we do to improve the service exactly at the moment of truth?

MEASURABILITY

> **Truism**: Most measurement systems are completely ineffective. They make us feel better, especially when printed on nice colored paper, but they might as well be used for wallpaper.

Measurement is extremely important to capability and visibility. For instance, to determine a system's capability, we need some way to measure it. To understand a system is to define it in mathematical terms. As most of us know, implementing an effective measurement system is hard work. First, we determine what to measure, and then we collect accurate data and try to sustain the measurement system over the long term. The setup is the most important part of the work. Effective measurement systems begin and end with what you measure, so the greatest challenge is deciding what to measure.

Lean teaches us about eliminating waste and reducing inventories through the use of pull replenishment systems. Six Sigma teaches us the importance of the customer's *voice* as well as how to design processes that will meet our customer's expectations. Consequently, our measurement system needs to address these focus areas, starting with the customer. This provides an excellent lesson in business. When in doubt, start with the customer.

From customer and logistics points of view, all measurements can be categorized into one of the following three areas:

1. Cost
2. Time
3. Quality (including service)

With these three categories in mind, we can construct a measurement system with visibility into the logistics network. Figure 16.2 defines the perfect measure. To begin, we start with the customer.

Voice of the Customer

Though hard to believe, it is true that companies often build and sell products without acknowledging their customers' thoughts and feelings. Fortunately, Total Quality Management and Six Sigma have emphasized the concept of the "voice of the customer."

The voice of the customer is about understanding your customer's expectations and current challenges. It is instinctive to develop your product or service to meet these expectations and challenges. Of course, we want to know if and how well we are achieving those critical objectives. Consequently, the first measurement system should represent the voice of the customer.

A simple interview with the customer will determine expectations and current challenges. Use the feedback from this interview to build a measurement system. For example, during the interview, you may learn that the customer is implementing Lean principles and reducing raw material inventories. Your measurement system will need to describe possibilities that increase deliveries and reduce lot sizes in an attempt to shrink inventories. Hence, in addition to measuring customer inventory (the dependent variable), we would measure lot

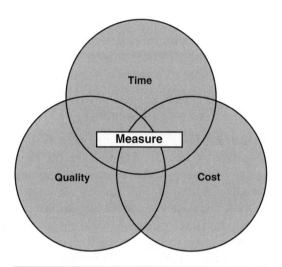

All measures can be categorized by time, cost, and quality. A balance of all three is required for full understanding of any process.

Figure 16.2.   The Perfect Measurement.

size and delivery frequency (independent variables that influence customer inventory). You may take the same approach to time and quality issues. What is important is that the measurement makes sense and that it passes the "so what?" test. The "so what?" test is a check to confirm that people and processes, operational priorities, and the measurement system are all driven by the voice of the customer. It is one way to verify that the focus on customer satisfaction, as indicated by the customer, is being maintained.

At present, many measurements do not pass the "so what?" test. For example, a manufacturer that is taking up Lean principles probably measures transportation providers by measuring on-time performance of inbound routes delivering raw material to the plant. Although the carrier is measured on yard arrival, it will probably not be measured on when the trailer was received at a door. More importantly, *when* the inventory was consumed in the manufacturing process is probably not measured. In some cases, the material may sit in the trailer in the yard for three weeks before being drawn into the manufacturing system. Clearly, measuring the overall flow of the inventory has greater meaning than simply knowing if the carrier arrived on time.

Our measured data should convince customers that we understand their business needs. For instance, our measurement system should articulate to the customers that we are meeting or can meet (perhaps even exceed) their expectations. Once this customer-centric measurement system is in place, we can focus on our internal measures. Listening to the voice of the customer is a critical driver of Lean Six Sigma Logistics and will be revisited in Section 4.

Creating Internal Measures of Meaning

A measurement system needs to accomplish at least two goals. It needs to articulate the performance of specific activities and provide information that generates guidance for future action. Relative to internal functional measures, we determined that all measures will fall into one of three categories. These categories are cost, time, and quality. In developing a measurement system, we need data representation for all three categories. No one measure can be allowed to define a system.

For example, for years the automotive industry has measured cost on a per-unit basis. Logistics cost per vehicle is the most common measure used for logistics cost in the automotive world. However, taken in isolation, this measure will not describe the performance of the logistics system accurately. This is due to the fact that the denominator in the equation does not have a direct relationship with the numerator. In this example, as soon as the plant loses production time and does not produce to plan, the logistics measure will be meaningless. This happens because the logistics system is fixed for the immediate period and, consequently, is a fixed cost in the short term. Therefore, the measure of logistics cost per unit built is wholly determined by how many vehicles are built. Yet, the measure does nothing to articulate the performance of the logistics system itself. This begs the question "What is the best measure or set of measures?" To answer this question, we need to know what drives the activity in the variable (i.e., the dependent variable) we want to measure.

In the above example, the automobile manufacturer is interested in a measurement that describes the performance of the logistics system. Although cost per vehicle built is one measure that can be used, we have argued that it does not tell the whole story. To develop a more accurate measurement system, we need to isolate the activity that drives the variable we want to measure. In our example, we want to measure inbound logistics costs. Therefore, we need to determine what drives these costs. After some discussion, we are likely to conclude that the purchase of raw materials actually drives inbound logistics costs. Consequently, an appropriate measure would be inbound logistics as a percentage of raw material value purchased. This measure will better articulate the performance of the inbound system. However, as already mentioned, multiple measures need to be used to ensure that the whole story is told. These measures should incorporate data concerning not only cost, but also time and quality.

Ultimately, a valuable measurement system leads to an action. A good measurement system provides sufficient visibility within the system, to turn visibility into action and action into an improvement opportunity. Once these improvement opportunities are executed, the measurement system is more likely to reflect and articulate operational improvement.

ACTIONABILITY

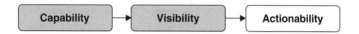

> **Truism**: Logistics visibility without action is like driving a race car that never gets out of first gear.

Lean logistics systems are capable. Capable logistics systems are predictable, stable, and visible. Visible systems are both understandable and measurable. Building a logistics system that is visible and measurable allows us to make improvements in our day-to-day activities.

Many organizations have developed logistics systems that do not enjoy built-in flexibility. In this situation, improvement opportunities will be known, but implementing a solution will be impossible. Even if the willingness to improve is there, the resources, skills, and time may not be available. For example, once visibility is achieved, an organization should be able to see if trailers are going out underutilized. In a perfect setting, a trailer will be fully utilized before leaving the yard. Trailer utilization solutions could involve redesigning particular routes, consolidating shipments, or calling the customer to increase the order size. Making adjustments requires people with time and skills. Actions require a system that has the capacity to change as needed. For example, some organizations have paperwork processes that do not allow last-minute changes. Even though you could add to the shipment on the trailer, you are blocked by the computer system that will not allow it. These types of constraints are unacceptable when action is the priority.

It should not surprise us at this point that making a logistics network actionable is more about communication than anything else. Setting the stage for action requires the development of communication channels. To begin, isolate the areas most likely to require action. Or, put another way, predetermine the areas that you want to act on or improve on a daily basis. These areas may be:

1. **Outbound trailer utilization**: Action is to ensure that trailers are fully utilized.
2. **Supplier shipping compliance**: Action is to ensure that suppliers only ship what has been ordered.
3. **Carrier trailer pool level**: Action is to monitor and immediately correct levels of dropped trailers.

As you can see from these examples, we have chosen the focus areas where daily changes are often necessary. Once these areas are highlighted, processes are put in place to ensure that the change is actionable. Our goal is to ensure real-time processes and resources to increase trailer utilization, deal with noncompliant suppliers, and increase or decrease the number of trailers in a trailer pool. Without formal processes in place, action will not happen. Without real-time action, the system will decline and the result will be increased cost. To be sure, continuous improvement is an ever-present challenge. Implementing processes for real-time action requires an extremely disciplined communication flow.

As described in Chapter 12, real-time communication needs to be well planned in advance. Internal communication and external communication with service providers must be designed, documented, and agreed upon by all stakeholders. Without this planning, real-time operational action will not happen.

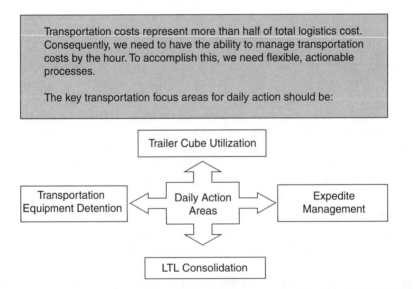

Transportation costs represent more than half of total logistics cost. Consequently, we need to have the ability to manage transportation costs by the hour. To accomplish this, we need flexible, actionable processes.

The key transportation focus areas for daily action should be:

Figure 16.3. Action and Transportation Costs.

Without disciplined processes, attempted action tends to result in confusion and operational service failures. When you focus on action areas, disciplined processes, and communication channels, waste can be eliminated on a day-to-day basis. When actions are integrated into an efficient measurement system, the logistician can articulate the value of improvements made each and every day. Figure 16.3 outlines that we need to take action every day in order to eliminate waste.

## 17

DISCIPLINE: COLLABORATION

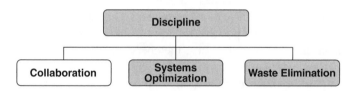

Integrated supply chain management is still unrealized because effective collaboration has not been realized. The implementer needs to collaborate internally with functional departments and externally with customers and suppliers. As with any other function, collaboration requires knowledge and planning. Effective collaboration requires commitment to the cause. The three strategic focus areas for logistics Collaboration are:

1. Teamwork
2. Strategic Sourcing
3. Project Management

These three areas will be discussed in this chapter.

TEAMWORK

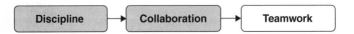

Truism: A company's success depends on teamwork. Functional silos are an out-of-date premise. Knowledge sharing and internal and external collaboration are necessities for survival.

It is troubling to see how little we understand the concept of teamwork, especially since most of us grew up playing or watching team sports. Although there are many definitions, teamwork essentially consists of a group of individuals, each with unique talents, working toward a common goal. Teamwork is a powerful force. The synergy that results from the melding of ideas and experience can often raise a company above its competition.

Too often, turf building and power brokering replace teamwork. Building teams and encouraging teamwork are difficult, but successful people understand that the payoff is worthwhile. A team that works well together can survive and even thrive when members have conflicting ideas. Distinctive — and sometimes conflicting — ideas create a positive force; remember that two (or more) heads are better than one. In creative teams, members are allowed to use their individual talents and are valued for their uniqueness.

For example, a typical manufacturing company's production unit wants to produce as few different products as possible, while the marketing unit wants to produce as many products as possible. In a typical environment, without teamwork, these departments begin to clash, and the tendency is to build walls and, in extreme cases, sabotage one another. In an enlightened teamwork environment, the units can learn to understand and work with their differences within a shared vision. Opening up a new point of view can maximize the capabilities of employees and, subsequently, the company's potential. Once this vision is agreed upon, team members will have stronger commitment and will enhance each other's talents as they work toward their goals. Working together teaches us that overcoming conflict is part of teamwork and ultimately worth the struggle.

Often, the best ideas are hatched during the early, stormy, stressful stages of teamwork development. Success will come to the person who strives to work cooperatively with colleagues who have opposing work styles, goals, and priorities. Building teams is not about who you like or what department you are in. Building teams is about a shared goal and who has what skill and talent to contribute to the team. Increasingly, in logistics and supply chain management, it is well known that more cross-functional teamwork is required.

Companies continue to suffer from a lack of cross-functional teamwork, which creates silos, stovepipes, and departmental barriers. Natural forces tend to create walls and maintain their existence. Excellence in supply chain management will not be reached as long as there are communication barriers. Hence, the significant question is "Why do departmental barriers exist and what can we do to break them down?" It can be argued that two of the key drivers of departmental barriers are a lack of understanding of internal processes and a lack of communication with the customer.

Processes and Knowing the Customer

Generally speaking, departmental dysfunction exists across two or more key groups in most organizations. That is, there are common sources of friction and lack of cooperation. The first is between sales and operations, and the second is between back-office processes and the rest of the firm. This includes critical functional processes such as sales, marketing, human resources, and finance. If we delve deeper, we find two groups of processes behind the issues that cause poor teamwork. These two categories can be called "core" and "enabling" processes.

Core processes are those that generate revenue for the firm directly. They are on the front line; they communicate and interact with the customer daily. In the case of manufacturing companies, the sales function typically manages the core processes, and in the case of service industries (third-party logistics companies, for sure), the core processes are managed by sales and front-line operations. You know you are part of a core process when your direct customer is the external customer who purchases your product or service.

Enabling processes are those that support the core processes. They are the functional areas where the immediate customer is the internal customer. Finance, human resources, and procurement all represent enabling processes where the "customer" is the sales or operations group whose job it is to satisfy the ultimate customer.

Herein lies the problem. Not all groups are in front of the real customer. For enabling processes, if there is no common understanding of the ultimate customer's needs, false perceptions of what is important can be created. Consequently, department heads responsible for core processes can make ineffective decisions that suboptimize the firm's potential.

Core-process employees are directly involved with the customer on a continuous basis. They can experience shell shock from a fierce customer who continuously demands price reductions and increased service. At worst, these employees suffer from the "Stockholm syndrome," where the captives slowly identify with their captors and, ultimately, become the enemy (e.g., the Patty

Hearst story). When this happens, the core-process employees become so focused on the customer that they can easily forget about internal realities and business factors that need to be addressed in order to serve the customer effectively.

Consequently, there needs to be a healthy balance between customer requirements and internal necessities. Bridging these two elements is the spirit of teamwork and strategic planning. Like many communication functions, bringing the core and the enabling groups together is easier said than done.

One approach that successful companies embrace is to provide senior managers and aspiring leaders with work experience in different departments throughout their careers. It is a sobering experience for a salesperson to work inside the company in order to gain a new appreciation for operations. It is equally sobering for a CFO to sit in front of an irate customer.

Bridging the gap between core and enabling processes leads to a common appreciation of internal business challenges and customer needs. In this way, all company employees deepen their understanding of the ultimate customer and internal realties. When this happens, we will be successful in aligning core and enabling processes in a systematic way. A holistic approach, like that offered through systems thinking, is required to break down functional silos further.

Building Teams

As professionals, our work is becoming more project based. As project managers, we must assemble teams in order to achieve our goals. This requires awareness of the following two key aspects of teamwork:

1. Effective teams have members with complementary skills and opposing views.
2. Teams go through natural phases of development before becoming effective.

Complementary Skills and Opposing Views

Any sports team would be hard-pressed to win a championship with only one type of player. Imagine a football team with only one wide receiver or envision a football team with no wide receiver at all. To be effective, teams need to have a cross-section of team members who bring a variety of skills and talents to the effort. Unquestionably, each of us brings diverse strengths and weaknesses to the team. Although it is always dangerous to categorize people, it is safe to say that a high-functioning team will need at least one member who can fulfill each of the following roles.

1. **Content specialist**: This is the team member who can help with science, mathematics, or specialized topic content.
2. **Driver**: This is the person who follows through on the steps needed for the completion of the project, who breaks down barriers, and strives for accountability from all team members.
3. **Visionary**: This is the person who thinks and dreams possibilities and ideas and is crucial in the brainstorming stage of teamwork where ideas and alternatives are necessary to generate a go-forward plan for the team.
4. **Analyst**: This is the person who can get the detailed work done, the grinder who can develop a work plan and manage the fine points.

At times, most of us are capable of stepping into any of these roles, although we are generally better suited for one in particular. Most people tend to migrate toward a particular function. For example, a visionary will find it difficult to perform in an analyst's role, although that may be necessary at times in the project. The key to effective teamwork is to have each role represented.

Natural Stages of Team Development

Most of us have had awareness training on the natural stages of team development, yet many of us continue to react negatively to team situations, seeming to ignore the progression of natural team-building stages. Teams evolve over time. The following words provide a humorous view of the natural stages of team development: forming, storming, norming, and performing. Figure 17.1 describes how team effectiveness will vary throughout the different stages of team development.

Of great interest to the team leader is the storming stage, which is typically the starting point where the team identifies itself and works through personality issues. All teams go through this stage. Therefore, it is important that the team leader know this and be prepared to manage the team through this critical stage as well as those that follow. This is particularly true in a Lean environment where members of the team may be from different functional areas of the organization. It is only natural that people want to understand exactly what role(s) they are expected to fill on the team. This activity often creates "storming behaviors," which cause discomfort in other team members. The good news is that this stage is extremely common and, in fact, is the catalyst to a high-performance team. In the end, the team leader needs to manage the transition of the team from one stage to the next to ensure that the team is continuously recalibrating and heading toward its goals. Collaboration is impossible without effective teamwork. Our organizations need to ensure that employees are trained on team principles and that discipline is used to manage teams and projects.

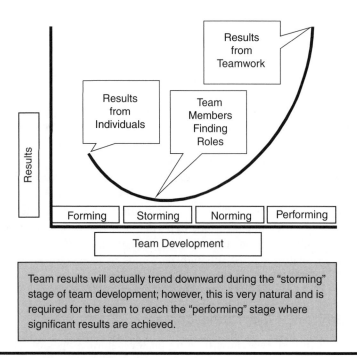

Figure 17.1. Team Development and Results.

STRATEGIC SOURCING

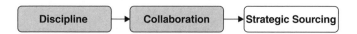

Truism: If we choose our suppliers as we choose our friends, we will have common goals, shared values, and implicit trust.

Embedded in the Lean lexicon is the concept of supplier partnerships. Lean theory suggests that supplier relationships should be based on long-term commitments to quality and cost reduction. Six Sigma theories suggest that the number of suppliers we have should be minimized in order to reduce complexity and the associated costs. Moreover, from a logistics point of view, strategic sourcing strategies have significant impact on logistics functions. Accordingly, all decisions regarding suppliers and sourcing need to be front and center on the logistics radar screen. The types of sourcing that logisticians are interested in are:

1. Raw material suppliers (choosing suppliers for purchased parts, components, raw material, and service parts)
2. Logistics providers (outsourcing logistics activities including, but not limited to, transportation, warehousing, cross-docking, packaging, and third-party logistics).

We will highlight the key discussion points relative to raw material suppliers, but our main focus is on the sourcing of logistics services.

Raw Material Suppliers

The logistics manager will, with any luck, participate in the selection process of suppliers for the manufacturing process. At the very least, the logistics manager should be involved with analysis when looking at sourcing strategies, especially reviewing supplier alternatives and locations relative to transportation and inventory carrying cost. This is particularly important as many organizations are moving their domestic supply base to offshore locations, with far-reaching implications.

When performing supplier selection analysis, the key elements to examine are:

1. Supplier location
2. Supplier order-to-ship lead time and reliability
3. Supplier to plant transportation lead time and reliability
4. Supplier quality of service compliance
5. Supplier quality of product compliance

From a Lean point of view, the focus of supplier selection is on how the decision impacts the manufacturer's inventory. This is one of the main reasons why partnerships and long-term relationships are so important. This may not be instinctive, but in reality, the better the relationship with our suppliers, the less inventory we should have in the system. The more we can trust our supply base, the fewer inventories we will need to carry. This lesson is embedded in Six Sigma theory: Variation is what causes the need for buffer inventory.

Safety stocks are carried to hedge against supplier lead time and supplier quality issues. The further a supplier is from the point of use, the more safety stock we need to hedge against the risk of supply interruption. We see this situation at work as U.S. ports become more of a risk in their ability to process offshore containers. Similarly, when we move to new suppliers that are untested, we will carry safety stock to hedge against risk of quality issues with material received. Long distances and variation in quality translate into high levels of safety stock. In most cases, organizations will hedge against the worst possible scenario, resulting in the buildup of significant inventories.

We are not suggesting that offshore supply bases are ineffective, but rather we are reminding logisticians to do their research and planning thoroughly before making the change. Far too many organizations make sourcing decisions without a complete understanding of the logistics issues. Transportation cost and inventory buildup are the two primary sources of costs to be considered in the equation, along with the prospects of poor customer service and lost sales that go along with supply chain disruption. When the cost estimates are available, your organization may find that the local or domestic supplier continues to be competitive. This is a positive point as local suppliers bring a number of benefits, including short transit times, short order cycle times, flexibility, and collaboration opportunities.

Standardization, Complexity, and Dual Sourcing

Standardization and complexity are key points that we have discussed extensively. The law of complexity suggests that the more suppliers that are engaged, the more complexity and cost associated with the supply base. With this in mind, we need to minimize our supply base. This is accomplished by challenging our best suppliers to take on new business. However, a healthy balance must be found between existing and new suppliers. Many Lean organizations embrace dual sourcing strategies as the optimal balance.

Dual sourcing means that we have at least two different suppliers to supply the same part or raw material. This is a valid strategy because it results in cost competitiveness and risk aversion. The cost competition arises when a company is able to negotiate with two suppliers for the same part, resulting in negotiations that resemble commodity purchasing, which ultimately drives down the price. By having two suppliers, we hedge against the risk of one supplier having quality or internal production interruptions. However, there is an administrative cost to dual sourcing. We may be reducing our possibilities for economies of scale by dividing up critical mass that one supplier may be able to leverage. This means that we need to choose wisely when deciding which parts to dual source. Typically, dual sourcing is used in cases of high-volume, high-value, and complex parts (requiring significant engineering). For example, we may dual source transmissions, but probably not office supplies.

Beware the Term "Partnership"

Collaboration and supply chain management both advocate close relationships with input suppliers and service providers. The term "partnership" is being used these days to represent a relationship where the goal is to strive for a win-win dynamic. While Lean and Six Sigma theorize the need and value of close partnering relationships, many suppliers feel that partnerships do not work to their advantage. Presently, suppliers of the world's largest companies believe cost reduction is the only thing that matters. This drive for cost reduction and the leverage our customers have over us is unprecedented in industrial history.

Whether or not this current business climate is healthy can be argued. On one hand, extreme pressures for cost reduction have forced manufacturers and suppliers to innovate and eliminate waste from their systems, yet on the other hand, quality and service may be engineered out of our products in order to meet cost pressures. The survivors will be those that maintain professional relationships with suppliers and customers and provide continuous and consistent quality of product and service. In order to provide service and quality, the logistics manager will need to collaborate significantly with logistics providers.

Collaboration and Logistics Services

All companies work with outsourced logistics in some way. Whether we are buying small-package delivery, truckload services, or warehousing, it is unlikely we can internalize all the required services. To meet our logistics challenges, we develop collaborative relationships with a number of suppliers, from trucking companies to freight forwarders to third-party warehouses. Economic conditions are changing the dynamics of these relationships, which typically have followed business cycles, especially in transportation services. To meet current challenges, many companies are moving toward hiring a third-party logistics company to manage the entire logistics function for the shipper. Although this third-party approach can bring significant benefits, it must be implemented methodically and with due diligence.

Collaboration with service providers is enormously important if we are to achieve our Lean goals and execute effective logistics strategies. In order to develop meaningful and successful strategies for a future within this changing environment, we must be persistent and determined to learn new ways.

In most industries, transportation costs typically represent the lion's share of total logistics cost. As a consequence, we tend to manage transportation cost above all others. That much said, there is tremendous need to focus on transportation issues.

Transportation costs follow the cycle of trucking rates, fluctuating dramatically with the variation in capacity. Although many companies talk about partnerships and collaboration, the unspoken reality is that capacity drives the price. This seems reasonable; the shippers win for a time and then the carriers and service providers win in a seller's market. The saying "make hay while the sun shines" would certainly describe the attitudes of shippers and service providers, each organization taking advantage of the situation, knowing full well that, in time, the tables will turn. However exciting this cycle may be for those who enjoy the roller-coaster effect, it is not compatible with Lean and Six Sigma doctrine. The logistics business environment is changing in so many ways that it will not return to what might be considered "normal."

For instance, there is a considerable shortage of commercial truck drivers in North America today. The life of a truck driver is not appealing to younger generations, and as a result, there are not enough qualified drivers succeeding the drivers who are reaching retirement age. This driver shortage has resulted in a capacity issue relative to availability of trucking resources — not a shortage of trucks, but a shortage of drivers. This capacity issue has resulted in a seller's market for the carriers and the rapid increase of rates. While not a new phenomenon, this situation is disturbing because there is no evidence of a solution to the driver shortage at present. Thus, our approach to transportation services will change significantly and permanently. The Lean Six Sigma Logistics organization recognizes these environmental challenges and works closely with carriers to help them in their driver retention efforts. The progressive organization realizes that the problems experienced by logistics partners ultimately become their own problems when left unaddressed.

Third-Party Logistics

There are as many transportation strategies as there are transportation providers. Each and every one has merits and challenges. Whether we subscribe to a private fleet, third-party logistics, asset-based trucking companies, or nonasset transportation intermediaries, we need to know who our transportation providers are and how to manage the relationship in a collaborative way. That is, we need to guarantee that relationships with carriers are being managed with respect and recognition of the significant services they provide. This is particularly true in the case of third-party logistics.

Choosing a third-party logistics company (3PL) is a serious strategic sourcing decision. In most cases, when a company considers outsourcing to a 3PL, it is making a decision to give a piece of its business to the 3PL. This decision has lasting impact, as the 3PL will have direct communications with the company's suppliers and customers. This direct contact means that the 3PL will be an agent for the logistics organization. As an agent, the 3PL must share the same values and customer service principles as the organization itself.

The third-party logistics industry is growing consistently at a double-digit pace each year. Unfortunately, as new third-party logistics relationships are born, existing ones are disintegrating in a milieu of failed promises. These failures tend not to be the fault of any one party but rather the result of poor planning and lack of effective strategies. The main reasons why these relationships are doomed from the start are:

1. The customer did not give accurate information from the beginning, which resulted in the 3PL unknowingly underpricing the contract in the initial proposal.
2. The 3PL was so eager to get the business that it did not consider all cost and operational components and therefore underpriced and overpromised.
3. The customer thought all aspects of the logistics function could be left to the 3PL.
4. The 3PL took on the new business without the resources to implement and operate the account effectively in the long term.
5. The customer did not set expectations, standards, and measurements to define success in the relationship.
6. The 3PL did not listen for or document the voice of the customer and consequently did not understand the customer's requirements or expectations.
7. The 3PL had no formal continuous improvement infrastructure in place, which resulted in a stagnant relationship after the initial start-up phase.
8. The relationship was based solely on cost-reduction goals, which are virtually impossible to calculate, confirm, or deny after the operation begins.

When we review this list, it is apparent that many third-party logistics relationships begin for the wrong reasons. Successful business relationships do not live and die by cost reduction. The successful relationship is driven by common goals, shared vision, and complementary expertise. Successful 3PLs bring skills and talents to the relationship. Skills and talents are not technology or trucks or trailers; they are the expertise of the people involved. Successful 3PLs will employ people who are professionals in their field, experienced and talented logisticians. This is crucial, in particular, for Lean organizations seeking to outsource logistics, as few 3PLs understand Lean.

Developing a Lean Third-Party Logistics Relationship

At some point, organizations embracing Lean Six Sigma Logistics will consider outsourcing many if not all of the external logistics activities to a third party. The selection process is the most important part of the initiative. In fact, it can be argued that the 3PL should be selected before any pricing negotiations take place. This point is counterintuitive, but it makes sense nonetheless. Choose the

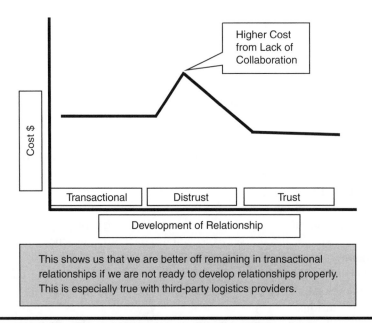

Figure 17.2.   The Cost of Unsuccessful Supplier Relationships.

partner first and then work on price. The relationship is what is most important. For example, Figure 17.2 tells us that poor partnerships are, in fact, more costly than staying in a transactional relationship with suppliers.

The logic is that if you choose the right partner, price will not be an issue as negotiations will be fair and equitable and will be indicative of market conditions. So, how do we choose the right partner? When choosing a 3PL to support a Lean initiative, the following should be taken into consideration:

1. What is the 3PL's knowledge level of Lean and Six Sigma?
2. Does the 3PL have a formal continuous improvement infrastructure?
3. What 3PL employees will work on your account, and what are their skills and talents?

The first question gets to the heart of whether or not the 3PL understands the value and operational dynamics of Lean. Sadly, there are 3PLs selling Lean principles without fully understanding them. It is important to ask "What process does the 3PL have in place to guarantee continuous improvement?" The lack of a continuous improvement initiative is the primary reason for failed third-party logistics relationships.

Just as important as continuous improvement is the capacity of the 3PL employees who will work on your account. Even though 3PLs may sell themselves as technology providers or problem solvers, the reality is that they are in a service industry. Inherent in the service business is that service is delivered by people. Therefore, the level of service is wholly determined by the attitude and capacity of the people delivering the service. It is crucial that we surround ourselves with team players who embrace Lean, Six Sigma, and the steadfast drive to eliminate waste. When logistics activities are outsourced to a competent 3PL that shares our values and hires highly skilled employees, there is no limit to the possibilities for positive outcomes of the relationship.

PROJECT MANAGEMENT

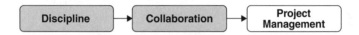

Truism: Work is changing. Logisticians are moving away from function-oriented activities to become project managers for process improvement and process accountability.

At one point, the logistics function was about negotiating freight rates, reading tariffs, and maintaining relationships with carriers. These were function-oriented jobs that went on in perpetuity. This is not the case for today's logistics professionals. In a Lean and Six Sigma environment, the role of the logistician is becoming that of a project manager. Implementing a third-party relationship, sourcing overseas, and opening a cross-dock are all examples of projects that are managed by the modern logistics professional. Certainly, Six Sigma companies using the DMAIC (Define-Measure-Analyze-Improve-Control) model (discussed in detail in Chapter 21) will have multiple projects going on at any given time. The logistician may be the champion of these projects or he or she may be a team member playing a key role in a project. Regardless of the role, effective project management skills are required to see a project through to successful completion.

A *project* is an initiative that has a clear objective and a finite start and end. Most projects will involve multiple people, many who may work in different departments or perhaps even different companies. Consequently, the success of any project will hinge on the ability of the project leader to manage the project from start to finish. This management is crucial because not all members of any given project team will have the same level of commitment to the project. This

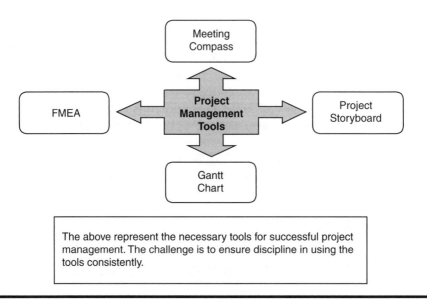

The above represent the necessary tools for successful project management. The challenge is to ensure discipline in using the tools consistently.

Figure 17.3. Project Management Tools: The Basics Are Crucial.

means that the project leader continuously directs others toward the ultimate goal. This requires project management and leadership skills, without which any substantial initiative will fail.

Project management is the backbone of any Lean Six Sigma initiative. It is so important that all respected Lean Six Sigma programs begin with training on team building, project management, and leadership. Experienced Lean Six Sigma professionals recognize that this so-called "soft stuff" is in fact the "hard stuff." You can train one hundred statisticians and can educate one hundred Lean engineers, but they will all fail if they lack the people skills to influence others positively to work toward a common goal. Luckily, managing projects does not need to be as complicated as some employees would indicate. Indeed, a large manual on project management has likely lost touch with the basics. Figure 17.3 outlines the basic tools used for effective project management.

Project Management: The Basics

Effective project management thrives when it concentrates more on the project itself and less on project management. Inundating ourselves with project management tools weighs down administration, which results in more time spent managing the project than getting the project done. It sounds odd, yet projects get bogged down when too much time is spent on the format of the project management tools themselves. This is an interesting aspect of human behavior. For example, workers spend huge amounts of time talking about formatting an approach to problem solving when they could be working on the problem itself. This is not to say that format is not important. The most powerful logic of Six Sigma is DMAIC, which is a model to follow that provides a format for solving a problem. It prevents wasted hours spent arguing about *how* to solve the problem and allows staff to begin work on the problem itself.

To accomplish the successful completion of projects, we need the following basic project management tools:

1. Meeting agenda (compass)
2. Storyboard (also known as A3 or tabloid)
3. Gantt chart with clear tollgate meetings
4. Failure Mode and Effects Analysis

Although project management purists will no doubt argue that many more tools are required, the average logistics professional will be well served by developing a disciplined use of these four tools.

Meeting Agenda (Compass)

Creating an agenda for meetings seems like an obvious and common sense thing to do; however, the reality is that many meetings go on without structured agendas. The lack of an agenda is the primary reason why meetings become dysfunctional and ineffective, yet completing a meeting agenda does not need to be cumbersome or complicated. First, the agenda simply needs to act as a "compass" to guide the meeting (see Figure 17.4). It should prescribe the "who, when, where, why, and how" of the meeting events. Second, the agenda needs to act as a document for action items to be captured. A meeting from which no action items result needs to be questioned seriously. Action items also need to follow the "who, when, where, why, and how" format.

Storyboard

The storyboard is known in Lean circles as the A3, which refers to the paper size used in Japan and Europe (called tabloid or 11 × 17 in North America) to sketch out the plan. The real charm of the storyboard is that it forces the project manager to describe the entire project on one piece of paper and will be the main document used to update people on the progress of the project. Items listed on the storyboard include the name of the project, the project leader and team members, a short description of the project, an analysis of the voice of the

Meeting Core Purpose:								

				start	stop			
Date:		Time:				Place:		

Attendees :							Prep Work
Leaders		Name			Name		
Meeting Owner			Minute Taker				
Time Keeper			Monitor				

Agenda:			
start	end	who	topic

Action items:			
#	who	what	when
1			
2			

Parking Lot	
1	
2	

Meeting Effectiveness								Safety
1	H M L	setting objectives	6	H M L	participation		
2	H M L	assigning roles	7	H M L	listening		
3	H M L	handling conflict	8	H M L	leadership		
4	H M L	decision making	9	H M L	outcomes		
5	H M L	on track					

Figure 17.4.   Sample Meeting Compass.

customer, current condition analysis of high-level measures, desired condition, high-level project time line, and ultimate goals. The storyboard is updated regularly and used as the compass throughout the entire cycle of the project. Figure 17.5 illustrates the storyboard approach.

Gantt Chart

The power of the Gantt chart cannot be overstated. Simple in design and use, the basic Gantt is what holds the project together. It is the vehicle that communicates project tasks, delegates responsibility, ensures accountability, and most importantly, drives the project forward. A Gantt chart is an XY matrix detailing the chronologically ordered tasks of the project (see Figure 17.6). Each task is listed with a clear line of responsibility attaching the task to a person. There will be clear starting and ending dates for each task. Once the Gantt chart is agreed upon by all project members, the stage is set and the players know what to do and when to do it. It is essential for successful project management.

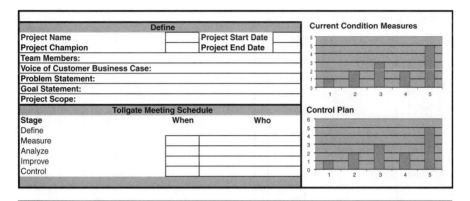

Figure 17.5. Sample Storyboard for Project Management.

Another aspect of the Gantt chart is the concept of *tollgate meetings*. Tollgate meetings are formal meetings with senior management to review the progress of the project. In Six Sigma, the tollgate meetings typically occur after the completion of each stage (D-M-A-I-C). In fact, the tollgate meeting is the meeting where the project manager is given the green light to move from one stage of the project to the next. This meeting serves many purposes, including:

1. Shows senior support for the project
2. Allows the project manager to ask for additional support or resources
3. Allows the entire group to discuss and review the original objectives
4. Highlights challenges or constraints being faced by the project manager
5. Highlights project members who are or are not supporting the project, if appropriate

These tollgate meetings drive the project forward and keep the project fresh in the minds of executives. If they are managed well, the project will see completion and implementation of new initiatives. To ensure a successful implementation of these new initiatives, we rely on the Failure Mode and Effects Analysis, described next.

Failure Mode and Effects Analysis

The Failure Mode and Effects Analysis (FMEA) is an implementation tool. It sounds more complicated than it is. At its core, the FMEA simply asks the project manager to brainstorm about what may go wrong in the implementation of the new initiative. The FMEA will be populated with all the possibilities for

Populate the chart with all required information to manage a project effectively.

Step	Sub Step	Step #	Action Step	Tool	On Time	Ownership	Output Required	M 1/5	T 1/6	W 1/7	TH 1/8	F 1/9
STRATEGY DEVELOPMENT	Define Vision	1	Meet	Communication Plan	Yes	Robert	Meeting Compass	▨				
		2	Plan	Gantt Chart	Yes	Tom	XY Matrix			▨		
	Measure Current Condition	3	Measure	SIMPOC, Flowcharts	No	Tom	Flowcharts				▨	
		4	Do	Operations Checklist	No	Robert	Control Chart					▨

(WEEK ONE)

Figure 17.6. Sample Gantt Chart.

Process:
FMEA Owner:
FMEA Date:

P = Probability or chance of failure occurring
S = Seriousness if failure occurs
D = Likelihood that failure will result in customer defect
R = Risk priority level = P x S x D

1 = Low Risk
5 = High Risk

Process Name	Process Purpose	Failure Mode	Probable Root Cause of Failure	Effects of Failure	Current Control Plan	P	S	D	R	Recommended Corrective Action	Action Taken
Outbound transportation	Deliver product to customer	Carrier did not show up	No truck availability	Product not shipped	Phone carrier to confirm dispatch	4	4	4	64	Have carrier allocate 10 trucks each day to our account	Carrier guarantees 6 trucks per day

Figure 17.7. Failure Mode and Effects Analysis (FMEA).

failure with respect to the operational implementation. For each failure, we then ask ourselves:

1. What is the likelihood or frequency of this failure actually happening?
2. What is the implication or severity of this failure if it does happen?

The FMEA allows us to look at every potential failure mode in order to prioritize the management of each possible failure. That is, we can decide where to assign precious management time in order to prevent possible breakdowns during implementation. Figure 17.7 illustrates the FMEA logic.

The way logistics professionals work has changed forever. They have become professional project managers and hence require the skills of a professional project manager. An additional and significant challenge to the logistician is to develop the soft or people skills in conjunction with basic project management tools. When this is accomplished, meaningful continuous improvement will be the result.

## 18

DISCIPLINE: SYSTEMS OPTIMIZATION

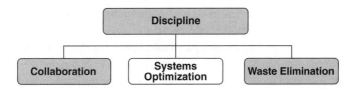

A fundamental of Lean Six Sigma Logistics is the goal of managing total cost. Lean teaches us that an organization works as an entire system. Even though the logistician does not always have total system authority or accountability, we must drive toward the goal of optimizing the entire system by reducing inventories and eliminating waste at all levels. The three strategic focus areas for logistics Systems Optimization are:

1. Total Cost
2. Horizontal Integration
3. Vertical Integration

These three areas will be discussed in this chapter.

TOTAL COST

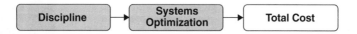

> **Truism**: Talk about total cost is everywhere; action on total cost is not so easy to find.

Lean teaches us that our business acts as a system. This system is a complex web of interdependent people and processes, where each has an effect on the others. To this end, we recognize that it is false to look at any particular activity in isolation. This is a fact for all business processes, but is particularly relevant in logistics. Logistics has inherent dynamics that make the concept of total cost confusing and frustrating. The main perplexing dynamic is a result of the less than obvious relationship between visible operational costs and inventory carrying costs. As well, organizations need to manage the concept of explicit costs as compared to implicit costs. Typically, most operational costs are explicit, whereas many inventory carrying costs are implicit.

Optimization is a term used to describe a situation where an entire system is performing at the optimal level, given all the variables, dynamics, and constraints with the system. Organizations should strive for optimal solutions in all processes. Least total cost is what results when we optimize the processes relative to the overall system inside the firm. For example, the most common area to manage total cost is developing inventory strategy. At its roots, inventory strategy is about balancing the cost of carrying inventory relative to customer service targets. In itself, this is a total cost concept. In other words, we need to determine how to spend carrying inventory to meet a targeted customer service performance level. However, the implication of targeted customer service levels can be far-reaching.

Explicit and Implicit Costs

Many opinions exist about how to calculate total cost. For example, how should we calculate the cost of capital in order to recognize the opportunity costs of holding inventories? Cost of capital will not show on a logistics manager's financial statement, so managing and including this aspect of the equation is troublesome. How many organizations are so progressive that they increase spending in transportation in order to offset a higher corresponding cost of holding inventory? To complicate this situation even further, the actual cost of holding the inventory may not even be visible! Because a cost is not visible does not mean that it does not exist. We need to recognize and understand the difference between implicit and explicit costs.

Explicit costs are defined as historical costs or actual costs that are tangible and visible on a firm's financial statements. With respect to logistics, these costs can be seen in items such as storage, transportation, and material handling costs including personnel, warehouse, and explicit freight costs. Explicit costs associated with holding inventory include those related to scrap, rework, shrinkage, obsolescence, taxes, insurance, and damages to the inventory.

Although many of these costs should be explicit and visible, in many organizations they are not. Even though firms recognize that explicit costs exist with inventory, many companies rationalize these costs as necessary for doing business. Even though reducing these explicit costs appears daunting, doing so can separate the top performers in a competitive industry.

Implicit costs are those costs that do not involve actual payment by a company, but do represent lost opportunity that results from allocating money in one area, thus abandoning other potential investments and projects. The opportunity cost of such decisions results in lost profits that an abandoned project may have returned on the invested capital. There are many schools of thought on how to calculate the cost of lost opportunity, but most financial managers will agree that the financial losses fall somewhere between the actual cost of capital and a firm's required risk-adjusted rate of return on its equity (the weighted average cost of capital). Regardless of how a firm calculates the opportunity cost of holding inventory, there is no doubt that the cost exists and must be taken into consideration when making strategic decisions. For example, what is the cost of setting a target of a 100 percent fill rate? Would 98 percent suffice? How much safety stock will be required to move from a guaranteed 98 percent fill rate to 100 percent? It certainly is a lot more than 2 percent! What is the overall or total cost to the firm in making this strategic decision?

As you can see, explicit costs are not reflective of the whole story relative to inventory. Implicit costs of holding inventory tell the true story of how inventory can have significant financial implications on a firm. As we can see from the inbound cost driver example presented earlier, it is essential for a firm to understand its total cost picture relative to these logistics activities. To this end, the goal must not be to optimize each activity individually, but rather to optimize the entire system using the sum of all costs together in reaching strategic decisions.

In order to do this, each activity driver must be analyzed relative to the cost drivers within the relevant system. To exemplify this philosophy, a firm can choose some of these logistics cost drivers to analyze and understand their interrelationships. One difficulty is that it requires cross-functional cooperation and high-level understanding of the issues because there may be instances where one area should increase its costs in order to reduce overall system costs. For example, even though many companies are aware of how much it costs to carry inventory, they continue to optimize transportation costs and try to move raw materials in truckload quantities. This is shortsighted, backward logic because the costs associated with holding the inventory will most likely exceed the savings achieved from optimizing transportation costs. For example, Figure 18.1 shows us that total logistics costs will far exceed just transportation costs.

Consequently, the valid challenge for companies is to develop an algorithm or management method that focuses on optimizing (i.e., minimizing) total cost.

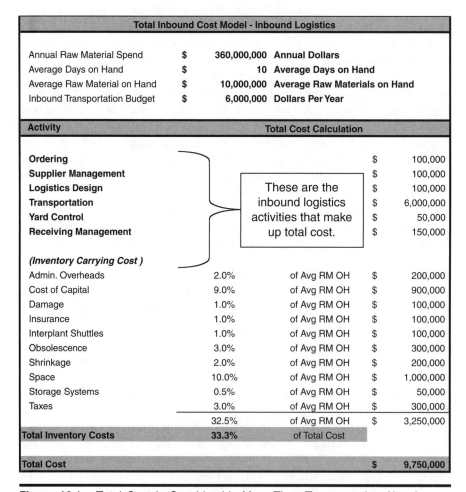

Figure 18.1. Total Cost Is Considerably More Than Transportation Alone!

To manage total cost will require excellent coordination and horizontal integration inside the firm. For successful completion, someone must take responsibility for the total logistics system. This person will be a vice president of logistics or supply chain management or someone higher in the organization and, in fact, may be the CEO in many companies.

HORIZONTAL INTEGRATION

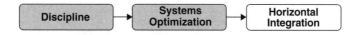

Truism: The vision of managing total cost will be realized when people can see the bigger picture and have some incentive to act in the interest of the system.

Most strategic planning textbooks define horizontal integration as a strategy that firms use to develop markets by growing horizontally, for example acquiring a competitor. From a logistics point of view, we describe horizontal integration in a different way. Logistics horizontal integration is concerned with using the full potential of an organization to maximize the total cost algorithm. Currently, horizontal integration is not widespread, and many opportunities exist for companies to realize substantial operating efficiencies and cost reductions. Why is it so difficult for companies to drive horizontal integration? Once again, the answer rests in poorly designed processes and people issues. Figure 18.2 outlines how processes and people issues flow in very different ways.

Driving horizontal integration will improve logistics operations for a firm dramatically. This is based on the premise that in logistics, volume drives opportunity; the more volume, the more opportunity. For instance, an organization may be using five geographically dispersed facilities in North America to meet manufacturing needs. The typical situation is that each plant creates and manages a logistics system. Alone, each plant may not have the volume required for Lean logistics principles such as milk runs or cross-docks. Consequently, the logistics system will be costly and will not support Lean principles that are designed to reduce inventories and focus on total cost.

One improvement opportunity is for the five plants to combine their volumes and allow logistics engineers to consider *total volume* when designing solutions. Clearly, the opportunity for milk runs and cross-docking would increase substantially. This combined volume would allow for significant flexibility to increase delivery frequency and level flow into the manufacturing plants.

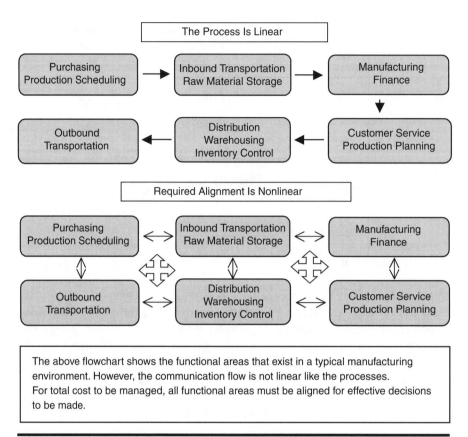

Figure 18.2. Incongruence in the Process and Communication Path.

A second example of horizontal integration is the assimilation inside a single-facility environment. As discussed previously, total cost is realized only when we optimize the sum of all of the parts. The parts represent functions, processes, and internal departments. This means that total cost will only be accomplished when internal departments work together. Purchasing needs to work with transportation, and transportation needs to coordinate with warehousing, and warehousing needs to cooperate with receiving and material handling. As easy as this appears, it is seldom executed in practice. Why is it so difficult to accomplish horizontal integration? Key hurdles to overcome are:

1. Perceived difficulty and system constraints
2. Poorly designed incentive and compensation programs
3. Teamwork, imperfection, and defensive behavior

Perceived Difficulty and System Constraints

Many organizations have opportunities for horizontal integration relative to aggregating shipping volumes. It is the challenge to cooperate and collaborate that is seldom met. While the primary hurdle is commitment to get the job done, there are practical challenges to meet. The main challenge is system constraints and the perception that they are impossible to overcome.

Many organizations have grown by way of mergers and acquisitions. Consequently, these organizations have a plethora of different processes, operational techniques, and computer systems. These constraints alone are used as an excuse summarily to dismiss any idea of horizontal integration. Survival of the corporation dictates integration. Combining and leveraging logistics activities simply makes sense; it is unequivocally the correct thing to do. It is helpful to avoid thinking of integration as a larger than life initiative. Computer systems do not need to be integrated, and all processes do not need to be identical. Although this would be ideal, it is not crucial to early integration initiatives. Simply commit to getting volumes in a standard format, and have logistics engineers analyze the data for possible integration opportunities. When opportunities arise, they can be executed operationally, one small event at a time. For example, you do not need to combine entire corporate volumes overnight, but you can implement one milk run or one less-than-truckload consolidation at a time.

Compensation and Incentive Programs

Poorly designed incentive programs could be the leading cause of logistics operations failure. There is no incentive for people to make changes based on horizontal integration. In fact, in many cases, people are financially motivated to do the opposite of what is smart or best for the organization. For example, why would a traffic manager reduce lot size and increase frequency of delivery if a bonus is based on transportation cost? Clearly, a traffic manager would want all shipments to move truckload. Or, for instance, why would warehouse managers want to reduce inventories to free up space when their bonuses are based on warehouse utilization?

Incentive programs need to be based on the total cost concept. The total cost algorithm needs to be completed, and incentives need to be linked to the goal of the total cost drivers. This will result in multiple people, from multiple functions and departments, all being responsible for a common goal. The common goal will be to increase operational efficiencies and optimize overall total cost. This results in doing more with less, eliminating inventories, and driving waste out of the system. Even under these circumstances, basic human nature will create walls that need to be broken down.

Teamwork, Imperfection, and Defensive Behavior

Organizational teamwork has become the fashion over the last decade. Many companies embrace the theory and wisdom of teamwork, yet true teamwork is often hard to find in mainstream industry. When one reviews the main points of teamwork, it makes sense. Consider working as a high-functioning group trying to reach a common goal through synergy, collaboration, and more. Indeed, teamwork could help us bridge core processes with enabling processes. Often, one functional area recognizes the weaknesses in another functional area of the company. That is, the employees from one area often see and recognize what needs to be corrected in other areas of the organization. Yet, communicating these weaknesses and solving problems in a team environment remains a difficult task. Why? The answer rests in the concepts of human imperfection and defensive behavior.

No human being is perfect; on this we all agree. Therefore, no CEO, vice president, or manager is perfect. As professionals, if we are not perfect, then we know that some areas in our jurisdiction need improvement. In a perfect world, we would embrace critical and constructive feedback from colleagues who more easily recognize our division's weakness. Alas, it is not a perfect world, and logical, effective implementation of cross-functional, horizontal feedback remains a challenge.

The irony here is that defensive behaviors exist because of the exact reason we need to overcome them. That is, because we are not perfect, as professionals, there are always areas in our span of control that can be improved. Our co-workers recognize these areas because they are not as close to the situation as we are. This describes the quintessential "fresh set of eyes" concept that is the winning formula for most consulting companies. However, our natural defensive behaviors do not allow us to be open or receptive to the feedback from our imperfect co-workers. Put another way, we are not willing to accept critical feedback from colleagues who may have many issues within their own departments. So, we think, "How dare you recommend improvements in my department when your department is a wreck!" Colleagues' comments about areas for improvement are probably accurate, and, in fact, their observations of our weaknesses have no relationship to how well they manage their own areas. They may be incompetent in their work, but from a distance they could be accurate in their assessment of another department.

For these reasons, it is crucial to embrace feedback in a positive manner. Getting over this destructive cycle requires a mutual understanding that we are not perfect, that others see the imperfections in our work, and that critical feedback is not necessarily negative, but rather constructive and can be valuable in reaching the combined goals of the company. That would be teamwork!

Breaking Down the Walls

If the Berlin Wall can be broken down, we can dismantle the invisible walls within our own organizations. Without silos or functional barriers, an organization will make more effective decisions and positive results will grow exponentially. The beginning is to understand and respect our imperfections and, consequently, to encourage and embrace critical feedback from colleagues. The successful company will complement this increase in corporate self-confidence with a total systems approach to measurement and effectively bridge core and enabling processes. When this is accomplished, teamwork will thrive, costs will go down, revenues will grow, and customers will be in awe.

VERTICAL INTEGRATION

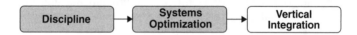

> **Truism**: The dream of supply chain management has yet to be realized, and it will not be realized until vertical integration, collaboration, and cooperation become second nature.

Lean theory talks extensively about supplier and customer relationships. The theory holds that Lean attempts to synchronize production to demand. The heartbeat of demand is defined as *takt time,* and takt time is the rhythm used to build product. The goal is to build only what the market is demanding, thereby avoiding the costs associated with building and carrying inventories that will not sell. As noted, overproduction can be considered a waste that creates many other wastes. Supply chain management theory then dictates that once we are producing to the beat of the customer, we should encourage suppliers to produce to the same beat. In theory, suppliers and manufacturers are totally synchronized in order that nothing be built until it is in demand by the ultimate customer.

Let's use a bag of potato chips as an exaggerated example. In a theoretical supply chain environment, when you buy a bag of potato chips at the local grocery store, you would set off the following series of events, all in real time:

1. The information regarding your purchase will be captured at the point of sale in the system at the grocery store.
2. The distributor of the potato chips would receive a signal to replenish the bag that was purchased. This bag would be shipped.

3. The manufacturer is signaled to manufacture a bag of potato chips to replenish the one shipped from the distribution center. It would order and receive raw materials just in time in the quantities necessary to manufacture one bag of potato chips.
4. The farmer (supplier) would pick one potato from the field and plant another one to replenish the one that was picked.
5. Every party would be paid electronically at the time that you purchase the bag of potato chips from the store.

Clearly, this example is utopian as it has some practical challenges that prevent successful implementation. Seasonality of raw materials, economies of scale of manufacturing, electronic communication constraints, and uncertain demand from the customer are a few of the many constraints we face in order to reach a seamless, waste-free supply chain such as this example. Even though utopia is unattainable, there are significant improvements that can be made relative to vertical integration.

From Customer to Supplier

Vertical integration attempts to look at the entire series of business processes as one business. That is, from end customer to the highest level of raw material supplier, we attempt to build systems that optimize the entire supply chain. One fine example of vertical integration was when Henry Ford owned every aspect of the supply chain to build automobiles. From iron ore mining straight through to the car dealerships, every aspect was owned by Ford. The goal was to integrate each step in the process to synchronize flow in order to optimize the total system. Certainly, if you own all the operations in the supply chain, you can attain your goal. This is because the main elements of successful vertical integration are communication, information sharing, and trust. To support these ideas, Figure 18.3 shows a simple approach to getting started on vertical integration.

Vertical Integration and Information

The bullwhip effect is a well-known operational hazard. Rooted in the theory of Industrial Dynamics offered by Jay Forrester in the late 1950s,* the bullwhip effect teaches us that inventories grow inversely in the supply chain as a function of the amount of information that is shared among supply chain (vertical) partners. This relationship is reciprocal in nature; the less the information is

---

* Forrester, Jay, Industrial Dynamics: a major breakthrough for decision makers, *Harvard Business Review*, 36(2), 37–66, 1958.

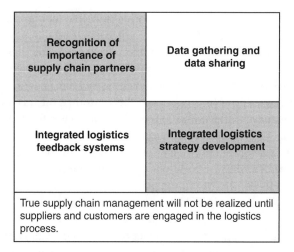

Figure 18.3.   Vertical Integration: Steps to Success.

shared, the more inventories are created in the system. The information that needs to flow includes forecasting, demand planning information, and actual sales. Certainly, it would be easier to optimize the system if we knew the exact demand that would be directed to each supply chain level. Starting with the customer, we could work backward to calculate the requirements for the supply chain. Indeed, this is the heart of Lean and pull replenishment theories. This is the Lean model: build only what is sold and replenish only what is consumed.

Unfortunately, modern business practice does not allow for effective vertical integration implementation. This is in large part due to trust issues and ineffective communications. It is also caused by lack of knowledge. That is, most organizations would be happy to share forecasts and information if only they knew what was going to happen, but they do not. Inefficiencies in their internal systems and processes create an environment where workers are so busy fighting fires that proper supply chain management is still a dream. When this occurs, variability results, and it is this variability that creates vertical instability in the supply chain.

Variability, Leveled Flow, and Vertical Integration

Six Sigma teaches us to understand and manage variation. Lean teaches about flow and leveling of processes and demand on resources. Once again, we learn how Six Sigma and Lean interconnect to find solutions to serious operations management problems. In particular, variability and leveled flow play a significant role in vertical integration.

Take, for example, a tier 1 automotive supplier that is serving multiple original equipment manufacturer (OEM) customers from the same facility. Even though they are serving the OEM customers from the same plant, the supplier will likely have very different operations in place to serve each customer. For instance, maybe one of its OEM customers is a Lean manufacturer that has leveled its manufacturing to the beat of the customer. In this case, the tier 1 supplier should have little or no safety stock in place for the OEM, as the variability in the OEM orders will be minimal. This low-order variability allows the tier 1 supplier to plan and trust what the OEM will need. The supplier can then plan its own systems to build what is required to be ready *just in time* for the customer delivery.

Now consider a second OEM customer being served from the same plant. This OEM is not practicing Lean manufacturing and therefore has unleveled demand and many changes to its production schedule. Although the customer may be giving the tier 1 supplier a forecast, it will change. This change could be as much as 20 percent on the day before an order is shipped. How is the tier 1 supplier to manage its own business with this much variation in customer orders? The only way is to carry safety stock because safety stock is the only way to hedge against uncertainty. Yet safety stock results in significant costs that, at some point and in some way, must be passed on to the OEM responsible for the expense.

Vertical integration is about communicating expectations and needs so trading partners in the supply chain can plan better systems and maintain more effective operations. This means that information, communication, and material must flow throughout the whole supply chain. This requires commitment and trust — commitment to share and trust that data are used for honest purposes. Mainly, vertical integration requires recognition that supply chain partners are an integral part of our business. Successful vertical integration requires a supply chain strategy based on total cost and a systems approach to supply chain management.

19

DISCIPLINE: WASTE ELIMINATION

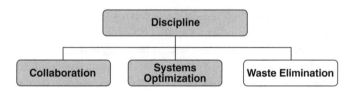

The buck may stop with the CEO, but waste elimination ends up on the desk of the implementer. No matter how successful the company, waste is still abundant, and the goal of all employees needs to be to eliminate this waste. Just like all important initiatives, implementing the solution can prove very challenging, but it must be accomplished. The three strategic focus areas for Waste Elimination are:

1. Quality at the Source
2. Continuous Improvement
3. Execution

These three areas will be discussed in this chapter.

QUALITY AT THE SOURCE

Truism: There is a significant difference between an operational error and a customer defect.

Initiatives are often doomed before they start because we fail to build quality into our products, services, and processes. The trick is to define quality up front and not allow design or operational errors to pass down the line, ultimately turning into customer defects.

A key Lean concept is that an error is very different from a defect. Errors happen because people and machines are involved. The exciting news is that errors do not have to turn into a customer defect. This is the foundation of the *quality at the source* concept. The challenge is to build error-proof processes into our procedures and manufacturing systems. Error proofing (or mistake proofing) allows us to catch errors before they turn into defects. To support this concept, Figure 19.1 describes the difference between an error and a defect.

To most people, quality is about manufacturing and the quality of products built. Most manufacturing companies use inspections and rework to fix quality issues before they reach the customer. What we want to emphasize is that quality is more than shipping a defect-free product. Quality is about having superior products, superior services, and superior processes. Quality begins at the source.

Before we design a product or service, we first need to define what "quality" means to that product or service, and then we need to ensure that quality is built in from the beginning. In the event of quality issues, we must make certain that poor quality is not passed on to the next step in the process. This is vital because quality issues compound in severity as they travel through an organization on their way to the customer.

For example, picture a salesperson doing a setup for a new customer. Assume, for the moment, that this salesperson takes no pride in the work and is careless when inputting the new customer information. Consequently, inaccurate data are recorded. In this case, the salesperson enters the customer's address incorrectly. The customer places the first order, which is sent out to the wrong address. The customer calls the salesperson, and the salesperson starts firefighting. A second order is sent to the customer, but it arrives late. When the company invoices the customer, the invoice goes to the wrong address, and the rest is a series of comical errors that are anything but comical

---

Error

Definition: A mistake made that could result in a defect to a product or process.

Example: Wrong customer address on shipping documents

Probability of errors happening: 100 percent

Probability of eliminating 100 percent of errors: 0 percent

Defect

Definition: A defect in process or procedure as defined by the customer (internal or external)

Example: Shipment delivered to wrong customer address

Probability of opportunity for defects occurring: 100 percent

Probability for defect free = Six Sigma = 99.999997 percent

An error is very different from a defect. Errors will most certainly happen. However, errors do not need to turn into customer defects.

Figure 19.1.   Error Versus Customer Defect.

to the customer. It sounds absurd, but it happens every day in business. Many big problems start with little mistakes. The challenge is to focus on quality and to integrate quality into all procedures from the very beginning. We need to do the following:

1. Understand that quality needs to begin at the source.
2. Look for processes that need quality improvement at the source.
3. Define what "quality" means and build it in at the beginning of any process.

The Benefits of Quality at the Source

Many aspects and features of Lean production address the capacity of a company to implement a quick response to defects and to develop processes that check the process itself or the immediate result of the process. This concept of self-checking is mistake proofing. Somehow, we need mechanisms that detect errors before they turn into defects. Mistake proofing, or poka-yoke (see also Chapters 12 and 22), is important in order to develop flow and it is a key to variation reduction.

The ambition of any business goal is to deliver 100 percent conforming product to every customer. This goal cannot be accomplished by inspecting each product after the fact. Quality must be built into the product by giving processes and employees the means to correct problems as they occur. Mistake-proofing designs and processes to prevent defects from occurring in the first place need to be implemented. If we can accomplish this, we will:

1. **Reduce rework**: Developing the ability to manufacture a product correctly the first time is a key component of continuous flow. It prevents interruptions in product movement and reduces the wasteful consumption of resources. It focuses resources on building just what is needed to supply the customer. In other words, quality at the source will eliminate the hidden factory.

2. **Reduce scrap**: The very purpose of quality at the source is to reduce scrap and rework. Scrap and rework are items that create process variation, diminish the ability to achieve standard work, and simply increase cost and lead time.

3. **Reduce risk**: Quality at the source reduces issues where the product is created (or the point where true value is added). This alleviates the potential for costly issues and disruptions further along the process of an operation or further down the total value stream. It reduces the risk of more cost and the possibility of the customer finding the defect. It also creates an environment where problems are discovered and dealt with at the point where they take place, which can uncover and remove the root cause or allow for the placement of a countermeasure.

4. **Reduce variation**: Variations of any type disrupt flow. Defects create significant forms of variation, resulting in inventories and additional resources. For continuous flow, the removal of variation from the system is critical, and this requires detection of defects as well as a speedy determination of root cause.

5. **Reduce complexity**: Implementing quality at the source reduces system complexity. The more defects that a system generates, the more complexity the system must maintain in order to deal with finding, fixing, and understanding the root cause of the defect. Applying quality at the source simplifies the system, which ultimately is a reduction in complexity.

Logistics and Quality at the Source

Initiating a quality at the source program can be intimidating. How to begin is the first question that must be answered. To develop a quality at the source implementation map, draw from the "perfect order" in logistics management. The perfect order is described as the five rights: The *right* part in the *right* quantity at the *right* time in the *right* quality at the *right* cost. With this definition in mind, we need to ensure that we have quality at the source or mistake-proofing methods in place to realize the perfect order. For practical purposes, we will examine an example.

For the perfect supplier order to come about in a Lean manufacturing environment, we need to ensure that suppliers are shipping the right parts in the right quantity and condition at the right time to the right place and at the right cost. One approach that Lean manufacturers use to guarantee quality at the source for the perfect order is to have order verification completed at the supplier *prior* to the order being loaded on the outbound truck. This verification process is completed by the truck driver who is responsible for picking up the parts. Acting as an agent for the manufacturer, the driver is trained to verify all perfect order components of the supplier order. To accomplish this, the driver is armed with a detailed manifest that outlines what the supplier is to ship that day. Prior to the freight being loaded on the truck, the driver verifies that the order staged for shipping has the right parts in the right quantity in the right packaging with the proper labeling and any other variables critical to quality of the process. By doing this, the driver recognizes any issues with the process. For example, if the supplier is supposed to ship twenty steering wheels and there are only eighteen on the rack, then the process is stopped immediately by the driver. Called *jidoka* in the Lean lexicon, this is the act of stopping the process immediately when an abnormality is detected. Hence, we uncover an error and avoid a defect. In this case, the driver would inform the supplier of the parts shortage and a solution would be developed right there on the spot.

Compare this process to one that has no mistake-proofing mechanism in place. The driver would arrive at the supplier and have the truck loaded with whatever the supplier had ready to ship at the time. The trailer would arrive at the manufacturing facility, where, upon inspection, it would be determined that two steering wheels are missing (if detected at all!). However, at this point, it is too late, and a parts shortage will likely result, possibly shutting down the manufacturing line, resulting in an expensive expedite at the very least.

Quality at the source teaches us to detect errors as quickly as possible. In logistics, this means that we need to have mistake-proofing tools in place for all critical processes. In practice, this means that we should look at processes as far up the supply chain as possible. The goal is to detect and resolve issues prior to their becoming a burden on the organization.

CONTINUOUS IMPROVEMENT

> **Truism**: Continuous improvement is neither an initiative nor a "flavor of the month." Continuous improvement must be the foundation of the organizational culture.

It is fair to say that the concept and principles of continuous improvement are not completely understood by many organizations. In fact, in multiple surveys, continuous improvement is one of the key deficiencies among logistics service providers (third-party logistics companies and carriers) when serving their customers. In other words, logistics providers need to improve on their improvement skills!

That much said, customers also need to improve their internal improvement capabilities. Why is it such a struggle to develop and sustain a culture of continuous improvement? The answer to this question is not simple, and as is the case with most difficult questions, the journey begins with more questions. A few of these are:

1. What is continuous improvement?
2. Why is continuous improvement so hard to understand and implement?
3. How can we develop an organizational culture that embraces and drives continuous improvement?

Continuous Improvement: The Bare Facts

Simply put, continuous improvement is about improving organizational performance. It is surprising that many companies do not have a formal process for improvement. In the absence of a formal process, continuous improvement is nonexistent.

These days, continuous improvement is part of the Lean Six Sigma lexicon. In Lean, it is known as *kaizen*, and in Six Sigma, the drive for 3.4 *defects per million opportunities* has continuous improvement imbedded and implied in the process of Define-Measure-Analyze-Improve-Control. Consequently, any initiative in Lean or Six Sigma will eventually lead to organizing around a con-

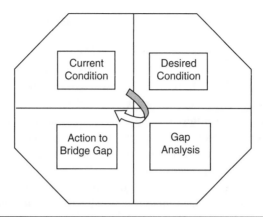

Figure 19.2. The Continuous Improvement Quadrants.

tinuous improvement infrastructure, which is instrumental in the development and sustainability of corporate continuous improvement. We will discuss this in more detail later.

The first thing to understand about continuous improvement is that it is not an event. The term "kaizen event" has damaged the principles and values of true kaizen. Although focused improvement initiatives are important and should be completed, continuous improvement needs to flow continuously through an organization, not in isolated, sporadic bursts of development. Figure 19.2 shows the simple, but powerful, quadrants of continuous improvement.

When continuous improvement flows through an organization, we immediately recognize that continuous improvement does not happen in larger-than-life re-engineering initiatives. Instead, improvements come from small, incremental upgrades. The paradox of true continuous improvement is that, at times, the improvements can be so small that they appear inconsequential. A tiny improvement may not be quantifiable; it may not have a return on investment or an operational dynamic that is obvious or even visible. However, these small incremental improvements will, over time, create processes and operations that are highly efficient and effective.

Over time, incremental improvements create best practices, and continuous improvement eliminates the challenges that come with change management around larger re-engineering initiatives. This is a critical point. Organizations that do not embrace continuous improvement will follow destructive patterns of reorganization, restructuring, layoffs, and other reactionary management techniques that make executives feel they are doing what is right. These executives do not understand their business as a total system, and consequently their actions are usually unwarranted tampering with the natural system at work.

To draw an analogy, consider that an organization is like a ferry trying to move from point A to point B by crossing a river. Clearly, the shortest and fastest way to reach point B is to move in a straight line. However, when traversing against a strong current, we are forced to adjust our course. These forces may be external or internal dynamics to the system. Uncertain economics, changing customer requirements, and staffing shortages all represent dynamics that change our course throughout a fiscal year.

An organization that embraces continuous improvement will see and act on these changing dynamics and, like a good ferry operator, will make small incremental adjustments to the course. These adjustments may go unnoticed. In keeping with our analogy, the ferry would appear to be continuing in a straight line. In contrast, organizations that do not have continuous improvement infrastructures will be blind to the force of change, and dramatic, reactionary changes eventually will be necessary. Now picture a sailboat attempting to cross the same body of water in a straight line by continuously tacking at forty-five-degree angles. Unfortunately, a perfect forty-five-degree angle is hard to sustain, and eventually the organization will be making ninety-degree turns or may be going in circles, if not going under.

The Challenges of Continuous Improvement Implementation

Leaders of organizations do not publicly state that continuous improvement is bad for their organizations, yet the harsh reality is that many fail to strive for improvement in the day-to-day activities. This is the continuous improvement paradox. We believe in continuous improvement, but do very little to achieve it. Leadership theory would suggest this happens for one of two reasons. The first is that we are capable (we have the skills and knowledge) of continuous improvement, but consciously choose not to improve. The second possible reason is that we truly want to improve, but do not possess the skills and knowledge to develop, implement, and sustain an effective continuous improvement strategy. Although the former may be true in environments with poor labor relationships and impoverished employees, the latter is by far the reason why continuous improvement does not flourish inside our organizations. We want to improve. We do not know how. Consequently, we need to uncover and address the key drivers that prevent us from reaching our organizational and personal potential.

Among the many reasons for the lack of continuous improvement are the following problems:

1. Lack of a problem-solving and continuous improvement model
2. Lack of time and trained resources to commit to continuous improvement
3. Lack of discipline and corporate infrastructure to sustain improvements

Bridging the Gap

In order to improve, organizations need a model that provides a common language that all members can use to articulate the value and work plan of any specific improvement initiative. Although there are many models available to us (such as *Plan-Do-Check-Act* from Lean and *Define-Measure-Analyze-Improve-Control* from Six Sigma), they all drill down to a similar approach to problem solving. This approach is to look at a situation where we intuitively know improvement is required and answer the following questions:

1. What is the current condition of this process?
2. What is the desired condition of this process?
3. What is the actual-desired gap?
4. What can be done to close the gap?
5. How can we sustain the improvement over time?

Depending on the complexity of the problem, answering these questions may be simple and require very few analytical tools, or we may require special skills and intricate analytical tools. However, the ultimate goal is to be able to communicate where we are today, where we want to go, and how we will get there. This takes time and resources. Executives can be misguided when they roll out continuous improvement strategies without taking into consideration the time, energy, and skill required to improve. Simply declaring that continuous improvement is the new way will undoubtedly result in frustration and failure.

Continuous improvement and problem solving require trained people with the proper tools and time. This is no different than any process inside our organizations. Indeed, continuous improvement is a process and needs to be managed in the same way as we manage other important processes. Consequently, if we expect people to work on improvement initiatives, they must have the time to do it. Far too often, managers will get a team together, sell the merits of continuous improvement, and then send the team back to the floor with the mandate to improve the operation. Yet the team members have full-time responsibilities that have not changed and no spare time to work on continuous improvement initiatives. This point is even more pronounced in the logistics industry, where many of our day-to-day activities require urgent and immediate attention. In this environment, it is virtually impossible to manage regular activities and complete any improvement projects.

Perhaps this is a self-fulfilling prophecy in that if you take the time to initiate improvements, you will prevent the firefighting or urgent issues from happening. This argument has merit in theory, but experience shows that we will never eliminate urgent issues, particularly in the logistics function. Consequently, for any continuous improvement program to be successful, employees must be given the time to work on continuous improvement projects. This is precisely why the Six Sigma movement has been so successful. In a true Six Sigma environment, companies will train as many as 2 percent of their employees and pull them out of their full-time jobs to work exclusively on improvement initiatives.

Getting People Trained

Training people for continuous improvement can be a daunting task. In what should we train them? What skills do they need? Do we need engineers and statisticians on staff? Although these are good questions, the reality is that the skills required for successful continuous improvement are often overprescribed. At first glance, we think we need process engineers and mathematicians to design processes and measure data to analytical limits. It is true that these skills may be required in complex problems, but most of the business problems that we are experiencing do not require that level of sophistication. In fact, in many cases, employees know the answers to a problem, yet they do not change the way things are done. This is not to say that rigorous analysis is not required or important. It surely is. However, in most cases, particularly in service industries (trucking and third-party logistics operations), the processes are not always so complicated that advanced statistics techniques are required to analyze a problem.

So, what *is* required? The training needed to sustain a continuous improvement program includes the development of people skills along with project management, teamwork, change management, and leadership. Working through any continuous improvement program requires project management skills. The ability to create and manage time lines and Gantt charts is crucial in order to keep a project on task and hold all stakeholders accountable. In-depth understanding of teamwork is required. People need to be involved to ensure that the initiative spans departmental and functional borders. Leadership skills are crucial in order for significant, sustained change to occur.

Sustaining improvement initiatives is the most difficult part of any continuous improvement program. The unfortunate truth is that people and processes are inclined to a natural resiliency that physically draws processes back to the old ways. One famous CEO said, "The system wants to be a bureaucracy. Every day, we need to fight to keep the bureaucracy from taking over." Although this may sound like science fiction, there is no question that natural forces are at work challenging the sustainability of continuous improvement. Consequently, all employees, from the CEO down, need to be educated in leadership and change management issues. Significant improvement will happen when all the stakeholders recognize, understand, and believe that continuous improvement has an important place in bringing success to the organization.

EXECUTION

Truism: Talk is cheap. In logistics, you have to get the job done!

We have all been involved in initiatives that seem like great ideas in the beginning, only to have a project die miserably in implementation. Indeed, Six Sigma and the DMAIC process highlight the importance of sustained improvement. Sustained improvement is accomplished only when we execute successfully and then sustain the improvements over the long term. This is not easy; the natural force of resiliency makes it difficult to change and maintain the new ways of doing work. The logistics profession faces these challenges. In fact, most logistics professionals know exactly what needs to be done inside their organizations; the actual challenge is to get corporate support for logistics priorities. Progressive organizations that are embracing Lean and Six Sigma fully recognize the importance of logistics and are doing something about it. However, overall as a profession, logistics has a long way to go.

At this time, our vision and dreams of world-class logistics and supply chain management have outpaced the operational realities inside most organizations. Let's call it an *ingenuity gap*, where our ability to execute is lagging behind our ideas, innovations, and recognition of what needs to be. Figure 19.3 describes the relationships of the key variables needed for successful execution.

We do not need to be surprised or overly concerned; all significant changes and mental model shifts start out with an ingenuity gap. As the adage says, "There is nothing like an idea whose time has come." Clearly, Lean Six Sigma Logistics' time has come. What is needed now is leadership.

Acting as Lean Six Sigma Logistics Leaders

There are literally thousands of books that promote their particular definition of leadership. They might emphasize vision, passion, drive, or the ability to

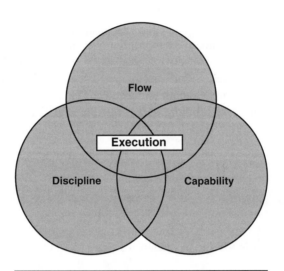

Lean Six Sigma Logistics can be successfully implemented by using the Logistics Bridge Model as a compass for the organization.

Figure 19.3.   Lean Six Sigma Logistics Execution.

influence others. These are all accurate; however, they amount to nothing without action. The ability to act, to get things done, is not just one aspect of leadership; it is the glue that holds it together. No leadership style can survive without action. Action is what drives logistics into the executive boardrooms of our companies. Assertive action followed by effective execution will champion the impact that Lean Six Sigma Logistics can have on organizational performance. Again, where do we start?

As leaders, we need to focus and then act on three key areas. That is, we need to ask the tough questions, seek the facts, develop strategies, and pursue the three principles of:

Logistics Capability: Is our logistics system capable?

Logistics Flow: Have we designed a logistics system that flows?

Logistics Discipline: Are the logistics processes grounded in disciplined principles?

1. Capability means that the logistics leader is focused on ensuring that the logistics system is predictable, stable, and visible.

2. Flow relates to the logistics professional's ability to describe and articulate how the system performs relative to asset flow, information flow, and cash flow.
3. Discipline is crucial to sustaining stability and flow, with major disciplines including collaboration, systems optimization, and a steadfast commitment to waste elimination.

When logistics and supply chain executives focus on capability, flow, and discipline, it will become clear that supply chain activities are indeed the corporate actions that bridge the organization successfully to the customer, rising above the wastes in which our competitors are quagmired. It will not be easy, but in the end, organizations that embrace Lean Six Sigma Logistics will be the victors. As logistics professionals, we have painted the vision and set the stage, and what is needed now is action, action, and more action.

Now that we have the vision, structure, and call for action set forth by the Logistics Bridge Model, let's continue in the next section by examining key tools that can help close the gaps between current and desired conditions in the logistics system. Tools and methods from Lean and Six Sigma will help to guide continuous improvement initiatives and measure their effectiveness.

SECTION 4.
BUILDING THE BRIDGE:
LEAN SIX SIGMA
LOGISTICS TOOLS

20

STRATEGY AND PLANNING TOOLS

SURVEYING THE TOOL KIT

Lean and Six Sigma are designed to be comprehensive programs. Embedded within the two initiatives are pervasive philosophical principles, values, models, and tools. This creates a challenge when trying to describe what Lean and Six Sigma have to offer when combined. As well, it can make training and implementation challenging because employees may get confused between theory and practical next steps. This is especially true in logistics, given its hands-on focus on operations. Consequently, it is important for the logistician to understand Lean and Six Sigma beyond theory, from a practical point of view. In order to be effective, the logistician must be armed not only with theory, but also practical knowledge and tools that will lend directly to improved operational effectiveness and reduced costs.

Many training courses and books will attempt to separate the Lean tools from the Six Sigma tools. For example, one may argue that voice of the customer is a Six Sigma tool, whereas value stream mapping is a Lean tool. Although the tools' origins may be traced to one camp or the other, the logistician simply needs to know what tools are available and when they are best applied. For that reason, we have interspersed the tools commonly associated with Lean and Six Sigma across four categories: (1) strategy and planning, (2) problem solving, (3) operations, and (4) measurement. Methods and tools associated with these four categories are reviewed in this section over the next four chapters.

Before introducing the tools of Lean Six Sigma Logistics, three points are critical to note. First, the tools are not "new." In most cases, it is only their common application to logistics and operations that is new. Second, the list provided is not meant to serve as a comprehensive catalogue of available tools, methods, and concepts, but rather as a representative sample of valued, tested tools used in Lean Six Sigma Logistics. Third, the discussion tied to each tool is intended to provide awareness and the beginnings of a working knowledge of the tool. Fortunately, volumes of reference books and Web content exist for each tool.

This chapter reviews key tools used for strategy and planning that aid in providing direction and scope for Lean Six Sigma Logistics implementation. It is here that the focus and priorities of the organization's efforts are established; for Lean Six Sigma Logistics is not just about doing things right, but doing the *right things right*. The Logistics Bridge Model emphasizes hearing the voice of the customer, and it is here that we start our discussion of valued tools.

VOICE OF THE CUSTOMER

The voice of the customer is, as its name suggests, a concept that embraces the input of customers toward the products and services provided to them. This belief is the Six Sigma manifestation of the "marketing concept," the realization that customers are the business's reason for being and that it is far more effective and efficient to identify customers' specific needs first and then develop products and services consistent with these needs. This runs counter to the conventional "production mentality" that suggests finding products and services in which the company excels and then passing those goods and services to customers. This distinction can be summed in a comparison of the statements "We make what we sell" versus "We sell what we make." Lean Six Sigma Logistics recognizes that understanding customer needs *must* come first. Pushing products and services to customers can only create waste.

When it comes to logistics services, it is easy to see that not all customers want the same services or expect the same level of service. Some customers seek value-added services like labeling and packaging, others call for transportation and storage, and still others seek only transportation. Among those calling for transportation services, one customer may expect 95 percent on-time performance, 98 percent for another, and 100 percent for yet another. Clearly, a uniform approach to service design and fulfillment will not accommodate customers' diverse needs.

Key aspects of the customer that the supplier must understand include answers to the following questions:

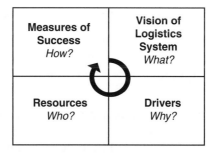

Figure 20.1. Voice of Customer Cycle.

1. What are the goals of the customer?
2. What are the motivating forces behind these goals?
3. What are the customer's challenges, constraints, and resources?
4. How can we help the customer meet these goals, given the challenges?

Figure 20.1 integrates these concerns in a cyclical framework. The purpose of a voice of the customer analysis is, ultimately, to better understand the real needs of customers, to "feel their pain." To deliver greatest value, one cannot limit understanding to what the customer specifically states, but rather must understand the bigger picture, including: (1) the goals of the customer and how the service offering contributes to specific objectives and (2) the drivers for the customer's goals. This level of understanding leads not only to an improved recognition of the goals and sense of camaraderie based on pursuit of a common objective, but also the prospect of achieving something greater than the customer dared to venture on its own. Solutions not thought possible (or not identified at all) might be possible.

Yet, recognizing goals and drivers stops short of having sufficient information to make the vision a reality. Resources and their constraints must also be recognized and considered in order to devise the plan of attack. Finally, capabilities should be developed to achieve the goals, with measures of success gauged to drive subsequent action. The cycle does not stop here, however. By the time goals are achieved, customer needs have changed and new goals are established, creating what seems like a constantly moving target.

Obviously, life gets complicated when trying to meet the specific needs of customers. For that reason, many companies have turned to segmentation as a method for grouping "like-minded" customers. Treating groups of customers as distinct segments can reduce the complexity of serving a multitude of customers and can also provide some degree of scale economies. The "right-sizing" of service to meet the needs of customers while also providing for the economic needs of the company is discussed next in linking voice of the customer to the voice of the business.

VOICE OF THE BUSINESS

Before addressing each customer's unique requests, one must understand the value that each customer offers the company in return for the effort. Too often, managers equate volume of sales with the profitability of the account. It is quite possible that the company's *largest customer* is the *least profitable* customer. This is particularly true when a large customer requires wholly unique services and inordinate amounts of handholding, causing the provider to incur exorbitant costs that offset the revenues generated in serving that customer. For this reason, it is critically important for the company to generate a profit and loss statement for each customer. It serves as an important "voice of the business." Without understanding the value delivered by each customer, it is easy to say "yes" to *any* customer request. When the costs of providing service to the individual customer can be measured, the manager can readily assess the level of service that is justified.

Figure 20.2 depicts a segment profitability analysis, illustrating the net income (revenues minus avoidable costs) generated with each of three key customers. The top-line revenues earned in serving each customer tell one story, but review of the bottom-line margins tells another. The "big" customer (C) proves to be the least profitable, showing a loss in the current analysis! It looks as though the supplier in this instance has jumped too high too often to see a positive return from this customer. The small customer (B), however, is showing a healthy margin. Concerns should focus on how the company can maintain customer A, grow with customer B, and make customer C profitable.

Recognizing that revenue does not equate with profitability is key for any business. Surprisingly, few companies employ profit analysis on a customer-by-customer basis. The challenge rests with accessing the proper data to populate the analysis. Revenue figures are easy enough to gather, but populating assignable costs (costs that can be applied to specific customers) is more complicated. The ideal solution is to capture information at the desired level of analysis (by customer or segment) to support the tracing of costs to customer- or segment-specific services. In the absence of such information, we must rely on a basis of allocating costs to customer activity. To date, activity-based costing offers the best (though not perfect) means for attaching costs to the activities driven by particular customers and/or products. Figure 20.3 provides a synopsis of the approach and the data required for an activity-based cost analysis.

	Customer A	Customer B	Customer C
Net sales	1,000,000	500,000	2,000,000
COGS (variable mfg. cost)	600,000	300,000	1,200,000
Manufacturing contribution	400,000	200,000	800,000
Variable marketing & logistics costs:			
Sales commissions	20,000	10,000	50,000
Transportation	100,000	60,000	250,000
Warehousing	50,000	10,000	100,000
Order processing	10,000	5,000	30,000
Chg. for investment in accts. rec.	5,000	2,000	15,000
Contribution margin	215,000	113,000	355,000
Assignable nonvariable costs:			
Salaries	100,000	50,000	200,000
Segment-related advertising	10,000	5,000	20,000
Slotting allowances	10,000	3,000	20,000
Inventory carrying costs	25,000	5,000	60,000
Controllable margin	70,000	53,000	55,000
Charge for dedicated assets used	40,000	15,000	80,000
Net margin	30,000	35,000	(25,000)

Figure 20.2. Segment Profitability Analysis by Customer.

Key considerations when conducting activity-based cost analysis include the following:

■ Only costs that would go away with the customer's business should be included in the analysis.
■ Determination of proper drivers of costs can be challenging; costs should rise and fall in direct proportion to the activity driver.
■ Collection of necessary data can be taxing the first time the analysis is conducted, but gets easier in subsequent efforts.
■ Economies of scale are largely ignored by linear expressions of cost.

While activity-based costing is, at its core, a way of allocating costs that are not easily assigned to specific customers, the feeling among most veterans of the method is that the analysis provides cost determinations that are "basically right." When the costs are then used as an input to a profitability analysis, the company enjoys a level of unprecedented business intelligence. Rather than relying on speculation and hunches that managers have regarding the value of a customer, the proof is presented in black and red ink. The company can now

The calculations

Resources ▶	$\dfrac{\text{Cost}}{\text{Driver}}$	X	$\dfrac{\text{Driver activity}}{\text{Cost object}}$	=	$\dfrac{\text{Cost}}{\text{Cost object}}$
Cost data from the general ledger or income statement	Overall driver activity level in records, observation & employee estimates		Documentation of cost object activity in customer/sales records, observation & employee estimates		Total service cost for a cost object (customer, service, product)

The data sources required for each calculation

Figure 20.3. Activity-Based Costing: Calculations and Data. (From Goldsby, Thomas J., Closing in on the true costs of service, *Transportation Trends*, 1, 2, 1999.)

gauge the level of service that is *justified* for a given account. One manager likens his experience to a hunting expedition: "Before conducting the profitability-by-customer analysis, we used to shoot in the dark, aiming recklessly at anything that startled us. Now that we have this information, it's like the lights have been turned on and we can plainly see the targets." The manager continued by noting how the "hit rate" improved for his company, providing right-sized services that met customer needs, but at the least total cost.

Clearly, the firm must employ voice of the customer and voice of the business insights in concert to determine the kinds of service and levels of service that are justified across the array of customers. Some customers will make justified demands based on the value they offer in return. Other customers will make demands for which there is insufficient justification. Knowing which customers are "worthy" of time and effort is critical in doing *the right things right,* the essence of Lean Six Sigma Logistics. Beyond the economics at work, it is important for the firm to develop flexible, robust processes to deliver on diverse needs *profitably*. Value stream maps help in this regard.

VALUE STREAM MAPPING

Many companies start down the Lean path by conducting a value stream mapping analysis. A value stream map uses flowchart techniques to capture visually the sum of activities performed in the sourcing, making, and delivery of a specific item or product. Value stream maps are similar to process maps, though a subtle difference is found in their focus. Whereas a process map focuses on a process

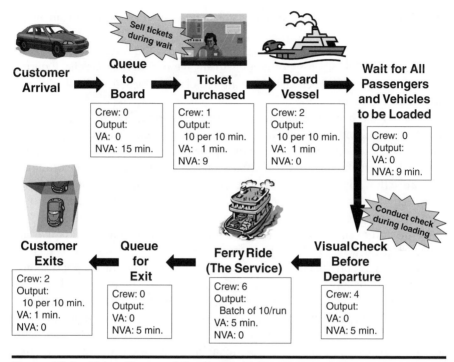

Figure 20.4.   Value Stream of the Ferryboat Experience.

that can apply across products and items, a value stream map is product centric and, therefore, likely to span across multiple processes. Process maps ordinarily serve as the first step in value stream mapping. Despite this difference in dimensionality, the general purpose is the same: to identify waste and opportunities for eliminating it. The specific purpose of the value stream map is to identify: (1) activities that create value in the eyes of customers, (2) activities that create no value yet are necessary steps, and (3) activities that create no value and are candidates for waste elimination.*

Figure 20.4 illustrates the value stream map for the ferry ride described earlier in Section 2. In this example, we see a fifty-two-minute experience for the passenger of the ferry service, of which only eight minutes (15 percent of the total time) lend any value to the customer. The action of purchasing the ticket only offers value if it serves as an opportunity for service inquiry or information gathering; the ticket purchase itself is not a value-added experience. Also note that the ride — what people are actually paying for — consumes only

---

* Womack, James P. and Jones, Daniel T., *Lean Thinking*, Simon & Schuster, New York, 1996.

five of the fifty-two minutes. Two immediate opportunities for improvement are noted in the figure. One is to sell tickets to customers while they wait rather than when they board the ferry, eliminating nine of the forty-three nonvalue-added minutes. The other opportunity is to engage in a continuous check during the loading activity, rather than after all vehicles are loaded. This would save another five minutes.

Much of the benefit found in value stream mapping is tied to the fact that activities associated with sourcing, making, and delivering product span functional boundaries, and the mapping effort and its output can open everyone's eyes to the waste created in the normal scope of business and the opportunities to improve flow. By providing a visual depiction of the value-added and nonvalue-added activities present in the "current state," achieving buy-in for the improvement initiative becomes less challenging and motivation for pursuing the "desired" or "future state" is reinforced. Though sourcing, making, and delivering product typically serve as the focus for value stream analysis, areas such as customer service, product development, and promotional product support should also enter the picture, given that significant waste can be eliminated through collaboration between these nonoperational business functions and operational areas like purchasing, production, and logistics. Waste is sometimes inherent when these two sides of a company fail to come together. Value stream maps are too often devoid of these nonoperational influences, perpetuating wastes that could be eliminated through internal collaboration.

The value stream map has two additional deficiencies that must be considered in its application. One, value in the eyes of the customer, cannot be fully appreciated without knowing what the customer really needs and is willing to pay to receive a particular service attribute. Companies often speculate on these bases in the absence of conducting a complete voice of the customer analysis. Second, as depicted in the ferry example, the remedy for reducing waste may not reside in simple improvements to the current process. The best solution might be a completely revised process (i.e., the bridge in the ferry example). Therefore, one should not feel captive to existing activities and processes depicted in the "as is" state. Despite these considerations, value stream mapping is a critical tool for supporting the continuous improvement culture of a company.

PARETO ANALYSIS AND ABC CLASSIFICATION

One reality associated with having a culture of continuous improvement is that perfection is never reached. At any given time, there are multitudes of processes to improve since perfection is the vision. What this amounts to is competition among the potential projects and initiatives in need of time and attention. Of course, time is the single most important resource for most companies and the one that can never be reclaimed. Therefore, selecting the improvement opportunities that will earn highest priority of our time and attention is critical.

Two tools that assist in prioritization are Pareto analysis and ABC inventory classification. Both techniques are based on the century-old writings of Italian economist Dr. Vilfredo Pareto, who recognized that approximately 80 percent of Italy's wealth at the time resided in the hands of 20 percent of the nation's population. Hence, the 80/20 rule was born. Despite its original interpretation, the 80/20 rule has found application to a widely diverse set of circumstances. In fact, Pareto charts can serve both strategic and operational planning purposes. They are sometimes applied to the overall business to illustrate how 80 percent of a company's revenue is generated by 20 percent of the company's customers or, alternatively, that 80 percent of revenue is generated by 20 percent of the company's products and services. When used in this way, a Pareto chart that details the volume of business generated by individual customers or segments of customers provides valuable insights for strategic planning.

Viewed generically, Pareto analysis describes how a relatively small set of inputs is responsible for the vast majority of outputs, whether those outputs are favorable outputs such as revenues and profits or unfavorable outputs like defects and costs. Quality guru Joseph Juran later referred to this critical set of inputs as the "vital few" among the "trivial many." The key is to identify those vital few (whether they drive positive or negative outcomes) and to prioritize future action around them.

In the case of Six Sigma improvement initiatives, Pareto analysis can serve as a way to highlight the root causes of problems that are most vital for resolution. Root causes that are generating the greatest variation in processes, leading to the greatest waste, will serve as the most fruitful targets for initial improvement. Several tools are identified in the next chapter to assist in linking problems to root causes. Pareto charts complement root cause analyses by displaying the relative importance of different sources of error. Figure 20.5 displays the results of a Pareto analysis conducted around the ferry experience. It depicts the frequency of customer complaints. The complaints that are leftmost on the scale present the greatest opportunity for improving customers' overall experience with the ferry service.

It is important that the improvement team consider the "value" of correcting the problem or error. In essence, what are the long-term cost savings or additional revenue generated minus the short-term costs incurred in tackling the problem? The consideration of value can sometimes adjust the prioritization of

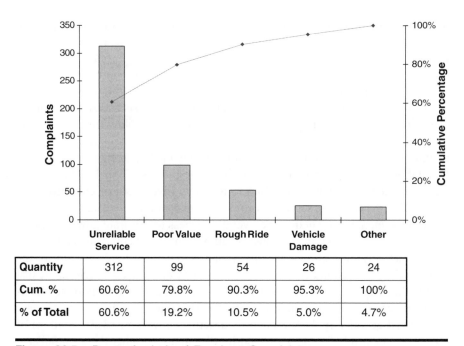

	Unreliable Service	Poor Value	Rough Ride	Vehicle Damage	Other
Quantity	312	99	54	26	24
Cum. %	60.6%	79.8%	90.3%	95.3%	100%
% of Total	60.6%	19.2%	10.5%	5.0%	4.7%

Figure 20.5.   Pareto Analysis of Ferryboat Complaints.

improvement initiatives from one based on frequency of error to one of *cost of poor quality*. By combining frequency with the cost per occurrence, one can generate a Pareto chart populated by total costs. Such a hybrid measure can shed greater light on the economic impact of the error than viewing frequency in isolation.

A related prioritization concept that attaches dollars to the opportunities for improved management is the ABC inventory classification. ABC classification is used to distinguish low- and high-value inventory. If an inventory reduction is to take place, the greatest return on the reduction effort will be found in the minimization of high-value inventory. ABC classification is often used to distinguish fast-moving ("A") inventory from slower-moving ("B", "C", and so on) inventories. Classifying inventory on the basis of throughput can lend value also. For instance, all other things being equal, slow-moving items would be prime candidates for immediate reduction. The greatest insight is gathered, however, by using a hybrid measure of inventory value and inventory throughput. Under these considerations, slow-moving high-value items would offer the richest opportunities for inventory reduction.

THE XY MATRIX

Another tool that can be used to establish project priorities is the XY matrix. The XY matrix drives priorities according to the voice of the customer and voice of the business considerations. While all opportunities for improvement might be regarded as worthwhile, some will prove more valuable than others. Likewise, some improvements can be harvested more easily than others. The XY matrix uses a simple input/output framework that considers both the *importance* of the prospective outputs and the *contribution* of inputs toward those outputs.

Figure 20.6 illustrates how an XY matrix can establish priorities coming away from the planning stage of analysis, pointing to opportunities where the greatest gain is achieved with initial continuous improvement efforts. The output variables (Ys) are listed across the horizontal axis and weighted, allocating 100 points among these criteria. The input variables (Xs) are then listed along the vertical axis. The organization would then populate the matrix by rating how a given input contributes to each of the desired outputs. A scale ranging from 0 to 10 is used to provide the relative contribution scores, with 0 suggesting no contribution and 10 representing great contribution to the output variable.

	Output Variables (Ys)	Growth	Customer Retention	Quality	Productivity	Cost		
	Output weight	30	25	20	15	10		Rank
Input Variables (Xs)		Association Table						
Space Utilization		5	3	7	8	8		565
Inventory Management		7	6	9	9	9		765
Receiving Cycle Time		7	7	6	10	7		725
Yard Management		1	5	5	7	5		410
Safety Management		3	5	8	9	9		600
Packaging Design		1	3	7	4	7		375

Figure 20.6. The XY Matrix: Establishing Priorities.

In taking a look at the sample matrix in the figure, the first input variable (space utilization) contributes little to customer retention but considerably to productivity and cost, relative to the other input variables.

Once the matrix is fully populated, the organization calculates the rank of each of the input variables by summing the products of each input's contribution times the weight of each criterion. In the case of space utilization, we use the following calculation to determine a rank score of 565:

$$(5 \times 30) + (3 \times 25) + (7 \times 20) + (8 \times 15) + (8 \times 10) = 565$$

After calculating the rank score for each input variable, we can compare values. The input variable with the highest value becomes the focal point for the organization's improvement efforts.

Ultimately, an organization should walk away from an XY matrix with consensus opinion about what issues to tackle, in what order, and which resources will be called on to generate results. A caveat attached to conducting an XY matrix analysis is the assumed independence of actions. That is, the opportunities presented among the input variables are all assumed to be feasible at the current time. However, after initiating the first action, the conditions may change such that other prospects listed among the possible inputs are no longer viable or no longer necessary. For that reason, interaction among inputs as well as between the inputs and outputs should be considered before taking any demonstrative action, realizing that one action could circumvent another or, more favorably, one action could capture multiple opportunities. For instance, in our example, the two highest ranking input variables (inventory management and receiving cycle time) can likely be pursued in unison to generate even greater value for the customer.

## 21

PROBLEM-SOLVING TOOLS

Once priorities for the organization are established using the strategy and planning tools highlighted earlier, the organization will then engage in improvement initiatives. Six Sigma, in particular, offers a wealth of methods and tools to assist with problem solving. In fact, its primary aim is in the structuring of problems and forwarding methods of analysis for solving them. The primary problem-solving method is DMAIC, described first in this chapter. Other tools include cause-and-effect diagrams, five-why analysis, and brainstorming.

DMAIC
(DEFINE-MEASURE-ANALYZE-IMPROVE-CONTROL)

Many refer to DMAIC as the roadmap for Six Sigma. Without question, it is the "backbone" methodology applied in Six Sigma improvement efforts. Some may question why DMAIC is recognized as a problem-solving tool rather than a strategy and planning tool given its comprehensive scope. Put simply, DMAIC is a means to an end. It does not necessarily determine the end, but rather provides, as indicated, the roadmap. The vision for a DMAIC endeavor is developed using the voice of the customer and voice of the business tools. The outcome of these strategic analyses should recognize the opportunities for improvement, and it is in pursuing these opportunities that the DMAIC method is employed. In addition, a focus on quality achieved through variation reduction can be a core element of a company's philosophy and strategy.

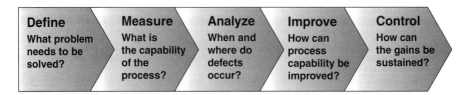

Figure 21.1. The DMAIC Method.

The stages of the DMAIC process are highlighted in Figure 21.1. Each step is reviewed next.*

Define

The strategy and planning tools described in Chapter 20 provide the logistician with a multitude of improvement opportunities. Voice of the customer highlights customer needs, voice of the business features the needs and the constraints of the company, value stream mapping illuminates the wastes, and the XY matrix helps to prioritize projects. The "Define" stage of DMAIC picks up where the XY matrix leaves off by defining the problem, selecting the project, and scoping the project. First, the problem must be stated clearly and succinctly. In turn, the project's purpose, scope, team members, resource requirements, and potential constraints must be delineated. It should be clear to everyone involved what is at stake, how and when the mission of the project is to be achieved, and who is responsible for what actions. Again, voice of the customer, voice of the business, and value stream mapping provide critical input in this stage of the process.

Measure

Precision in defining the problem should facilitate the next stage, measurement. Measurement refers to assessment of the current state. Should the focal problem for a DMAIC project be "improved reliability in delivery," transit time would serve as the primary measure. True to Six Sigma's concern with variation reduction, one would look not only at the average transit time but also the variance around it. We would be concerned with the accuracy in measurement as well. How is "transit time" determined? When does the clock start and stop? Who is currently measuring transit time? Can we trust the timekeeper? Ques-

---

* An excellent treatment of the DMAIC method can be found in Gardner, Daniel L., *Supply Chain Vector*, J. Ross Publishing, Boca Raton, FL, 2004.

tions of this sort come into play in this stage of the DMAIC process. Should multiple measures be necessary to assess a particular area of performance fully, all measures should be reviewed with the same scrutiny. In addition, they should be prioritized so that everyone knows which measures are most important. Common areas of measurement include cost, time, and quality.

The best measures will prove to be those that are:

- Quantifiable
- Easily measured
- Robust
- Reliable
- Valid

In the absence of valid measures, we are sure to experience "GIGO" (garbage in/garbage out), though we are unlikely to realize that bad information is driving our decision making. As noted in previous discussions, too often we become complacent with measurement, relying on measures for which we have long-standing history that enables the company to track "progress." However, careful analysis often suggests that we are measuring the *wrong things* or measuring the right things in the *wrong way*. The DMAIC process provides the perfect opportunity to correct errors in measurement. Though it can sometimes lead to separation anxiety, we must part with measures that act as bad compasses, telling us consistently to walk in the wrong direction.

Analyze

Given a clear statement of the problem and identification of focal measures, the DMAIC process proceeds with the "Analyze" step. This is where DMAIC borrows significantly from the scientific method in its pursuit of truth — to find what lies at the root of the problem that is leading to dissatisfied customers, unnecessary costs, dwindling margins, and frustration. The scientific method guides the researcher through three basic steps:

1. Observation of a phenomenon or a group of phenomena
2. Development of hypotheses that seek to explain and predict the phenomenon or phenomena
3. Testing of the hypotheses for causal relationships

These are the same basic steps employed in the analysis stage of DMAIC.

Six Sigma's borrowing from the community of scientists does not end with application of the scientific method itself, however, for it is in analyzing problems that Six Sigma practitioners look, act, and sound most like physicists, chemists, and statisticians. Six Sigma commonly employs tools like Design of Experiments to understand the cause-effect relationships among two or more factors, much like the biologist would test the effect of light on plant species in a lab setting. The logistician might examine the variance in delivery reliability by controlling for different factors associated with shipments of interest including, but not limited to, the way in which the shipment is tendered, dispatched, and scheduled; the way in which the order is physically prepared, staged, and loaded; the carriers and drivers used to fulfill the delivery; the time of day for pickup and delivery; weather conditions; and the processing of documentation associated with the shipment. Multiple factors may be to blame for the inconsistency of delivery and some factors may interact with others to complicate and worsen the problem.

Inferential statistics are often tapped to provide critical analysis of observations. Parametric techniques such as analysis of variance and regression analysis, along with nonparametric tools such as chi-square tests, are used to generalize findings from a sample of observations. The purpose of all methods is, again, to better understand the phenomena at work such that the cause-and-effect relationship can be realigned to provide improved outcomes: satisfied customers, minimized costs, healthy margins, and harmonious operations.

Improve

Unfortunately, recognizing the root cause of the problem is not sufficient for correcting it. Action must be taken. That is the concern of the "Improve" stage of DMAIC. Another way of looking at this stage is that it offers the opportunity for competitive advantage when many companies in an industry are staring at a common problem; it is the firm that deals with the problem swiftly and most effectively that achieves valued differentiation. Being the first one to solve the problem does not account for much unless the solution is acted on.

Making effective change is not an easy thing for any organization. Most good ideas never see the light of day given the challenges they face in this stage of implementation. And what is more pathetic than a good idea that fails to be recognized and implemented? The Lean Six Sigma organization is less prone to this disconnect between good ideas and good implementation because bringing effective ideas to the fore of the organization and pursuing them relentlessly is what Lean Six Sigma thinking is all about. It does not start with the good idea itself; it starts with discipline, developing a culture that relishes opportunities for improvement. Key to establishing a culture that is flexible and poised for opportunities is an orientation favoring teamwork. An organization with individuals not only interested in but, in fact, vested in the success of the whole is far more likely to meet change with favor than those that force change to resistant bands of employees. That much said, teamwork alone can be misguided in the absence of leadership. Therefore, vision must guide the team effort for anything worthwhile to be accomplished.

Once the culture for embracing change is in place (and this is no easy feat), the opportunities themselves must be seized using a structured approach. The approach involves open communication of what is at stake, how the improvement will be managed, and what is expected of all team members. Not all team members will necessarily be involved in every improvement opportunity, yet providing open communication to everyone establishes "communal understanding" and an environment of support, while minimizing suspicions that inevitably surface when efforts are made to manage change in a cloistered or underhanded manner.

Along with the communication of the change and expected contribution of team members is communication of the critical measures used to judge the success of the effort and to assess the contribution of each individual. The individual measures hold team members accountable for contribution, though the measures must correlate directly with the bigger goal of the change. Too often, measures ensure the busy-ness of people, but the efforts of the people do not translate into *meaningful* productivity — actions that fulfill the organizational vision. Lean Six Sigma Logistics and the DMAIC process embrace the belief that every action taken by every team member contributes to value in the eyes of the customer and, in turn, success for the company. Improvement efforts are pursued to rid the wastes and distractions that get in the way of meaningful productivity.

One key point relative to the Improve stage is that Six Sigma in and of itself does not provide the actual solution to the problem. That is, the Six Sigma DMAIC model provides a problem-solving method, but we need to rely on our Lean tools in order to generate possible solutions to the problem.

Control

Despite the challenges presented in bringing a good idea to light in the "Improve" stage of DMAIC, what can prove even more challenging is sustaining the effort. "Control" is the final stage of the DMAIC process, and it focuses on this aspect of improvement projects: avoiding complacency when the project is going well and goals are being met and taking corrective action when either the project strays or the environment changes. Clearly, elements of sustained or corrective action should be part of the improvement initiative from its outset, though it might be regarded as pessimism by some. Despite best efforts and well-established plans, the team must be ready to adapt with the situation. Robust, flexible processes will be those that prove most adept at accommodating change. Processes should be designed such that they can meet not only the immediate challenges of day-to-day fluctuation but also the dramatic or perhaps unthinkable challenges that might be revealed. The Lean Six Sigma organization must be ready for anything associated with these most critical aspects of the service.

Primary considerations in this phase of the DMAIC process center around issues of motivation and measurement. The Lean Six Sigma organization must be sure that the right performance is being measured and recognized. Performance that fails to correlate perfectly with the desired outcomes is waste. Unfortunately, inconsistency between expected and desired outcomes does not become apparent until the improvement project is under way. It is on this basis that many companies engage in a limited trial with each DMAIC project before full-scale rollout. The trial allows for a more comprehensive understanding of issues involved such that any misjudgments can be corrected before they derail the larger effort.

In sum, the DMAIC method is the backbone of Six Sigma methodology, offering a roadmap to improvement projects from conception to completion. As noted, critical to any effort to bring about meaningful change are the cultural attributes of discipline and teamwork. The DMAIC process will only lead to frustrated effort in the absence of these organizational prerequisites. Given the comprehensive nature of the DMAIC method, subsequent tools in this section offer insights that support the "Analyze" stage.

CAUSAL ANALYSIS TOOLS

Many tools are available in the Lean and Six Sigma domain to assist with root cause analysis. Some are very basic and can be conducted with little training and no formal data collection. These include brainstorming, cause-and-effect diagrams, and five-why analysis. These tools provide preliminary analysis but, perhaps more importantly, serve as a starting point for discussion and subsequent analysis. Other tools are more technical, quantitative, and call for extensive data collection to feed the analysis. In return, these tools offer deeper insights that should be free of the biases often found in qualitative approaches. Tools that belong to this more technical category include Design of Experiments and inferential statistical methods. Both qualitative and quantitative types of tools will be reviewed briefly.

Brainstorming

Brainstorming offers a general-purpose way to initiate conversation and gather ideas. Brainstorming sessions are likely to occur throughout the DMAIC process as a way to not only gather ideas but also get team members involved in problem recognition and resolution. Though the sessions should encourage free and open conveyance of ideas, they need not be devoid of structure. In fact, brainstorming sessions that lack structure may prove confusing and unproductive, defeating the improvement effort before it begins. First impressions often serve as lasting impressions. If the kickoff session for an improvement initiative is characterized by chaos rather than order, all confidence in the effort may be lost before it ever has a chance to be built.

One way to structure a brainstorming session is to ask everyone to focus on a single question or problem and then gather the input of participants in sequence around the table. This prevents a free-for-all scene that is commonly experienced in brainstorming sessions. Ideas should be captured on a white board with as little paraphrasing as possible. Ideas that are not relevant to the focal question or beyond the purview of the current scenario should be captured as well in a "parking lot" list. Parking lot items can be revisited later, as necessary. Ideas are gathered until no one has anything new to offer. Once ideas are documented, the leader might engage the group in a "mind-mapping" exercise, a technique used to organize the ideas by displaying them visually and drawing the interconnections that exist among the set. Mind maps help to provide synthesis to the brainstorming exercise.*

Cause-and-Effect Diagrams

Cause-and-effect diagrams (sometimes referred to as fishbone diagrams or Ishikawa diagrams) provide a structured, though qualitative, approach to problem solving. The main purpose of these diagrams is to generate discussion that can close in on the root cause or causes of a focal problem. The cause-and-effect diagram often provides structure to causal analysis brainstorming and serves as a good starting point for deeper analysis. Rarely is the diagram sufficient in and of itself to justify action. Rather, the diagram is a preliminary analytical tool that narrows the scope for subsequent analysis.

Common categories to look toward as potential sources of root causes include people, process, technology, equipment, material, and environment. Though these categories are often used in a manufacturing environment, they find application in logistics as well. Figure 21.2 organizes possible sources of customer dissatisfaction with the ferry service described in Section 2. Discussion should focus on a specific question, such as "Why is the ferry service so

---

* An interesting read on mind mapping can be found in Buzan, Tony and Buzan, Barry, *The Mind Map Book: How to Use Radiant Thinking to Maximize Your Brain's Untapped Potential*, Plume, New York, 1996.

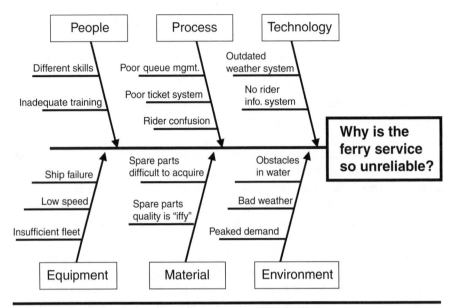

Figure 21.2.   Cause-and-Effect Diagram for Ferry Service.

unreliable?" A brainstorming session conducted around this question might generate the list of possible causes depicted in the diagram.

Like all forms of brainstorming, cause-and-effect diagrams are qualitative in nature and rely on the imagination of the team members involved to populate the diagram. Two caveats of cause-and-effect diagrams are the prospects of not working on the *real* problem and failing to identify the true cause of a problem. Yet another concern associated with diagram efforts is the fact that the possible causes identified in the diagram are not necessarily ranked as likely culprits of the problem. These concerns reiterate the need for additional analysis.

Five-Why Analysis

Five-why analysis is another technique that is commonly used to ascertain the root cause of a problem. The belief is that by focusing on a key problem, we can get to its core by asking the question "Why?" in succession. By asking "Why?" up to five times, one can usually feel as though the essence of the problem is understood and the root cause should also be readily apparent. The five-why approach ensures deeper investigation than that typically associated with fishbone diagrams.

A favorite tool of Lean practitioners, five-why analysis is a convenient way to explore cause-and-effect relationships. We can gain a better appreciation for how it works by returning to our ferry example and its unreliable service. Using the cause-and-effect diagram in Figure 21.2, let's assume that the consensus opinion is that service varies most based on personnel. The line of inquiry might proceed as follows:

Why #1: Why is the ferry service so unreliable?

Response: Because different people are working at different times and the skill levels vary.

Why #2: Why do the skill levels vary?

Response: Some operators are veterans, but many others are newcomers; it takes time to learn the job.

Why #3: Why do we have so many newcomers?

Response: Turnover has been quite high among ferry operators.

Why #4: Why has turnover been high among operators?

Response: Ferry operators have complained about the long hours and erratic shift changes.

Why #5: Why are operators asked to work long hours and erratic shifts?

Response: Poor scheduling has led to unusually long hours and demands for frequent shift changes.

What is interesting to note from this line of inquiry is that the response to the fifth "Why?" points to a potential root cause that was not identified in the cause-and-effect diagram. While poor scheduling is probably not entirely to blame for unreliable service and dissatisfied customers, it seems like a viable problem to tackle in the near term. Can the ferry operator expect service reliability to close in on perfection by making this one simple change? Probably not, but marked improvement should be expected as the cause-effect chain operates in reverse of the five-why questioning: Improved scheduling should lead to more reasonable, steady hours, which should reduce turnover, which should eliminate the need for newcomers, which should provide a more consistent level of experience among "veteran" operators, which should improve the reliability of service. You get the idea.

Something that should not be lost on the ferry service provider, and should not be lost on anyone pursuing Lean Six Sigma Logistics, is that a demonstratively inferior service offering is unlikely to attract significant volumes of new business in the presence of a superior alternative. That is, even with improved reliability in service, the ferry cannot reasonably expect to steal customers away from the bridge, at least not under normal circumstances. This is why companies are challenged to identify the best way to serve customers and not simply improve existing, conventional means. This calls for out-of-the-box thinking that can be spurred by the causal analysis tools presented here, if the company encourages team members to avoid "captive thinking."

Design of Experiments

As previously indicated, the qualitative causal analysis tools like brainstorming, cause-and-effect diagrams, and five-why analysis are excellent ways to help define a focal problem or initiate analysis, but they are limited in the depth that they can provide. Their value is tied to bringing the parties together for the sake of further investigation of problems and highlighting likely candidates for root causes. Subsequent, in-depth analysis might include Design of Experiments (DOE) methods described earlier. DOE can provide an unbiased, empirical method for root cause examination.

In technical terms, DOE is based on the controlled isolation of cause-and-effect relationships. Experiments involve the application of carefully crafted manipulations to random sets of a sample. In doing so, the researcher can observe how changes to the input factors result in different outputs. By then using inferential statistical methods (described next), the researcher tries to generalize the observed findings to a broader set of circumstances. This basic approach to experiments is used widely in physical and social sciences.

In recent years, Six Sigma practitioners have embraced DOE as a critical element in the DMAIC process. Its power as an analytical tool has gained wide acceptance among operations-oriented personnel, many of whom have relied historically on heuristic (nonquantitative) methods of analysis. Given the precision with which one can determine cause-and-effect relationships through direct observation of controlled conditions, people are cracking open those long-forgotten yet trusty textbooks on research design and statistics to learn (or relearn in some instances) how tried-and-true techniques like experiments can help to solve everyday problems. While a thorough discussion of DOE is beyond the scope of our current effort, worthwhile references are available.*

---

* For a good, quick reference on DOE, see *The Black Belt Memory Jogger*, Goal/QPC and Six Sigma Academy, Salem, NH, 2002. Other references include: Anderson, Mark J. and Whitcomb, Patrick J., *DOE Simplified: Practical Tools for Effective Experimentation*, Productivity Press, New York, 2000; Barrentine, Larry B., *An Introduction to Design of Experiments: A Simplified Approach*, ASQ Quality Press, Milwaukee, 1999; and, Breyfogle, Forrest W., *Implementing Six Sigma: Smarter Solutions Using Statistical Methods*, 2nd ed., Wiley, New York, 2003.

Inferential Statistics

Coupled with the widespread adoption of technical research methods like DOE is the common usage of inferential statistics. Six Sigma and its pursuit of variance reduction is to credit for bringing statistical methods to prominence in the analysis of everyday operations. In order to understand variance, one must realize that variance is simply an expression of dispersion. If everything happened the same way all the time, we would have no dispersion in our observations and, hence, no variance. The fact that variance does, in fact, happen leads us to examine *why* it happens.

The basic premise of statistics is to use sample data to *infer* what is occurring in reality. We develop models composed of observable, measurable variables to represent inputs in our prediction of some output. A good model is an efficient model — one that has much to say about reality using a few predictors. Some models may use only a single predictor (univariate analysis), while others rely on multiple predictors (multivariate analysis) to explain what is happening in the output variable (or "dependent" variable). Regression analysis is the primary method used to assess the influence of predictor variables on a dependent variable.

Predictor variables may be either number based (continuous) or label based (categorical or discrete). Continuous variables are those that can be measured using numerical scales that reflect the degrees present in a condition of interest, whether that condition is time (hours), heat (degrees Fahrenheit), weight (pounds), happiness (1 = very unhappy, 7 = very happy), or any other condition that can be quantified in some way. Categorical variables refer to those that are not expressed in numbers, but rather in labels. Examples include gender (F = female, M = male), professional certification (yes, no), and work shift (first, second, third). A much-heralded tool in the Six Sigma tool kit is analysis of variance (ANOVA). ANOVA is a special case of regression where one or more categorical variables, rather than continuous variables, are used to predict behavior of an output variable. Both continuous and categorical variables may be combined in a multivariate regression model to predict a single output variable.

To illustrate the various kinds of regression analyses, let's revisit our ferryboat example. The output variable of interest is ferry service reliability. Should we decide to use only a single predictor variable to explain variance in service reliability, we can elect to perform simple regression analysis by selecting a continuous variable (say, years of experience for the boat operator) or t-test analysis by using a single categorical variable (weather: good or bad). These relationships are expressed mathematically using the nomenclature of the output (Y) as a function of the input (X), or in our case:

Basic expression of relationships: Y (output) = A function of X (input)

Simple regression analysis:
Service reliability = f (Experience of the boat operator, in years)

t-test analysis:
Service reliability = f (Weather: good or bad)

When multiple predictors are added to the mix, we should see added explanatory power in the model. If the model is composed entirely of categorical predictors, we use ANOVA. If the model uses continuous variables or a combination of continuous and categorical variables, we use multiple regression. A multiple regression analysis might take on the appearance of the statement below:

Multiple regression analysis:
Service reliability = f (Experience of the boat operator [years],
weather [good/bad],
age of boat [years],
time of day [peak/off-peak],
season [tourist/nontourist])

By including the different predictor variables in the model, we are stating that we expect that each one will contribute to our understanding of the outcome variable (service reliability), that a relationship exists between each predictor and the outcome. When we expect a relationship to be present between two factors, we have a hypothesis. Our success in developing a good regression model is measured by finding predictors that appear to influence our output variable or, put another way, finding support for our hypotheses. Success is also measured by the amount of variance in the output variable that is explained by the predictors. This measure of variance explained is known as the R-square (R^2) statistic or coefficient of determination. For example, if the R^2 equals 0.82, then that means that 82 percent of the output can be explained by the inputs.

Figure 21.3 illustrates the concept of explained variance by using Venn diagrams. The first diagram shows that approximately half of the variance in the output variable (ferry service reliability) is explained by the predictor variable (operator experience). The second diagram shows that even more variance (67 percent) is explained when the age of the boat, weather, time of day, and season are added to the mix. Adding predictors to the model improves the explanatory power of the model, but at the expense of efficiency or "model parsimony" as scientists call it.

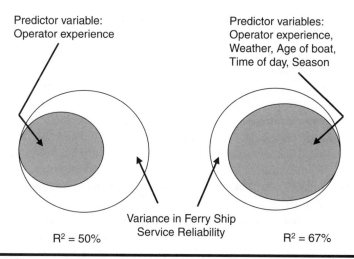

Predictor variable:
Operator experience

Predictor variables:
Operator experience,
Weather, Age of boat,
Time of day, Season

Variance in Ferry Ship
Service Reliability

$R^2 = 50\%$

$R^2 = 67\%$

Figure 21.3. Variance Explained in an Output Variable.

To reiterate Lord Kelvin's observation, "When you can measure what you are speaking about and express it in numbers, you know something about it; but when you cannot express it in numbers, your knowledge is of a meager and unsatisfactory kind." Inferential statistics provide us with tools to measure and quantify our understanding. Once we understand the sources of variation in the output variable, we can take action to control it. Six Sigma pioneers are to credit for turning operations practitioners into physical and social scientists by demonstrating the relevance of proven tools to the problems faced every day in the supply chain domain.

One caveat when using regression analysis and ANOVA is tied to the realization that these methods rely on correlations, or the "traveling together" of data. *Causality* cannot be tested using correlations, though it can be inferred given observation of the phenomenon of interest. Correlation analysis is prone to the problem of common underlying causes, sometimes referred to as "spurious effects." This problem seems to rear its head regularly in studies conducted within the medical community, such as suggesting that regular flossing of teeth leads to longer life expectancy when, most likely, flossing is one part (though not an inconsequential part) of a larger regimen for good health and long life expectancy. To suggest that failure to floss regularly is the root cause of shortened life expectancy is an overstatement, to say the least. Therefore, great consideration must be given to the selection of predictor variables used in analysis such that the root cause is represented somewhere in the set of predictors. Brainstorming, cause-and-effect diagrams, and five-why analysis help to ensure that root causes will be represented in the analysis.

Another caveat is related to the fact that many statistical methods rely on the assumption of normally distributed data, representative of a "normal population" where the mean, mode, and median are equal, with half of the distribution below the mean and half above the mean. A case in point resides in the fact that Six Sigma quality, resulting in no more than 3.4 defects per million opportunities, assumes a perfectly normal distribution. The truth is that most data, and the populations from which data are drawn, are not perfectly normal. Some may be somewhat skewed (asymmetrical) or laden with kurtosis (flatness). Other samples may demonstrate dramatic departures from normality (e.g., bimodal distribution).

The point is that on collecting data, one must engage in preliminary data analysis, reviewing the characteristics of the data set, checking for completeness of the data, assessing reliability and validity of the data and, finally, the distribution of the data. Data that violate the assumption of normality can often be standardized or corrected. In other cases, statistics packages offer adjusted statistical tests or tests appropriate for non-normal data. So, one must not simply assume that the data are complete, reliable, valid, and normal. It is up to the individual conducting the research to ensure that the findings are valid based on sound science. If the data are junk or not fully considered in the choice of statistical test, Garbage in/garbage out makes a repeat appearance. The effort is wasted and perhaps misguiding in its result.

A final caveat worth mentioning here is tied to the ease with which complicated statistical analysis can be conducted today with the aid of PC-based statistics packages. On completing data collection, analysis is a few points and clicks away. The danger is in not understanding the underlying logic at work when models are unwittingly put together and tested. A sound review of statistics is strongly suggested before venturing far down the path of using inferential statistics as a viable problem-solving tool. However, Lean, Six Sigma, and eliminating waste are not only about statistics, so we should not let our natural phobia of mathematics and statistics stop us from doing what is right.

## 22

OPERATIONAL TOOLS

Tools that support strategy and planning as well as those that help solve problems are great, yet the manager needs an equally capable set of tools to help with day-to-day execution of the operations. This chapter illustrates more than just tools — an assortment of concepts, methods, and even beliefs that can help the manager execute the work of logistics and supply chain management more effectively. They are divided into two broad categories: flow concepts and organization concepts.

FLOW CONCEPTS

Several key concepts that shape the operational aspects of Lean Six Sigma Logistics are rooted in the management of physical flows in the supply chain. Most of these concepts find their basis in Lean theory. These concepts include just-in-time and the pull system of replenishment; lead-time management, speed, and flexibility; leveled flow; and delivery frequency and lot size. Each will be discussed in turn.

Just-in-Time and the Pull System

Just-in-time replenishment is a fundamental aspect of Lean implementation. The idea is to replenish only what the customer needs, *when* the customer needs it. The "customer" may be an internal customer (a work cell on the shop floor or a distribution center within the company's logistics network) or an external customer. The obvious benefit is the reduction of inventory that comes with reserving commitment of inventory until demand is known. Hence, customers pull the inventory rather than having it pushed on them. We have discussed the many forms of logistics waste that tend to be created when companies speculate on what customers will demand, the quantities they will demand, and the specific location of that demand. Speculation leads to opportunities for error, and in fact, we *know* that there will be error. The relevant issues become how far off our judgments will be and in which direction. Using a pull system removes speculation of demand from our day-to-day execution. As a result, we not only achieve inventory reductions but also benefit from reductions in the other six forms of logistics waste. For instance, transportation waste is reduced by not sending goods out into the field that may or may not sell, goods that may have to be reclaimed or repositioned in the market for another chance at sales. As for storage and facilities, less is needed because the company is only handling product that is sold or will be sold in the near future. The other wastes are similarly reduced when we act on *certainty* rather than *guesswork.*

How is a pull system operationalized in the supply chain? One way is through the use of kanban cards in both their paper and electronic format, which serve as visual cues of demand. The kanban signals when a small quantity of supply is consumed downstream and needs to be replenished. Toyota used the card-based kanban method to introduce North American suppliers to the pull orientation of just-in-time after setting up operations in the United States and Canada. After getting suppliers up to speed, the system has since converted to electronic kanban communications, but the returnable containers in use today throughout the Toyota system continue to serve as visual cues of demand.

While kanbans are typically believed to only find application in the inbound side to manufacturing, the same basic concept is employed in vendor-managed inventory (VMI) systems. In VMI, the vendor company (usually a manufacturer) determines the inventory level that a customer downstream should maintain, either at the distribution center level or perhaps at the point of retail. By having visibility of inventory on a real-time basis, the vendor can determine when to replenish supply and the quantity of the replenishing supply. The supply chain and end customer benefit from better matching demand with ready (and fresh) supply with little or no speculative inventory. In addition, by not committing inventory to customers in advance of demand, the vendor is free to determine where inventory should be deployed in real time based on current needs.

Very few supply chains operate on a pull basis from beginning to end. Even Toyota, the epitome of Lean, only relies on a true "pull" in feeding its manufacturing plants. On the outbound side from the plants, Toyota Motor Sales continues to forecast the supply of finished automobiles that dealers will need to meet the subsequent needs of customers. This essentially reflects a "push" to the market as dealers and Toyota speculate on what consumers will buy on the lot. This is a fact of life for auto manufacturers given that few consumers are willing to wait the several weeks (and for some automakers several months) that it takes to produce and deliver a customer-spec vehicle. Most consumers would prefer to show up on the lot and drive home that same day or soon thereafter in a new vehicle that closely, though not perfectly, matches expectations. In response, automakers flood the market with sedans, coupes, trucks, minivans, SUVs, and hybrid vehicles that they *hope* will meet the needs of the market.

There is no question that operating on a pull basis is tough. Operations must be synchronized with demand, flexible enough to accommodate whatever might happen in the marketplace, and quick in response. This forces most companies to simply say "It's not possible." These are also the companies that will be standing on the sidelines when their competition demonstrates that pull systems are possible. These challengers will certainly understand the economics of operating on a conventional basis, but will develop capabilities (along the lines illustrated in the Logistics Bridge Model) that change the economics — achieving flexible market accommodation at a lower cost than staid competitors stuck in speculate-and-push modes of operation. Anyone with an eye toward the personal computer market, among others, has seen this very dynamic at work in recent years. The next three areas to be reviewed are key ingredients in the transition from push to pull replenishment.

Lead-Time Management, Speed, and Flexibility

If a company is ever to have aspirations of delivering on customer promises at anything close to real time, then lead-time management, speed, and flexibility are critical. In order to reduce lead time, the processes performed in capturing, fulfilling, and delivering an order must be scrutinized and, more fundamentally, questioned. Significant lead-time reductions usually call for dramatic process redesigns. Redesigning logistics-related processes must also take into consideration how the process should interface with other internal functions, suppliers, customers, and service providers given logistics' boundary-spanning presence in the company and the supply chain.

Recall that logistics is the thread that links the supply chain system. The challenge of lead-time reduction efforts is to make the companies that compose the supply chain collectively recognize process elements that add value given the time consumed and to compress the nonvalue-added elements from the process. In the end, we have a lean, synchronized system that reduces lead time to its absolute minimum but also makes all involved parties more efficient and competitive.

Once unnecessary and nonvalue-added steps in a process have been eliminated, we can focus on performing the remaining steps with speed and accuracy.

Like eliminating unnecessary steps in a process, the organization must seek to remove bottlenecks in flow, wherever they might exist. Consistent with Theory of Constraints thinking,* the speed of any flow is going to be regulated by the speed of the constraint. This is as true in process flow as it is in the flow of a dammed river. Lean-ing out internal operations does not necessarily improve flow when the bottleneck exists outside the four walls of the "Leaned out" operation. Yet again, we see why one must take the mission for improvement outside the company in tackling constraints to optimal flow.

Obviously, we cannot look past the accuracy or reliability of the process, for a fast process that only delivers half of its anticipated yield is not worth much. The challenge of building fast yet reliable processes is not enough because they must be flexible as well. Processes must be able to handle whatever comes their way. Too often, this aspect of Lean processes is overlooked. Unfortunately, Lean practitioners often feel that in order to create a fast, reliable process, they must fix it, whereby "fixing" the process makes it rigid. But we cannot afford to have "fixed," rigid processes, for they must be ready for anything. Even the most finely tuned sports car makes for a poor off-road vehicle. Lean processes must be able to accommodate the bumps and rugged terrain that comprise today's marketplace.

Processes that reflect desired characteristics of speed, reliability, and flexibility must then be fed by real-time information to leverage the benefits of the system. It is information that conveys not only the market needs but also the operational status of the system that must be captured and consumed by a company to make the vision of Lean Six Sigma Logistics a reality. The goal of these efforts is to create a system with a high level of readiness, one that is ready to respond to whatever challenges and opportunities are presented. Lead-time management, along with the costs incurred in providing quick response, represents the supply chain's tangible, holistic measure of readiness. Total cost paired with revenue implications should drive a company's pursuit of fast, reliable, flexible processes.

Leveled Flow

Despite our focus on flexibility and readiness to take on anything, we cannot look past the importance of planning. We must have an ability to look ahead to sense what might be in store for the company and perhaps the entire supply chain. Looking ahead on a strategic basis helps to ensure the company's lead-

---

* To read more about Theory of Constraints, see Goldratt, Eliyahu M., *Theory of Constraints*, North River Press, Great Barrington, MA, 1990.

ership position, introducing the right products, and working with the right customers and suppliers, among other endeavors. Looking ahead operationally is important too. Though we should develop processes and capabilities to accommodate "uncontrollable" variation in demand, it does not mean that we should not try to rope in the variation.

Oftentimes, it is the company itself that *creates* the variation. Most companies stir up demand by engaging in promotions and temporary price reductions that surge demand in the short term, generating artificial peaks in demand. Generally speaking, these peaks are followed by long, deep valleys in demand as the excess inventory must be depleted before customers are ready to buy again. Yet, the company (and, indeed, the supply chain) must be prepared for the peak, having capacity and people on hand to fulfill the heightened volumes when such artificialities are present. In place of these man-made ebbs and flows, the logistics organization should work with internal and external parties to level the flow, minimizing the so-called bullwhip effect that leads to overreactions with changes in demand and the inevitable waste created by these overreactions.

The benefits of leveling flow are fairly obvious. You do not need capacities to cover the peaks, but rather to cover the average demand over the course of the planning horizon. You do not need to have people ready to accommodate the peaks, but only the smoothed demand. You will be less prone to paying premium prices for materials in high demand as well as constrained capacities in warehouses and transportation assets. In sum, by reducing variation in the activity level, the company will only pay for assets and processing necessary to cover the averages rather than the peaks.

The challenge of leveling flow involves more than having the ability to respond to demand as it happens; it involves an ability to foreshadow the near term. The only way to foreshadow with any accuracy is to collaborate — collaborate with the forces creating demand, namely marketing, sales, new product development and commercialization, and customers. We should not limit our focus to next-stage customers, but also focus on tier 2 customers and beyond if we find ourselves separated from end customers by multiple tiers in the supply chain. Only to the extent that we can have some idea of what end customers might have in store for us can we have any hope of foreshadowing the future with any accuracy. The collaboration need not only provide foreshadowing benefits; by sharing capabilities and working through constraints with these outside parties, opportunities can be realized to make greatest use of what Lean Six Sigma Logistics has to offer the company and the entire supply chain. Therefore, leveled flow can serve not only as a way to achieve lowest total logistics cost, but also as a means of collaboration between logistics and other functional areas in the company and between the company and its trading partners in the supply chain.

Frequency and Lot Size

The frequency of delivery and lot size determination are intimately related to pull replenishment, lead-time management, and leveled flow. As discussed in the Logistics Bridge Model, delivery frequency is among the most powerful Lean tools for reducing inventory levels. In one example, we examined how high frequency and small lot sizes supported by milk runs and cross-docks resulted in leveled flow into manufacturing plants, allowing the manufacturing line to synchronize demand with real-time supply.

Despite the attraction and quantifiable benefits, there is inherent resistance to increasing frequency and reducing lot size. Large lots are encouraged and rewarded in purchasing, production, and logistics in many companies given the basis on which these functions are typically measured: cost per unit. Unfortunately, most cost-per-unit measures do not capture the indirect costs attached to buying, making, or shipping more volume than the company needs in the here and now. Costs like inventory carrying costs, increased warehousing costs, and the cost of repositioning unsold inventories may not be taken into account, not to mention the hard-to-measure damage to brand equity that comes with price discounting used commonly to move excess inventory.

While it is true that per-unit purchasing, production, and transportation costs are likely to increase (at least in the short term) with smaller lots delivered more frequently, a company should rely on *total cost analysis* to determine whether it is a good idea and to determine what the ideal lot size should look like. This calculation should take more into consideration than annual inventory carrying cost and annual ordering cost found in simple economic order quantity logic. It should truly reflect all costs affected by the lot size, such as transportation and warehousing. In turn, measurement and reward systems must be devised such that purchasing, production, and logistics management are not held accountable for functional or per-unit costs, but for contribution to the collective effort captured in total cost. The value of matching supply to demand becomes apparent when total costs are determined.

ORGANIZATION CONCEPTS

Whereas some operational concepts are associated with the management of flow, others help to organize the work environment to support optimal work flow, free from error and hazard. Like the concepts of flow management, the organization concepts are rooted in Lean theory. These concepts include the standardized work plan, 5S organization, and visual controls. Each will be discussed in turn.

Standardized Work Plan

Standardization has served as a consistent theme throughout our discussion of Lean Six Sigma Logistics. It was one of the twenty-seven tenets associated with the principle of capability. A standardized operation is one in which we know the input requirements, the procedure of the process, the time for each step in the procedure, and the expected output of the operation. Standards are essential for understanding the current condition of a process, supporting continuous improvement, and measuring improvement. Not only must the work be standardized, but the expected inputs, procedure, and outputs must also be clearly documented. The documentation should be so clear that an outsider should be able to step into the process, understand the process, and soon operate as a fully functioning team member, making appropriate contributions to the process.

The reason that standardized work is so important is that it allows us to understand variance in our processes and to make appropriate corrections. You may recall the example of the novice golfer trying to improve his swing by making one modification at a time to an established method. Without standardization, the source of the variation is uncertain and cannot, therefore, be corrected. For that reason, standardization serves as a fundamental platform for continuous improvement.

The SIMPOC Model

To answer the question "What does a standardized process look like?" we need to break down the process itself. The good news is that all processes are made of the same basic variables. The SIMPOC (Supplier-Inputs-Measurement-Procedure-Outputs-Customers) model* defines the key variables and provides a framework for documenting standardized processes by answering the following questions:

1. **Supplier**: Who supplies the inputs for the process?
2. **Inputs**: What are the inputs required for the process? This may include material, people, or information.
3. **Measurement**: How do we measure the process to ensure success?
4. **Procedure**: What are the procedures for the process? This includes documenting the process steps and the timing of each step.
5. **Outputs**: What are the expected outputs of the process? These can include actual products, information, or documentation.

---

* The SIMPOC model is often referred to as the "SIPOC" model in the absence of the "measurement" component.

The SIMPOC is a valuable tool to compare the current condition of processes and to develop standardized operations.

Sample Process: Receiving Function of Two Divisional Manufacturing Facilities.

SIMPOC – Receiving Function	Plant 1	Plant 2
Supplier to the process	Ordering Department	Purchasing
Input for the process	Receiving Schedule	ASNs
Measurements	Receiving Time	None
Procedures	Documented	None
Output	Part to Line Side	Parts to Stores
Customer	Line Side	Stores Area

This high-level example of a SIMPOC shows how the tool can be used to compare processes in different facilities. Clearly, these two plants have very different processes in place to receive material.

Figure 22.1.   Standardized Operations and SIMPOC Analysis.

6. **Customers**: Who are the customers of the process and what do they expect?

These questions are addressed in the example illustrated in Figure 22.1. If we can document the SIMPOC for each process in our operation, the result will be a set of documented standard operations. Once this is accomplished, the standard is set. As noted, a standardized, documented process is one that new team members can quickly understand and contribute to immediately. Even though a process becomes standardized, however, we should not become content with it. The vision is to always seek new, better ways to perform the work.

5S Organization and Visual Control

Fundamental to Lean-ing out any operation is to eliminate clutter and complexity. Clutter and complexity in the workplace lead to chaos, and chaos leads to waste. The organized workplace is one in which team members are fully functional, efficient, comfortable, and safe. 5S is a method used to organize the workplace. The terms of 5S are presented in Table 22.1, in both original Japa-

Table 22.1. The 5S Approach to Workplace Organization.

Japanese Expression	English Equivalent	Meaning
Seiri	Sorting	Identify unnecessary items in the workplace and remove them (example: red tagging).
Seiton	Straightening	Organize the workplace for safety and efficiency (example: taping and labeling).
Seiso	Scrubbing	Maintain tidiness with accountability and regularly scheduled cleanups (example: TPM).
Seiketsu	Standardizing	Document expectations and procedures to ensure consistent performance.
Shitsuke	Sustaining	Maintain the discipline with good work habits and problem-solving mind-set (example: poka-yoke and workplace kaizens).

nese expressions and the English translations. Put simply, 5S suggests that there is "a place for everything and everything is in its place." This concept applies to operations environments like the shop floor, loading docks, and storage areas, but it also applies to office environments. The idea is that when team members know where to find the physical tools they need to do the job and clutter is minimized, the work will be done safely and efficiently.

Maintaining order is a key cultural element of the Lean Six Sigma organization. An orderly work environment conveys a message of discipline to team members and portrays an image of quality to all outsiders, whether they are customers, Malcolm Baldrige Award reviewers, or health and safety inspectors. The work environment that condones 5S principles is never shy about introducing new or prospective customers to the operations or nervous about the next drop-in inspection because the environment is always under the inspection of the team members. Maintaining a clean, safe working environment is the responsibility of all team members and can serve as a starting point for a broader total productive maintenance (TPM) program, where members not only maintain order in their work are, but also perform basic maintenance (e.g., inspecting, cleaning, tightening, lubricating) of the equipment and assets they use.

Red Tag Initiatives

One tool highlighted previously in the book is the red tag initiative, where team members are given the opportunity to "red tag" items throughout the workplace for their potential removal. Should an item be tagged, someone has forty-eight hours to justify its presence. Red tagging has proven to be a simple, fun, and effective way to eliminate clutter, improve the work environment, and gain team member involvement in the cause.

Red tagging is one form of visual control. Visual controls are creative means to make work not only visible but understandable. When paired with standardized work and 5S organization, visual control highlights variation from the expected condition, the difference between the expected condition and the actual condition. Essentially, visual control provides many eyes and ears in the workplace, all trained to recognize variation, report it, and respond to it.

Poka-Yoke

Beyond recognizing defects in processes after they *have* occurred is the effort to *prevent* mistakes from occurring in the first place. Originally developed by Shigeo Shingo, poka-yoke methods are devised to make it difficult for errors in work to take place and be passed along in a process. Like all methods of work flow improvement, mistake proofing is not merely the domain of industrial engineers, those who design optimal work flows for a living. Anyone with a good idea to lend that leads to less waste, greater efficiency, and enhanced safety should be encouraged to bring that idea forward. Team members who are empowered to improve the process take ownership in it. Ownership is tied to pride in quality execution. Poka-yoke was introduced previously in our discussions of data flow (Chapter 12) and quality at the source (Chapter 19) in the Logistics Bridge Model.

## 23

MEASUREMENT TOOLS

At the cornerstone of Lean Six Sigma Logistics is one's understanding of the processes that deliver value to customers and generate returns for the company. Central to gaining an understanding of the processes is measurement. Given careful design of a process and expectations regarding output, we must be able to assess its relative performance. This chapter reviews valuable measures of Lean Six Sigma Logistics performance and emphasizes the importance of valid inputs to measurement. In fact, we start with a discussion of the data collection plan before surveying measurement tools, including those associated with process capability, priorities, and output.

DATA COLLECTION PLAN

Data collection is the critical, though unglamorous, step in solving any problem. As indicated in the chapter on problem solving, the validity of the analysis inputs is critical toward having valid outputs to guide intelligent decision making. Too often, managers become so focused on tackling a problem that they forget to direct much mental energy to this critical middle step in problem solving. Measures that are populated with the wrong data or data riddled with holes provide little meaningful insight.

While there are tools like XY matrices, cause-and-effect diagrams, and five-why analysis to help identify the right problem to solve, less guidance is available to help identify what data are necessary for solving the problem. A few key questions must be addressed before engaging in the data collection:

1. What is the purpose of the data?
2. What data are needed?

3. Where are the data?
4. In what format do we need the data?
5. What is the cost-benefit tied to the data collection?

The final question is important given that the "ideal" data will not always be accessible or might prove more taxing than the value of the solution. Therefore, we must consider the costs and value of the data before embarking on the collection effort. Once these concerns are satisfied, the plan for data collection can develop.

An important aspect of the data collection plan is to assign responsible, unbiased individuals to the task of collecting the data. Again, where the quality of the analysis rests with the quality of the inputs, one must not view data collection as an unimportant task. The collectors of the data should be trained to ensure that the right data are collected correctly. Tasking the summer intern with these responsibilities is fine as long as sufficient guidance is provided.

As indicated, it is also important that the data be gathered in an unbiased fashion. If the data contain any real or perceived biases, the findings of the analysis will (justifiably) be met with resistance. Therefore, all interested parties should have an opportunity to participate in the data collection plan to provide "veto" votes at this preliminary stage of the analysis rather than after the analysis, when considerable time and energy have been directed to the research effort. This chapter continues by examining tools that can be used to provide valuable knowledge given sound data inputs.

PROCESS CAPABILITY

While Lean offers great insight toward designing efficient, effective processes, Six Sigma puts great focus on measuring the capabilities of processes and guiding their improvement. The term "Six Sigma," in fact, refers to quality in execution, with six sigmas implying fewer than 3.4 defects per million opportunities. The term "sigma" is Greek notation for "standard deviation," a statistical measure of dispersion, or deviation from the mean. Figure 23.1 illustrates the appearance of standard deviations (sigmas) around the mean of a normal, bell-shaped distribution. The area under the curve is measured by what is called the z-score. The z-score represents the proportion (area) of the sample that falls within two boundaries. Given that the mean is in the middle of the bell-shaped curve, half of the curve's area is to the left of the mean and the other half is to the right. Within the boundaries of one standard deviation to the left of the mean and one standard deviation to the right ($\pm 1\sigma$), we have just over 68 percent

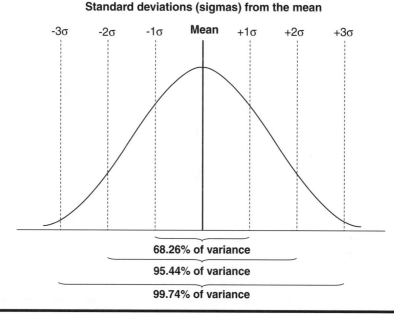

Standard deviations (sigmas) from the mean

68.26% of variance

95.44% of variance

99.74% of variance

Figure 23.1. What Is a Sigma?

of the curve's area. If we extend the reach out to ±2σ, we have over 95 percent, and out to ±3σ, we have over 99.7 percent of all observations represented in the normally distributed curve.

The idea is to pursue perfection in execution. "Perfection" is measured by having no variation from the expected outcome of a process. One way to look at the standard deviation (or sigma) as a measure of performance is to ask "How successful have we been in reducing variation, in pushing defects out of the process?" This is opposed to letting defects close in on you.

Figure 23.2 illustrates how a process with the same mean can have two different levels of variation. Though the curve at the top of the diagram has the same mean as the one below it, the dispersion of observations is greater; hence, this curve reflects greater variation in performance. The values for standard deviations will be greater as a result. Therefore, the same performance indicated on both curves might be deemed acceptable in the high-variation setting, but unacceptable in the low-variation setting, where tolerances are less. In the process illustrated in the top curve, the highlighted observation rates between the second and third sigma, and might be deemed "acceptable," whereas that same observation in the process depicted below occurs right at the fourth sigma.

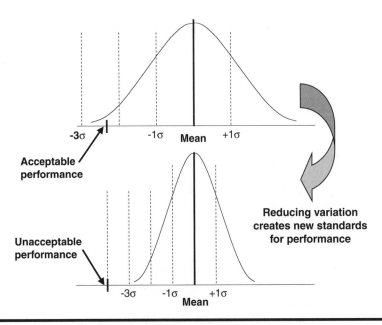

Figure 23.2. What Is Six Sigma Quality?

Imagine tightening the distribution further such that this same observation would occur at the *sixth* sigma. This illustrates the pursuit of perfection embodied by Six Sigma, pushing variation out of the process.

Lean theory complements Six Sigma by suggesting that the tolerances should not only tighten but that the mean should move in the proper direction as well. For example, daily on-time performance might be 96 percent, but might range from 68 to 100 percent on a daily basis over the course of a month. Not only do we need to deal with the variation, but we are not happy with the 96 percent average. Improvement initiatives will focus on reducing the variation as well as taking the average to a more reasonable level. Getting rid of not only the 68 percent on-time days but also the 78 and 88 percent days will help greatly to move the average closer to 100 percent.

While perfection and Six Sigma quality should serve as the goals of process execution, this level of quality can rarely be achieved in the pursuit of "perfect order" logistics execution. Six Sigma concepts and methods find their roots in manufacturing, where Six Sigma quality is conceivable given the level of automation and volume processed in a manufacturing environment. Given that logistics remains a largely manual function prone to errors of human involvement, Six Sigma quality is not always viable at the aggregate output level of the order where cumulative probabilities suggest that 100 percent perfection must be achieved in all contributing activities and processes. It is more viable at the individual activity level, however. That much said, the sigma methodology continues to hold relevance whether the goal is four- or six-sigma achievement. We will continue with an overview of useful concepts and tools in the assessment of process capability toward sigma achievement.

Defects per Million Opportunities

Performance toward Six Sigma objectives is measured in defects per million opportunities (DPMO). DPMO can be applied at any one of several different levels of analysis. While we are ultimately concerned about satisfying customers at the lowest total cost, analysis at this high level may not provide sufficient information to guide process improvement efforts. All process improvements should drive performance in valued service and cost reduction.

Before one can measure DPMO, there must be agreement on what is defined as a "defect" and what is defined as an "opportunity" for defect. Unfortunately, this discussion can sometimes stop an improvement project in its tracks. Although the definitions are important, an organization should not lose sight of the bigger picture — to improve processes so that greater value is generated, returns are enhanced, and company competitiveness is improved.

"Defects" should be defined in the eyes of the customer. Anything that a customer finds unacceptable or inconsistent with expectations is a defect. Obviously, one cannot know what the customer considers a defect unless there is an understanding of needs as well as recognition of what the customer dislikes or finds "defective." Documentation of customer complaints, explanations of product returns, and damage claims are examples of easy ways to recognize inconsistencies between expectations and actual performance. These are initial sources of customer feedback. Additional information is gathered by *asking* customers what they consider to be a defect. The list of possible defects should be conceived broadly, including not only areas that customers currently find lacking or unsatisfying but areas in which the company currently excels (though fault might be attributed in the future in these areas).

"Opportunities for defects" can then be defined as conceivable ways that the process can go wrong. Here again, the unit of analysis and level of detail become important considerations when determining the meaning of "opportunity." For instance, would an opportunity for defect occur when picking the individual case or is it building the pallet composed of several cases? It is helpful again to think about this in the eyes of the customer. Would the customer complain about a problem occurring at the case level? Most likely, the customer would. Would the customer complain if the case packaging showed signs of wear, like a puncture to a box (even though the contents might be fine)? Some customers would complain while others would not. These are the conversations that must transpire regarding definitions of "defects" and "opportunities for defects." The goal is to reach consensus and to proceed with the analysis.

After agreeing on the definitions, the organization can set out to collect data in the appropriate areas and at the appropriate level. Again, the integrity of the data must be ascertained before conducting the analysis. Once satisfied with the quality of data, the DPMO calculation can proceed. DPMO is expressed simply as:

$$\text{DPMO} = (\text{Defects/Opportunities}) \times 1{,}000{,}000$$

or expressed another way:

$$\text{DPMO} = [\text{Defects/(Defect opportunities per unit} \times \text{Units measured)}] \times 1{,}000{,}000$$

where units measured refers to the volume of activity observed during the period for which we have data.

Sigma Calculations

DPMO can be used to calculate "sigma performance." Sigma performance can be used as a benchmark comparison against a predetermined standard or across different processes. With regard to comparing different processes, the sigma calculation can serve as a common metric for processes that may vary in the degree of complexity, particularly when the level of activity flowing through each process is the same. However, it must be recognized that defects occurring in simple processes (processes consisting of few steps) will naturally carry more weight than defects in complex processes, given the proportional differences in opportunities for defect. A simple process with three steps might have only three opportunities for defect per process iteration, yet a thirty-step process would have at least thirty opportunities in each iteration. The first process would have to run through ten iterations to have the same number of opportunities for defect as the second process. If the processes run through the same number of iterations, the simple process will tend to have a greater penalty placed on it for any single defect. That much said, simpler processes are easier to manage and *should* incur fewer defects.

The most common usage of the sigma calculation is to mark achievement against an established standard (e.g., Six Sigma quality). Given the value for DPMO, we can convert this value into a sigma score by simply using a trusty sigma calculator or translating the DPMO into a z-score and consulting a z-table

Table 23.1. Converting DPMO to Sigmas.

DPMO	Sigma Level
841,300	0.5
691,500	1.0
500,000	1.5
308,500	2.0
158,700	2.5
66,800	3.0
22,700	3.5
6,200	4.0
1,300	4.5
230	5.0
30	5.5
3.4	6.0

From Gardner, Daniel L., *Supply Chain Vector: Methods for Linking the Execution of Global Business Models with Financial Performance,* J. Ross Publishing, Boca Raton, FL, 2004, p. 113.

found in any statistics textbook.* Sample conversions are found in Table 23.1. In examining the numbers in the conversion table, it is worth noting that the proportionality of the DPMO number changes with each incremental improvement in sigma. For instance, defects must only decrease by 18 percent to make the jump from 0.5 sigma to 1.0 sigma. However, to improve from 3.5 sigma to 4.0 sigma (a similar 0.5 sigma improvement), defects must decrease by almost 73 percent from the 3.5 level. To go from 5.5 sigma to 6.0 sigma, defects must drop by almost 89 percent from the 5.5 level. It becomes increasingly difficult to achieve gains in sigma levels the further one pursues precision and quality in execution.

A quick illustration takes us back to the ferryboat example. An earlier Pareto analysis reviewed reasons why customers complain. The purpose of this analysis was to identify and prioritize opportunities for improvement. However, if we now wish to assess performance against a standard, calculating DPMO and sigma would help. The first task is to define the unit of analysis, defects, and opportunities for defect. Management of the ferry service determines that the rider experience is the proper unit of analysis, so the number of passengers handled over the past three months represents the volume of activity under analysis. Management also realizes that mistakes leading to customer-perceived defects can occur in any of seven different ways. These defect opportunities are listed in Table 23.2. The observed defects are determined based on the ship's

---

* A sigma calculator can be found on-line at http://www.isixsigma.com/tt/calculators/.

Table 23.2. DPMO and Sigma Performance for the Ferry Service.

Defect Opportunities	Data Source	Defects
Early departure	Ship's log	1,915
Late arrival	Ship's log	10,550
Damaged vehicle	Customer service	26
Personal injury/sickness	Customer service	54
Mischarged price	Complaint file	32
Miscommunication of service	Complaint file	67
Rude personnel	Complaint file	29
Total defects		**12,673**
DPMO		**75,434**
Sigma level achieved		**2.94**

log, passenger tallies, customer service records, and customer complaints and total 12,673 over the three-month period. This is considered relative to the ferry's 24,000 passengers and seven opportunities for defect per passenger, or 168,000 defect opportunities. The following calculation provides us with a DPMO:

$$\text{DPMO} = 12{,}673 \text{ defects}/(7 \text{ opportunities} \times 24{,}000 \text{ passengers})$$
$$\times 1{,}000{,}000 = 75{,}435$$

This DPMO value of 75,435 translates into a sigma level of 2.94. If the ferryboat company was pursuing three-sigma quality, it is falling short, and even shorter if pursuing four-sigma quality. The obvious concern when pursuing a target sigma level is not to overlook the small-quantity, high-impact defects, like vehicle damage and personal injury. These defects may register as few, but they represent much larger concerns than passengers receiving tardy service.

Data for DPMO and sigma calculations should be collected over extended periods of time in order to be representative of the sum of experience found in the process under examination. A single day is ordinarily not reflective of this sum of experience. The frequency with which the activity is performed will provide some bearing on how long the process must be examined in order to generate generalizable findings. Activities performed infrequently will need to be observed over a longer period to generate sufficient experience for conclusive findings. A *power of analysis* calculation should be conducted to determine how many observations are sufficient for generalizable findings.* Most basic statistics textbooks will provide a complete explanation of important

---

* Power of analysis logic is embedded in sample-size calculators. One such calculator can be found at http://www.isixsigma.com/tt/calculators/.

sampling considerations and techniques. In the absence of long-term data, adjustments are often made to the sigma value by subtracting 1.5 from the value generated by using short-term data. This adjustment is a common rule of thumb, although long-term data are best for assessing long-term performance and process capability.

CONVENTIONAL MEASURES OF LOGISTICS PERFORMANCE

Conventional measures of logistics performance, such as on-time performance, fill rates, and billing accuracy, among others, should not be lost in the mix of Lean Six Sigma Logistics measurement. In fact, many of these transactional measures of cost, time, and quality will serve as the focal points for improvement, particularly when performance in these areas falls short of customer expectations. More and more companies are using scorecard methods to evaluate supplier performance. This is actually very helpful for the supplier because the customer's priorities are clearly set forth, especially when service attributes are weighted in terms of importance. The key is to develop capabilities that match the priorities of the customer. On that basis, service priorities must be established and, in turn, performance measures must be prioritized to reflect what matters to customers.

Once the priorities for measures are established, we must focus on how to track the measures consistently. Consensus definitions for each measure and the means of collecting the necessary data must be established. Data collection may require the effort of individuals in other functions, other locations, and other companies, depending on the measure. Therefore, the responsibilities for all involved parties must be delineated clearly.

Once the ability to track measures is developed, the measures should be recorded and referenced regularly. *Control charts* can aid in this effort, providing a visual depiction of performance for an activity or process over time. Figure 23.3 illustrates one such control chart. The upper control limit (UCL) and lower control limit (LCL) can designate the acceptable range of performance, driven by customers' specifications. As well, the UCL and LCL need to be described statistically to describe whether the process is even remotely capable of meeting customer expectations. This is a key point. A process can, in fact, be in control and not be meeting customer expectations.

While control charts have been in use for several decades as a means of statistical process control, they remain an important diagnostic tool, particularly in their ability to track common and special cause variation. The key is to avoid complacency when performance remains within "acceptable" tolerances and

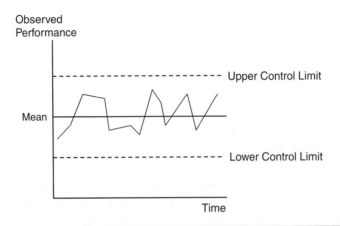

Figure 23.3. Tracking Performance with Control Charts.

instead continuously improve the process by shifting the mean in the desired direction ("up" for service and "down" for costs) and narrowing the tolerances (i.e., reduce the variation).

Transactional measures must be linked not only to customer preferences but also to the company's overall corporate performance. Corporate measures include metrics of a more global nature, including total cost, quality, time, and revenue. Corporate measures are not derived by single events, but are the aggregate (or result-effect) of multiple transactional events. Consequently, all managers need to be responsible for transactional measurements and accountable for contribution to corporate measures. In other words, a traffic manager's performance should be measured by reviewing on-time performance and traffic's contribution to overall corporate success. This corporate success reflects the ultimate performance of the entire system. The challenge many organizations face is to understand how each department contributes to overall corporate success. Only through full understanding of the entire system will this goal be accomplished, and that is where total cost enters the picture yet again.

TOTAL COST ANALYSIS

We would be remiss in our survey of measurement tools if we did not include the ultimate measure for Lean Six Sigma Logistics, total cost. This book is, in large part, dedicated to renewing the focus on total logistics cost. The concept of total cost has been around for several decades, but receives little attention from most logistics organizations. While many companies are turning attention to supply chain management, too often they are leaving their own houses in disarray by not properly organizing the work of logistics. After all, you must walk before you can run.

Lean theory fully embraces the concept of systems thinking and total cost. A typical inbound logistics process will have the following activities and cost drivers:

1. Parts ordering and supplier management
2. Transportation
3. Warehousing
4. Receiving and material handling
5. Inventory management and associated inventory carrying costs

In an effort to manage total cost, the logistics professional must understand how the processes and their associated costs interact. The goal is to optimize the entire system, not a single activity. As we engage in total cost analysis, we will develop a list of questions, including:

1. What are our purchasing policies relative to purchased lot size? Do we wait for truckload quantities from suppliers or do we make multiple daily deliveries? Are the purchasing discounts and incentives designed to motivate large shipments resulting in high inventory levels?
2. What are the transportation strategies? Are we minimizing transportation cost relative only to transportation cost or do we consider warehousing and inventory carrying costs when making transportation decisions?
3. Do we calculate inventory carrying costs? Are these costs visible? Are they captured on our financial statements? What is the relationship between inventory carrying costs, ordering policies, transportation, and warehousing?

Answering these questions begins the journey of managing total cost. Challenge rests with understanding how the activities and associated costs interact. To overcome this challenge, and to embrace total cost as a strategy, we must understand the concept of systems thinking and the trade-offs inherent among the logistics activities. A word of caution, however: it will be neither simple nor trouble free. One roadblock is invisible costs. This is because some costs are explicit and others are implicit. The explicit costs such as those associated with transportation and warehousing are easy enough to tabulate, particularly if a company hires out for these services (simply add up the bills!). Inventory carrying costs and the costs of poor service are typically opportunity costs, however. These implicit, intangible costs can be substantial and must be articulated and measured.

Determining costs on a customer-by-customer basis for segment profitability analysis can also be challenging. Activity-based costing, described in Chapter 20, can prove helpful to this end. Though it remains a subjective basis for allocating costs, activity-based costing runs away from averages and other arbitrary bases for allocation.

This section was intended to serve as a high-level survey of methods and tools common to Lean and Six Sigma implementation. It is not intended to be a comprehensive listing or provide sufficient depth for execution. Additional methods and tools are highlighted throughout the book, including those associated with measurement and action in Chapter 16 and project management in Chapter 17.

## 24

CASE STUDY: GOLDSMART PRODUCTS, INC.

LEAN SIX SIGMA LOGISTICS: A REAL-WORLD STORY

Case studies offer an effective way to comprehend new concepts fully. Unfortunately, case studies in logistics and supply chain management can be very *hit or miss* because logistics is such a broad function with diverse activities. It is virtually impossible to write a case that will satisfy all students or customers of the case.

Notwithstanding the above, it is important that we apply some of the lessons described in this book. To this end, we are calling the following case an *implicit case study*. This means that there are no definitive answers, no *right number* to be calculated, and no absolute strategy to adopt. Instead, we have provided:

1. A narrative that describes a typical corporate situation
2. A random sample of data and information that realistically may be available to the logistics professional
3. A list of responsibilities, or job description, for the Lean Six Sigma Logistics professional
4. A list of guiding questions to generate thought and guide discussion, drawn from the Logistics Bridge Model

The data provided in the case will supply clues as to where the logistics professional needs to concentrate time. Some of the clues are explicit and others implied. If, for some reason, you find yourself asking "What about this point?"

we suggest that you simply close the information gap based on experience in your own organization and environment. The value of this example is not for the reader to complete the case study in and of itself, but to begin thinking about his or her own organizational challenges.

It is our hope that the reader will spend a reasonable amount of time reviewing this case. However, our true motivation is for the logistics professional to spend more time using the tools and concepts within his or her enhanced knowledge base. Readers should use the principles outlined in the book as a compass to guide their way through this exercise, but should also use them in everyday management of strategy and operations.

Note: All case events, characters, names, conversations, and data are completely fictitious.

GOLDSMART PRODUCTS, INC.: A CASE IN LEAN SIX SIGMA LOGISTICS

The Calm Before the Storm

It was a cold Monday morning when Bob Murphy drove the familiar route from his suburban home to GoldSMART's downtown offices. Today seemed no different from so many other mornings as he ran through a familiar routine: the same morning talk show and the same traffic and weather reports, the sluggish traffic lights, and even the same annoying billboards. It was all the standard fare except for the hour. On this morning, Bob had convinced himself that he should hit the road an hour earlier than normal to make up for his early departure from the office on Friday afternoon. He would not have missed his daughter's school program for anything in the world, but the joy of the weekend had settled into the reality of another Monday morning.

Bob knew that the first half of the day, if not the whole day, would be consumed with playing catch-up in the form of returned phone calls, e-mail inquiries, and any number of hot issues around the office — to make up for those few measly hours he missed on Friday. It was a shame that he could not knock out a few calls on the way into the office, but a dead Blackberry battery was not helping the cause. Bob rationalized the situation by telling himself that the people he needed to reach would not even be in the office for another hour. "Why not relax and enjoy the drive?" he mused, staring down the license-plate-clad bumper easing through the construction zone a few feet ahead of him.

The sun was breaking through the morning sky just as Bob entered the parking lot at GoldSMART Products. Expecting to see an empty lot, he was surprised to see a handful of cars already stationed near the entrance. He instantly recognized that they belonged to some of his colleagues on the senior management team. As soon as Bob put the car in park and turned off the radio, he noticed that Lisa Romanowski of Corporate Affairs was pulling up alongside his parking space.

"I guess you got the message too!" Lisa smiled reservedly as they both reached for their bags.

"What message? What's going on?"

"Apparently, TriMagna has decided to end its courtship of FantastiCo," Lisa explained.

"You mean number one in the industry and number four are joining forces?" Bob asked, still incredulous to being in the dark on such a big event.

"Yep, those are the two. Looks like they're getting married," Lisa quipped as they approached the front door.

"Combined, they would pretty much double our market share now, wouldn't they?" Bob reasoned as the security guard nodded politely to the two as they strode toward the elevator.

"That's about right, Bob. TriMagna would go from a thirty-six share to forty-eight. You're right, that doubles our twenty-four share. We just went from second to distant second on this news. I'm sure I'll be seeing you in the boardroom in a bit," Lisa surmised as she exited the elevator on the fourth floor.

"You got it," Bob answered as the door closed and the elevator accelerated again, taking him to his sixth-floor office. "So much for catching up this morning," Bob muttered against the whirring sound of the elevator's pulleys.

The Approach of Ominous Clouds

As soon as Bob hung up his coat and approached his desk, he noticed the little orange light blinking on his phone. "Sure enough, it's begun," he thought to himself as he lifted the receiver and played the message. "Eight o'clock boardroom" he jotted on the desk calendar as the words of the CEO's assistant were relayed to him.

Rather than digging into the backlog of messages from the weekend, Bob decided to take inventory of the company's situation and that of his logistics organization going into the meeting. Logistics and the supply chain functions of purchasing and manufacturing had long been viewed as bastions of cost savings by the company. Logistics, in particular, had been recognized as a consistent contributor to the company's cost-cutting exercises and the logistics organization had delivered reliably year after year. "Where are we going to find the savings that we need now?" Bob wondered aloud as Susan, his assistant, appeared in the doorway.

"I figured you might be clocking in early this morning," she said. "What can I do to help for the eight o'clock meeting, Bob?"

"Gee, where to start? Can you pull together the last twelve months' metrics reports and our 'Big Five' customers' scorecards?" Bob asked, knowing that the task would be accomplished easily by his able assistant. "Oh, and throw in the 'budget versus actual' charts that we put together last week," he added.

"No problem. Anything else?" Susan replied.

"That should do it. You might order us lunch if this thing runs into the afternoon!" Bob joked half-heartedly.

"Let's see, where was I?" Bob resumed his train of thought. "If the big dog is getting bigger, that means we have to do something different, something bold, or else we're going to get trampled...as if we weren't already! How did this business get to be so complicated anyway? And to think that it all started fifty-five years ago with one simple product. Look at us now; the portfolio of products is so broad and deep that our catalogue looks like a big-city phone book. The product line has grown almost exponentially. It seems like we add five new products for every product that we should drop. And the sales and distribution networks seem to grow just as quickly. Who would've thought five years ago that we'd need a sales office in Thailand or a distribution center in Shanghai? The price we pay for success...but where will we find the growth and savings we need to stay in the game?"

Just as Bob found himself completely lost in thought, Susan strode confidently into the office, her arms full of binders and folders. "Here are the reports, Bob. The rumble gets under way in twenty minutes."

In the Eye of the Storm

As Bob made his way to the boardroom, he was joined by several of his colleagues from the upper ranks of GoldSMART management. There was Linda McNeely from accounting, Larry Davis from North American manufacturing, and Elisio Salazar from marketing and sales. Already in the boardroom were Randall Knight, the company's CFO, and Sridhar Agarwal, the CIO. The two seemed to be engaged in deep conversation sprinkled with occasional light laughter. A few more senior management team members joined the scene. However, as CEO Roger Atkins entered the room, the mood turned serious as everyone assumed their places around the long table. Before he could put down the cup of coffee he had carried into the room, Roger got the meeting under way.

"Does anyone *not* understand why I've called you all together this morning?" Roger reasoned that the ensuing silence reflected not only an understanding of what was apparently taking place, but also recognition of the magnitude of the event. "We find ourselves in the midst of a great transformation in the industry. I think that you can all grasp the enormity of what TriMagna is proposing and the challenges that will be before us should this thing take root. And all indications point to this thing, in fact, happening. There had been talk of a merger for some time and the analysts have been encouraging it. It looks as though FantastiCo shareholders are going to receive a handsome premium and it could be approved by the end of the second quarter. And, no, there's no chance that the Department of Justice will step in on this one. It's looking more and more like a done deal. Without question, we must act as if it is a done deal."

"It seems like we need to fight fire with fire. Why don't we look into buying Grantham Holdings? That would bring us within ten points of these guys?" offered Elisio.

"That is something that we examined in the not so distant past," Roger replied. "On the surface, it's an attractive proposition, but when you peel a few layers, it looks not only unattractive but unreasonable for a couple of reasons. The first is the substantial debt Grantham has incurred over the past two years with hefty R&D investments that have generated, well, pathetic returns, not to mention its hyper-expansion over the same period, both contributing to its debt burden. The other reason is our own cash position. We simply cannot justify investing significantly in anyone or anything right now."

"But won't the board's knee-jerk reaction be to respond in kind?" Linda interjected. "Won't we have to get big too, even if it means taking on some unwanted debt, so that we don't become TriMagna's next target? After all, we could use the international assets that Grantham has developed, couldn't we?"

Randall picked up where Roger left off. "There is just no way we can pull that off right now. As Roger pointed out, we prospected a Grantham deal just two months ago, and we wanted it to make sense, but it simply doesn't."

"Well, if the growth must be organic, we need to unleash our own new product development to get the next 'killer products' on the market before TriMagna can beat us to it!" Elisio fired back.

Bob and Larry sighed in unison at the very idea of launching more products in rapid-fire succession. Larry finally spoke up. "We have gained quite a bit of flexibility in the plants over the past year and made product changeovers a lot less painful, but we cannot afford to dilute our production economies any more. I lost count of the stockkeeping units that each plant makes a long time ago. Bob can speak to the same phenomenon at his warehouses."

"It's true," Bob agreed. "We had to introduce six-character alphanumeric codes this year to keep up with the proliferation of SKUs." It's gotten downright messy."

"It would be great if we only had to make products that enjoyed healthy margins, but we have to make 'winners' and 'losers' alike," Larry added.

Sensing that the meeting could very quickly become one reduced to an exercise in finger pointing, Roger regained control. The dialogue continued for another ninety minutes, with suggestions for growth coming from all sides and corners of the boardroom. When conversation turned to aggressive cost savings, Bob thought to himself, "Here we go again; the supply chain functions will be looked toward us for all of these savings." His fear was only fueled when Roger looked in the direction of Larry and himself when speaking of the need to "tighten the belt" and "drastically cut costs."

It was about then that Bob interrupted an exchange between Linda and Sridhar. "Might this TriMagna-FantastiCo venture actually represent an opportunity for us?" he pondered aloud.

Appearing puzzled at first and then intrigued, Roger encouraged Bob to explore the thought.

"I mean, TriMagna clearly thinks that efficiency gains will be achieved through the consolidation and that there are synergies to merging operations with those of FantastiCo. But how long will it take them to find these synergies...to tap into the benefits...if they can find them at all?" He had gained the undivided attention of the group. "There is a good chance that they will be so preoccupied with each other over the next several quarters that we can invade their turf."

"You know, there is some truth to that," Randall agreed. "If you track the history of many of these large-scale acquisitions, they often do not pan out. The anticipated benefits fail to be realized. Wall Street rarely rewards companies over the long term for taking on weaker partners."

"We might actually gain some traction with the customers of TriMagna and FantastiCo if we can prove that these two suppliers are getting distracted with each other and stumbling over the consolidation effort," Elisio pointed out.

"The last thing the market would like to see is a significant reduction in their alternatives, it seems," added Linda. "Although I suspect they will expect lower costs through better economies of scale."

Building confidence in what at first seemed like an errant train of thought, Bob continued. "It just seems like we need to be smarter than those guys. We need to do everything better than them. WE NEED TO BE SMART! It's in our company name for crying out loud!"

"You're right, Bob," Roger agreed. "It's time that we live up to our name again. Can I count on you to head up the effort, to figure out how we can be the smartest player in the game?"

Bob knew that there was no taking back his idea now, so with a growing lump in his throat, Bob offered a relegated response. "Of course, Roger, I'd be glad to do it."

On hearing Bob's anticipated agreement, Roger instructed everyone in attendance to participate in the cause and to be responsive to Bob's inevitable requests for input and data. When everyone agreed, Roger called the meeting to a close.

Still lost in the moment, Bob accepted the back-pats and condolences of his peers, along with the reality that the company's future just might rest squarely on the shoulders of his newfound responsibility. "It seems like only yesterday I was kicking boxes around the warehouse," he thought, "and now it feels like the weight of the whole company is riding on me."

Bob made his way back to the office, where Susan met him with an expression laced with both anxiety and curiosity. "Let's clear the schedule for the afternoon," he told her. "Please alert the team members that they should do the same. We'll meet in the conference room at one o'clock."

"You got it," Susan replied, knowing that the events of the meeting would unfold soon enough.

Riding Out the Storm

Bob was pleased to find that all but a few of his team members from the logistics organization were in the conference room when he arrived. He opened the meeting with an explanation of the likely merger between TriMagna and FantastiCo. He was not at all surprised that most of those in attendance were already aware of the news. Before allowing the meeting to explode into a frenzy of questions, Bob reiterated the sentiments of the senior management team and the nature of the dialogue that had taken place a few hours before. He also relayed the fact that the logistics organization was being looked toward for significant leadership in determining how the company would not only survive the crisis but thrive and grow in the face of it.

While many of the issues that needed to be addressed by the company were beyond the direct scope and responsibility of the logistics organization, Roger felt that Bob's connection with constituents within the company, as well as the reach he and his organization enjoyed with suppliers upstream and customers downstream, provided a unique opportunity for dramatic change as it applied not only to the physical flow aspects of the business but the entirety of the business. Bob knew that these facts had motivated Roger to call on the logistics organization to serve as a "virtual think tank" within the company. It was also based on Roger's confidence in Bob, who had somehow managed to generate consistent cost savings over the years despite strong inflationary trends throughout the industry. Bob was also recognized for having developed a progressive team made up of both industry veterans and talented young employees who were bringing leading-edge ideas from their universities and putting them to work in the organization. Bob would now need the collective strength of this group to devise innovative strategic and operational plans.

Rex Carnes, the company's traffic manager, got the dialogue started. "We can't expect to go after the carriers for cost savings this year. In fact, I expect carrier rates to stick for the first time in quite a while. Everyone in the industry is crying out about how rates are on the way up and there may be no way to fight them off."

Import/export manager Maria Sanchez echoed the sentiment. "It's going to be next to impossible to find savings from the steamship lines too. With the tight-capacity market and growing imbalance of freight flows from Asia, rates are likely to go up before they tick downward again. My fear is that service levels might nosedive simultaneously. It's entirely possible that we will be paying more for poorer service in the future."

Harley Johnson, the company's private fleet manager, failed to brighten the tone of the conversation. "I'm having a hard time keeping drivers around as it is. We've had to increase the driver wage three times over the past two years to keep them on staff. The big trucking companies keep trying to lure them away. And, as you know, we never used to have to pay drivers on an hourly rate, but that's what they've demanded when they have to sit and wait for hours on end at many of our big customers."

Dave Jones, logistics manager of the U.S. eastern region, only added to the woes. "My warehouses are full of product in anticipation of the fourth-quarter sales season, so much so that I'm searching for some public space to cover the need for the next few months. Unfortunately, that space is not going to come cheap, if I can find it at all in a few of our key markets. I probably wouldn't need the space if I didn't have to house all of those product take-backs from last season's customer overstocks. Has Salazar indicated what he wants to do with that stuff?"

"No, not yet," Bob replied with a sigh.

"Bob, if I can comment," injected Kathleen Boyd, one of the newest among the bright set of recent hires to the organization.

"Of course," Bob replied with an air of encouragement, hoping that the dialogue might somehow turn positive.

"It doesn't seem like we are going to make the critical impact that we need by going after the low-hanging fruit. It sounds like Roger has given us the green light to do things new and different around here, to create a revolution rather than an evolution, I guess."

"That's exactly what we've been asked to do," confirmed Bob. "In fact, Mr. Atkins expects us to work smarter, to outthink the competition. It might sound cliché, but that's exactly what we need to do. We need to step back and question why we do things the way we do them and, in fact, why we do many of the things."

"I see a new campaign slogan in our future," chided Andy Wilson, the undisputed "class clown" of the organization.

"What do you mean by that, Andy?" Bob inquired.

Andy sat up to respond. "Well, we all must have a desk drawer full of pens and buttons and closets filled with golf shirts emblazoned with the slogans of the day. I prefer the caps, myself. But the point is that we have all been bombarded with gimmicky efforts for everyone to work harder to produce more. And even if the efforts are important, they're often viewed as gimmicks. It sounds like we *really* need to make change happen now and we need to sustain improved performance. But I'm not sure how we'll able to do it given our past history of pushing people to get what we need out of them."

"Andy's right," Sarah Davies added. "We often push to get what we need out of the people. Though we often do see a temporary performance improvement, soon after the shirts and pens are handed out, everyone goes back to their old ways of doing things and performance reverts back to the norm. People have gotten cynical. How can we make it stick this time?"

"If the line workers smell another so-called 'efficiency study,' then we'll never get the buy-in we need of employees, especially if they think they might lose their jobs," added Michael Gregory, the organization's customer service manager.

Bob nodded in agreement, knowing that Michael, Andy, and Sarah were right. The changes that were about to take place would have to become a way of life, not a flash-in-the-pan proposition.

"Back to Bob's point though," offered Dave, "we have to question the very essence of what we do around here. Doing the wrong things very well won't count for much. It only assures us of generating unneeded costs and becoming increasingly irrelevant to our customers."

Kathleen spoke up again. "I know that I have only been here a short time, but I am not sure that I fully understand what it is that we do. I mean, I know what I am responsible for doing day to day, but the 'big picture' isn't crystal clear to me."

"Don't worry, kid," said Harley, "most of us don't understand it either."

"It's true!" Rex added. "I know how to find trucks and trains to move product, but to be honest, what takes place before and after the shipment is something of a mystery to me. I would be hard-pressed to tell you how Maria arranges for our import and export movements or how Dave finds that public warehouse space he needs."

When it became clear that the full scope of logistics activity was not well understood by the newcomers and veterans alike, Bob suggested that they work

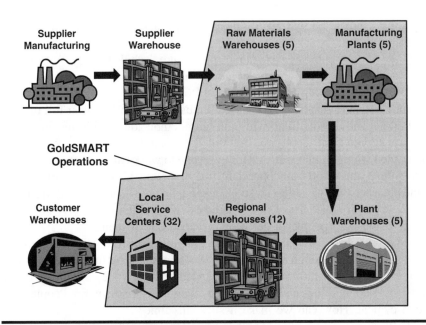

Figure 24.1. High-Level Value Stream Map.

immediately to remedy the situation. Having worked his way through the organization over the course of his career and ultimately assuming responsibility for the organization, he only now realized how he had taken his knowledge for granted. He had assumed that everyone around him possessed a similar knowledge base — an assumption that proved to be anything but sound.

To start, the group sketched out a cursory value stream map (Figure 24.1) as well as a map of the order process in its current state (Figure 24.2A and B). The mapping exercises themselves seemed to engender more questions than answers, but Bob was encouraged by his team's curiosity and enthusiasm for the task. With successive maps drawn of other logistics-related processes, Bob even found himself asking "We do what?" when the activity steps were explained by a person close to the process. What also became apparent in the presentations was that the work was not often performed in the same way for any two situations.

Bob decided that it was time to wrap up the day, although no one seemed to mind that the meeting was running into the early evening. "This has certainly been an eye-opening day for us. It's clear that we, including myself, didn't know what we didn't know when we walked in here this afternoon. Hopefully, we're asking the right questions. Undoubtedly, we're getting smarter. Let's continue to dig and look for the critical questions and the answers to those questions that

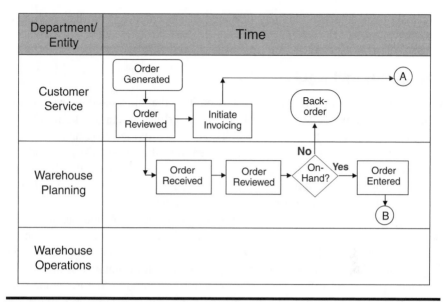

Figure 24.2A. The Order Process: Current State.

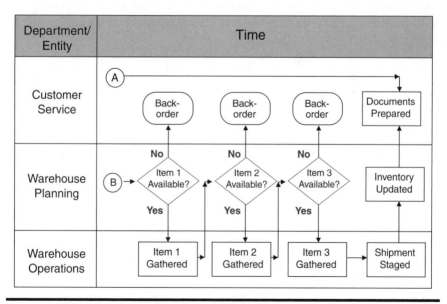

Figure 24.2B. The Order Process: Current State.

will make us the smart company that we must become." With that, Bob sent his staff home for the evening.

Seeing Daylight Again

Over the next few days, Bob and his staff built on the understanding established in that first meeting. They were able to gather critical operational data (Table 24.1) and financial data (Table 24.2). These data provided Bob and his organization with a better sense of the current health of the logistics system and the business in general. Breezing over the numbers, he could sense that both cost reduction and service improvements could be found, but exactly where and how would involve deeper investigation and understanding.

Using the principles of the Logistics Bridge Model, Bob and his organization developed statements of key focus areas (Table 24.3) and several significant questions for a high-level review for current condition analysis (Table 24.4). Bob examined the guiding principles along with remnants of the necessary data and found some sense of satisfaction in knowing that everyone was focused on the job at hand. What comfort he enjoyed was tempered, however, by the realization that tough decisions and volumes of work were ahead. If the company were to become the "smart company" that he envisioned, he would have to know what information must still be gathered and how to turn that information into knowledge that could guide the company out of crisis and into prosperity.

Table 24.1. GoldSMART Operational Data.

GoldSMART Data Collection Results

Operations Data

% common customers each plant	35%	
% common suppliers each plant	40%	
# of suppliers paying transportation (prepaid)	65	
% distribution centers being used for inbound	0%	
# of carriers (trucking companies) used	82	
% of spend with top 10 carriers	65%	
# of truckload carriers	64	40% Transportation spend
# of less-than-truckload carriers	10	28% Transportation spend
# of couriers	2	2% Transportation spend
# of expedited carriers	6	10% Transportation spend
Private fleet trailer/tractor ratio	3.5:1	20% Transportation spend
Total outside warehousing space	375,000 sq. ft.	
Total space used for finished goods	800,000 sq. ft.	
Total space used for raw material storage	250,000 sq. ft.	
Available cubic meters per trailer	70 m^3	

Weekly Summary of Plant Information (Plants 1 and 2 Only)

	Monday	Tuesday	Wednesday	Thursday	Friday	Total
Inbound trucks serviced						
Plant 1	40	10	25	5	20	100
Plant 2	50	5	40	0	30	125
Outbound trucks shipped						
Plant 1	10	20	0	40	80	150
Plant 2	5	40	15	5	90	155
Cubic volume (m^3) received						
Plant 1	2,000	300	1,000	50	800	4,150
Plant 2	2,500	100	1,600	—	1,800	6,000
Cubic volume (m^3) shipped						
Plant 1	500	800	—	1,200	4,000	6,500
Plant 2	200	2,800	750	300	6,300	10,350

Part # Lean factor analysis
Attempts to see whether there is flow and pull relative to ordering of parts and consumption of parts

Part #A12345 — usage per unit built

Parts used	600	500	600	550	600	2,850
Parts received	4,000					4,000
Parts in transit			3,000			3,000
Parts ordered					2,500	2,500

Table 24.2.   GoldSMART Financial Data.

GoldSMART Data Collection Results			
			Average On-Hand
Financial Data			
Sales	$ 787,500,000	Annually	$ 250,800,000
Cost of goods sold	$ 511,000,000	Annually	$ 26,250,000
Raw material spend	$ 273,750,000	Annually	
Average finished goods inventory	105 days		
Average raw material inventory — work in process	35 days		
Total Logistics Cost Components			
Ordering	$ 400,000	Fully allocated	$ 400,000
Supplier management	$ 325,000	Fully allocated	$ 325,000
Logistics design	$ —	Fully allocated	$ —
Transportation spend outbound	$ 48,500,000	Fully allocated	$ 48,500,000
Transportation spend inbound	$ 18,750,000	Fully allocated	$ 18,750,000
Company warehousing — distribution centers	$ 15,750,000	Fully allocated	$ 15,750,000
Outside warehousing	$ 2,850,000	Fully allocated	$ 2,850,000
Yard control	$ 325,000	Fully allocated	$ 325,000
Receiving management	$ 1,275,000	Fully allocated	$ 1,275,000
Inventory Carrying Cost			
Administrative overheads	0.5%	Average inventory	$ 1,160,250
Cost of capital	6.00%	Average inventory	$ 13,923,000
Damage	1.00%	Average inventory	$ 2,320,500
Insurance	1.00%	Average inventory	$ 2,320,500
Interplant shuttles	1.00%	Average inventory	$ 2,320,500
Obsolescence	3.00%	Average inventory	$ 6,961,500
Shrinkage	1.00%	Average inventory	$ 2,320,500
Space	6.00%	Average inventory	$ 13,923,000
Storage systems	0.50%	Average inventory	$ 1,160,250
Taxes	3.00%	Average inventory	$ 6,961,500
		Inventory only	$ 53,371,500
		Total Logistics Cost	**$ 141,546,500**

Table 24.3.   Logistics Professional's Key Focus Areas.

A. Logistics Professional Key Focus Areas

The logistics professional will lead the development of logistics and supply chain practices that result in industry operational excellence. This includes driving initiatives forward to support the organization's vision of quality, reputation, and customer satisfaction.

Through teamwork and collaboration, the logistics professional will develop and execute strategy for development of systems and practices that will continuously produce the "perfect order." This is defined as "the right product to the right place at the right time in the right quantity and condition at the lowest possible cost."

Key Focus Areas	*Includes design, planning, implementing, and control of:*
Logistics	Transportation, facilities and warehousing, security, packaging, and order processing
Procurement	Supplier development, supplier quality assurance, purchasing, global sourcing
Inventory control	Stratification, plan for every part, inventory placement, forecasting, order processing
Strategic support	Budgeting, strategic planning, human resource development, mergers and acquisitions support
Operational support	Sales and operations planning, training and development

---

B. Strategic Responsibilities

Voice of Customer	**Logistics Professional Responsibilities**
Customer expectations	To ensure supply chain structure is designed to support customer expectations
Customer perceptions	To ensure supply chain practices add value to customer internal strategies
Customer challenges	To ensure supply chain flexibility to meet customer and market changes
Voice of Business	**Logistics Professional Responsibilities**
Company expectations	To ensure supply chain practices meet organizational vision of success
Company perceptions	To ensure supply chain practices add value to internal customer
Company challenges	To ensure supply chain practices deal with internal challenges

---

C. Logistics Professional Responsibilities: Flow

Logistics Flow	
Asset Flow	***Effectively develop and utilize all organizational assets***
People	Recruiting, training, developing, and building of highly effective teams
Inventory	Implementing sound inventory control practices
Fixed resources	Rationalizing and managing effective use of plant and equipment
Information Flow	***To ensure information is shared and utilized for optimal corporate impact***
Data	Understanding and implementing effective use of technology and data management

Table 24.3. Logistics Professional's Key Focus Areas (continued).

Knowledge	Development and facilitation of "best practice" sharing
Communication	Implementation of effective management review processes
Financial Flow	*Development of logistics practices to support corporate financial objectives*
Income statement	Elimination of waste and execution of operating efficiencies
Balance sheet	Asset utilization and rationalization
Cash flow	Reduction of "cash-to-cash" operating cycle time

D. Logistics Professional Responsibilities: Capability

Logistics Capability	
Predictability	*To design and implement a logistics system that is predictable to all stakeholders*
Organization	Ensure facilities and processes are clean and organized
Coordination	Develop logistics and supply chain practices that are planned and proactive
Complexity	Simplify processes and attack sources of waste caused by variation
Stability	*To design and implement a logistics system that is stable to all stakeholders*
Standardization	Develop and implement standardized operating procedures and policies
Flexibility	Create flexible processes and technologies to meet changing market demands
Control	Implement control mechanisms to manage planned versus actual condition in real time
Visibility	*To design and implement a logistics system that is visible to all stakeholders*
Understandability	Create a supply chain that is understandable to all users
Measurability	Develop "corporate dashboards" and effective "measurement systems"
Actionability	Effectively implement change and improvement as required from feedback mechanisms

---

E. Logistics Professional Responsibilities: Discipline

Logistics Discipline	
Collaboration	*Create an environment based on teamwork, internal and external collaboration*
Teamwork	Develop highly functional teams with internal and external participation
Strategic sourcing	Understand and implement sound practices relative to "make versus buy" decisions
Project management	Implement and drive structured "project management" disciplines
Systems Optimization	*Execute sound practices based on a "total systems approach"*
Total cost	Design and implement decision support tools for total cost analysis
Horizontal integration	Ensure horizontal integration for optimal productivity and waste elimination

Table 24.3.   Logistics Professional's Key Focus Areas (continued).

Vertical integration	Ensure vertical integration for optimal productivity and waste elimination
Waste Elimination	*Develop and execute relentless initiative toward waste elimination*
Quality at the source	Design and implement "error-proofing" and "quality at the source" initiative
Continuous improvement	Develop and drive formal continuous improvement programs
Execution	Develop and drive effective problem-solving and operational execution practices

Table 24.4.   High-Level Review for Current Condition Analysis.

A. High-Level Review for Current Condition Analysis

	Questions
Voice of Customer	
Customer expectations	What is the customer's definition of "quality"?
Customer perceptions	What is the customer's perception of quality received?
Customer challenges	What are the customer's own internal and external challenges?
Voice of Business	
Company expectations	What are company's expectations of quality?
Company perceptions	What are company's perceptions of quality produced?
Company challenges	What are company's current internal and external logistics-related challenges?

B. Logistics Bridge Model Review Process: Flow

Logistics Chain Flow	Questions
Asset Flow	
People	What people are in place? What are their skills and responsibilities?
Inventory	What is the inventory management infrastructure?
Fixed resources	What is the plant and equipment infrastructure?
Information Flow	
Data	What technologies and data are available and how are they used?
Knowledge	What are the best practices and how are they shared?
Communication	What is the management review process?
Financial Flow	
Income statement	What is the income statement telling us?
Balance sheet	What is our balance sheet strategy?
Cash flow	What is our cash flow strategy?

Table 24.4. High-Level Review for Current Condition Analysis (continued).

C. Logistics Bridge Model Review Process: Capability

Logistics Capability	Questions
Predictability	
Organization	Do we have clean and organized facilities and systems?
Coordination	Are logistics and supply chain activities planned and documented?
Complexity	What are the sources of significant variation?
Stability	
Standardization	Do we have standardized processes and procedures?
Flexibility	Are processes flexible to manage contingencies effectively?
Control	How do we manage planned versus actual conditions?
Visibility	
Understandability	Can management clearly see and understand logistics-related processes?
Measurability	What dashboard and measurement systems are in place?
Actionability	What tools are in place to act on immediate and future action items?

D. Logistics Bridge Model Review Process: Discipline

Logistics Discipline	Questions
Collaboration	
Teamwork	How does teamwork flourish in the current environment?
Strategic sourcing	What should be insourced and what should be outsourced?
Project management	What project management skills and tools are in place?
Systems Optimization	
Total cost	How do we design and measure "total systems cost"?
Horizontal integration	How do we establish cross-functional expertise?
Vertical integration	How are we managing external supply chain relationships?
Waste Elimination	
Quality at the source	How are we error proofing our processes?
Continuous improvement	What formal procedures are in place for continuous improvement?
Execution	How do we ensure effective execution of new initiatives?

25

SUMMARY AND CONCLUSION

The topic of Lean Six Sigma Logistics is far from being concluded. In many respects, we are just getting started on what will eventually become a driving force in logistics and supply chain management. As we go forward over the next decade, our initiatives may not be called Lean or Six Sigma. Perhaps the initiative will simply be called *Business Excellence*, but the guiding principles of Lean and Six Sigma will be embedded in whatever initiative it happens to be. The principles and tools of Lean Six Sigma Logistics are all that is necessary to design and sustain a formidable logistics system. This means we can stop looking for *what* to do and start focusing and *how and when* we will do it. The Logistics Bridge Model provides the compass and sets the stage; one must only add the commitment and perseverance. In the end, success will be granted to the organizations that recognize that Lean Six Sigma Logistics is not a "nice to have" but rather a "must have."

As the authors of this book, we hope that we have been able to articulate the vision of Lean Six Sigma Logistics. We fully recognize that the reader may be left with more questions than answers. At some level, that is a desired output of the book. The reality is that many of our organizations do not have a solid understanding of logistics and the importance of fundamental logistics practices. We attempted to highlight this fact in the hope that we would motivate logistics professionals to drive their agendas into the corporate boardroom. We fully recognize that this will take time; however, the drive must start today. Logistics and supply chain issues are the last great frontiers for strategic management. Logistics and supply chain management need to embrace the science to complement the art form that it has become.

We developed this book with the intention of designing a compass or model that the logistics professional can use to develop an internal logistics strategy. We began this challenging task by recognizing the driving forces of Lean, Six Sigma, and logistics. This allowed us to realize the obvious and powerful relationship shared among variation, waste, costs, and customer value.

We then began a dialogue on the wastes that exist in most logistics systems. This set up the framework for us to begin our *awareness* campaigns, emphasizing the brutal fact that wastes exist throughout our logistics systems and supply chain networks. In particular, inventory, transportation, and warehousing provide a raging river of waste that must be addressed. To this end, we made every attempt to drive home the point that inventory is the *king of waste*. Inventory in the form of overproduction and safety stock covers up for variation and is the seed for many other forms of waste. To manage inventory is to manage variation. They are one and the same.

Completing our discussion on logistics wastes, we introduced the Logistics Bridge Model. This model is the compass that can be used to develop strategic and operational vision for the organization. Indeed, to develop a model for a topic as broad as logistics is a daunting task. We have no doubt that many readers will be left with questions. What about global sourcing? What about transportation capacity issues? What about the change management side of implementing these principles? These are all very good questions, and each could certainly be a book topic in its own right.

Our motivation was to provide a compass that can be used to develop the solutions to the multitude of challenges that exist in logistics and supply chain management. It is our hope that the reader will document his or her current challenges and integrate the challenges into the Logistics Bridge Model. The ultimate goal of any logistician is to link the organization to suppliers and customers efficiently and effectively. The Logistics Bridge Model provides the foundation for this to happen. The Logistics Bridge Model is designed to act as a catalyst to drive critical thinking inside the organization, for critical thinking is the element most lacking in many organizations. Before we can begin to implement solutions, we must have rigorous debate and develop common understanding of goals and objectives as they relate to the logistics function. This debate can begin by analyzing the three major principles of the Logistics Bridge Model. Significant progress will be made by asking the tough questions surrounding Logistics Flow, Logistics Capability, and Logistics Discipline. It is our belief that any logistics challenge will find its inherent solution with the aid of these three main principles.

Next, we introduced and examined several tools that will be helpful for the logistician to achieve results. It is virtually impossible to list all available Lean and Six Sigma tools, and therefore, we were challenged to select what we considered to be the *vital few* for the logistician to begin the Lean Six Sigma Logistics journey. Any logistician ready to engage Lean Six Sigma Logistics seriously will surely need to be versed on available tools and their uses. However, it is important to note that tools are simply tools. Tools are not strategy and they are not principles. Although the tools will help us to determine the *how* to accomplish our goals, they do not provide the answer to *why* we want to reach these goals. We need to understand the "why" in order to ensure that the organization is synchronized and heading in the right direction.

Finally, we provided the reader with a real-world example to be used as a working case study. The purpose of the GoldSMART case is simply to show the reader that logistics issues are extremely important to organizational success. Most organizations suffer from the same challenges: lack of data, lack of teamwork, and lack of focus on total logistics cost. Our hope is that, together, we can alter the course of time and strive for meaningful, significant change in the way we view and manage logistics.

At a minimum, we hope that you found this book worthwhile. At best, we are thrilled at the prospect that our book and the ideas herein will provide the catalyst and compass for you and your organization to embrace logistics fully and truly drive for perfection in all that matters.

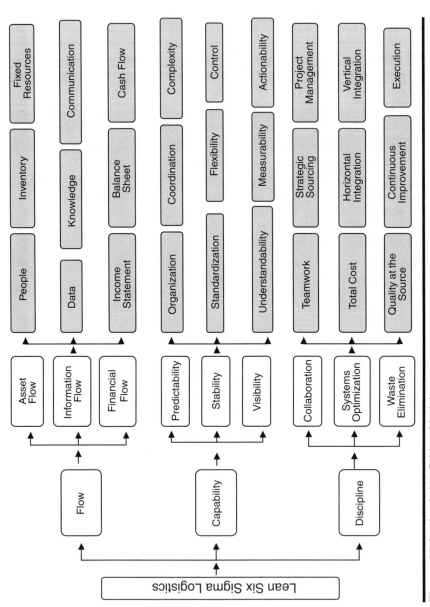

Figure 25.1. Logistics Bridge Model.

INDEX